Foundations German 1

Tom Carty
**Formerly Principal Lecturer in German and IWLP Leader
at Staffordshire University
and the University of Wolverhampton**

Ilse Wührer
Teaching Fellow in German, Keele University

Series Editor
Tom Carty

palgrave
macmillan

First published 2003 by
PALGRAVE MACMILLAN
Houndmills, Basingstoke, Hampshire RG21 6XS and
175 Fifth Avenue, New York, N.Y. 10010
Companies and representatives throughout the world

PALGRAVE MACMILLAN is the global academic imprint of the Palgrave
Macmillan division of St. Martin's Press, LLC and of Palgrave Macmillan Ltd.
Macmillan® is a registered trademark in the United States, United Kingdom
and other countries. Palgrave is a registered trademark in the European
Union and other countries.

ISBN 1–4039–0236–4 book
ISBN 1–4039–0256–9 cassettes

This book is printed on paper suitable for recycling and made from fully
managed and sustained forest sources.

A catalogue record for this book is available from the British Library.

Audio Production: University of Brighton Media Centre
Produced by Brian Hill
Voices: Monika Lind, Ulla Spittler, Gerd Knischewski, Andreas Hoecht, Ilse Wührer

Original design by Wendi Watson

Formatted by The Ascenders Partnership, Basingstoke

10 9 8 7 6 5 4 3 2 1
12 11 10 09 08 07 06 05 04 03

Printed and bound in Great Britain by
Ashford Colour Press Ltd
Gosport, Hants

CONTENTS

Acknowledgements

All photographic illustrations were supplied by Ilse and Bernd Wührer, except for page 1 (Anne) and page 3 (Kirsty), which were supplied by Colette Carty.

Every effort has been made to trace all copyright holders, but if any have inadvertently been overlooked the publishers will be pleased to make the necessary arrangements at the first opportunity.

Ein herzliches Dankeschön an meinen Bruder, Bernd G. Wührer. Bernd und seine Freunde haben viel Zeit damit verbracht, Fotos für dieses Buch zu machen – und es war kalt in Darmstadt!

Ilse Wührer

INTRODUCTION

Mainly for the tutor

Foundations German 1 is a course for beginners aimed at students taking a language option or similar module on an Institution-Wide Languages Programme (IWLP).

Many of the textbooks used on beginners' and intermediate language courses in higher education were not designed for that purpose. Tutors and students particularly complain of inappropriate topics (too much on food and drink or shopping, for example) and excessive length (with units and sections having to be skipped or the book not completed). Tutors often also find they have to supplement the textbook to make up for deficiencies in the coverage of skills, tasks or grammatical topics required by university module descriptors.

The Foundations languages series is specifically designed for IWLPs and similar provision in HE. Its structure and content are informed by market research and consultation. All the authors are experienced tutors on IWLP-style university courses.

This textbook is designed to fit the typical 20/24-week teaching year and assumes two or three hours of class contact per week. There are ten units, each structured in the same way.

Element	Pages	Function	Skills
Core	6	Introduces, practises new material.	LSRW
Extra!	1	Extension work (e.g. unscripted dialogues, more demanding reading).	LR
Grammar	2	One page exposition, one page exercises.	
Vocabulary	1	German–English, listed by exercise.	
Partnerarbeit	2	Consolidation, in or out of class.	S
Weitere Übungen	2	Consolidation, private study.	LRW(S)

For more details on the book's structure, see the 'Mainly for the student' section of this Introduction. Encourage your students to read the tips on learning a language which follow it.

Various approaches are taken to the introduction of new material but most involve listening and of these the commonest is **Hören und Lesen**, with the student listening to the dialogue while following the script before tackling input exercises, with exercises then developing and applying the input material.

To facilitate the use of German in the classroom, the exercises in the unit cores are marked with an icon indicating the linguistic activity or activities involved. The icons are listed and explained at the end of the 'Mainly for the student' section on the page viii.

Central to the situations in the book is the student experience and student expectations (e.g. first job). The second half of the book has material on Frankfurt, Berlin and the consequences for Eastern Germany of German unification. Holiday adverts feature Ostfriesland and Holstein.

There are two cassettes to accompany the course. The purchase price includes a site licence which allows free duplication within institutions (some conditions apply). You should fill in the registration form which is included with Cassette 1 to obtain your licence paperwork. Digital licences are also available. Contact the publishers Palgrave Macmillan at the address given on the cassettes for more information or via www.palgrave.com/foundations/languages.

The first three sides of the cassettes cover Units 1–10 proper. The **Weitere Übungen** section is all on Side 2b. It might be that this is the only side of the cassettes which you need to make freely available to students.

Mainly for the student

What follows is a guide to the textbook. Take time to read it so you get maximum benefit from your course. There are ten units. These have the same clear, consistent structure, which you will soon get used to. Each unit is focused on one or more topics or situations in which the language is used. The short **summary** at the start of the unit tells you what the topics are and describes what you will be able to do with the language once you have completed the unit. That's a key word ('do'): while language-learning requires and develops knowledge and understanding, it means above all developing the capability of using the language.

The half dozen pages that follow are **the core** of the unit. The core contains the input (new language) for the unit and various tasks designed to help you master it and make it your own. For ease of reference, each unit is divided into numbered items, each with an icon indicating the language skill or skills you will be using (listening, reading, speaking, writing). Each item has a German title, with an English translation where necessary.

There are boxes highlighting and explaining grammatical points as they occur. Answers to the various tasks and exercises set can be found on pages 171–88.

The key inputs are carefully designed to introduce new vocabulary and/or structures. They take various forms (such as *presentation*, when you are given numbers, days of the week or how to tell the time etc., or *matching exercises*, where you are introduced to new words or structures by matching up the German with its English equivalent or a picture), but *listening items* in the form of dialogues on the audio cassettes predominate. In some, you will be asked to listen and repeat or listen first and fill in gaps, checking the script afterwards, but in most you will listen and read, following the script in the book. Then there may be *questions* to answer in German; *true/false* statements; *wordsearch* exercises.

Whatever form the input takes, it is absolutely vital to spend time and effort on this material. Be guided by your tutor. He or she will introduce it in class or ask you to prepare it in advance. If there's a word or phrase you're unsure of, turn to the vocabulary page for the unit and check. Use the recorded dialogues for listening and pronunciation practice.

The material introduced in an input exercise flows into exercises in the section(s) immediately following, enabling you to practise and master this language. After you have done these exercises in class (or gone over them there, having prepared them in advance), make sure you revise the input material and key structures in your private study time.

When you have practised and mastered material on a given topic, you will want to produce your own German (especially in speech but also, where appropriate, in writing). There are exercises to enable you to do this, simple *role-plays*, for example.

The unit core is followed by a page headed **Extra!** As the heading implies, this material makes extra demands, is that bit more challenging. It gives you the opportunity to develop further your understanding of German, taking listening and reading skills beyond the confines of the core input material while staying on related topics. Vocabulary from this page is given in the overall vocabulary list at the end of the book.

Two pages are then devoted to the **grammatical structures** you have encountered in the unit. The first gives you a clear overview of the grammar, the second provides a set of short exercises so you can test yourself (answers at the back of the book). Don't skip these pages: they simply clarify and check off grammatical structures you have met with and used in the course of the unit. This is how you become aware of the German language as a system. The **vocabulary** page gives the new words occurring in the unit core, exercise by exercise. Learn and revise them.

Each unit has two **pair-work pages** giving prompts for each partner in a structured dialogue. This material can be used in or out of the classroom to develop communication skills. The scenarios are always based on the material in the unit core, so you are securely in a known context. The challenge is to use the language you have learnt to communicate information your partner needs and to respond to what he or she says.

The **supplementary exercises** beginning on page 123 give further practice on a unit-by-unit basis and are designed to be used in private study. Answers are given at the back of the book. Work outside the classroom, both that set by the tutor and that done on your own initiative, is an essential part of a taught language course.

For reference, as well as the **answers to exercises**, there is material on using numbers and on spelling/pronunciation, both supported by recordings, and there is an overall **grammar summary**, supported by a **guide to grammatical terms**. There is also an overall **aphabetical vocabulary list** or **glossary**.

Introduction

These symbols appear next to exercises and indicate the skill or activity involved.

 Hören (listening)

 Lesen (reading)

 Sprechen (speaking)

 Schreiben (writing)

 Partnerarbeit (pair-work)

 Wortsuche (wordsearch)

 Hören und wiederholen (listening and repeating)

The word **Fragen** indicates questions. The appropriate symbol will tell you whether you are to answer in speech or writing.

 indicates that either can be chosen.

LEARNING A LANGUAGE

The introduction on the previous pages outlines the structure of this book and indicates how it is designed to be used: make sure you read it. The aim here is to give more general guidance on language learning. You should read it before you begin your course and refer to it regularly.

The advice which follows takes into account that you are beginning a taught course rather than a course of self-tuition. The good news is you will probably find it refreshingly different from the rest of your studies. The language learning programme revolves round sessions in an active language classroom rather than an anonymous lecture theatre. These regular classroom sessions will involve you in a range of social interactions, small-group activities such as pair-work and simple role-play, for example, as well as in answering questions and working through exercises individually. Feeding into these classroom sessions and flowing from them is what is called directed study, set by your tutor but allowing you a lot of scope for organising your work in ways that suit you. Beyond that is private study, where you decide the priorities.

Increasing attention is being paid in higher education to what are called transferable skills. These are skills acquired in one context which can be used in another. Successful language learning is recognised as particularly rich in transferable skills valued by employers, such as communication skills and self-management.

So your language course will be a stimulatingly different learning experience giving you both CV-enhancing competence in a language and a vehicle for developing useful transferable skills. What should you do to get maximum benefit from the course?

1. Know in advance exactly what's expected of you. Check the course or module guide and/or **syllabus** and, in particular, find out how it is assessed. Is it a semester-based or a year-long course? Is there an exam? What assessed coursework is there? When are the assessments? The course guide and assessment information will probably be expressed in terms of the four language skills of listening, speaking, reading and writing. The relative importance of these skills can vary between institutions.

2. Remember you're not on your own. You are on a taught course and **your tutor** is there to guide you through it. You benefit from his or her experience and knowledge. Using the material in the book, he or she will introduce new structures, ensure you practise them in class and then enable you to produce

similar language as you develop the capacity to use German autonomously. The tutor will also answer your questions on language and language-learning. The first rule of a taught language course, then, is to follow your guide.

3. Of course a guide can't travel for you. While your tutor will show you the way, **only you can do the learning**, both in the classroom and outside the timetabled hours.

4. **Regular attendance** at the language class is vital. Don't miss out on it. A language class is a workshop, not a lecture. The classroom is a place of performance: you *do* things that can't easily be done elsewhere. Or to put it more formally, you take part in structured activities designed to develop your linguistic competence.

5. It follows that you benefit from the language class by being active, by **participating**. This means listening carefully, working through the exercises, answering questions, taking part in simple dialogues, contributing to group work, taking the risk of speaking without the certainty of being right. It also means preparing before classes and following up afterwards ...

6. ... because what you do **outside the classroom** is vital, too. While new topics will normally be introduced in class, your tutor will also set tasks which feed in to what you will be doing in the next session. Classroom contact time is precious, normally no more than two or three hours a week, and it's essential to use it to the best effect, so make sure you get the most from each session by doing the preparation. Similarly, the tutor will ask you to follow up work in class with tasks designed to consolidate or develop what you have done.

7. You should take time to **review** and reflect on your language-learning, regularly going over what you have done in class, checking back, testing yourself. This will also enable you to decide your priorities for private study, working on aspects which are particular priorities for you (see point nine below).

8. This assumes that you are **organised**: keep a file or notebook, in which you jot down what you have done and what you plan to do. Take charge of your learning. It's a good idea to work for several shortish bursts a week rather than for a long time once a week.

9. While a lot of out-of-class work will be done at home, your university or college will probably have a Learning Centre, **Language Centre** or similar facilities in the library. Check this out and use what is on offer to reinforce and supplement what you are doing in class and from this textbook. Make sure any material you use is

suitable for your level: it will probably be classified or labelled using categories such as 'Beginners', 'Intermediate' and 'Advanced'.

Possible resources are: audio cassettes, videos, satellite TV, computer-based material, the internet, books (language courses, grammar guides, dictionaries, simple readers), magazines and newspapers, worksheets. Possible activities include: listening comprehension, pronunciation practice, reading comprehension, grammar exercises, vocabulary exercises. Worksheets and computer-based materials will usually have keys with answers.

It's possible your tutor will set specific work to be done in the Language Centre or that you will be expected to spend a certain amount of time there, otherwise you should find times during your week when you can drop in.

You can use private study to work on areas which need improvement (such as a point of grammar), to develop increased competence at a specific language skill (such as reading) or to find out more about a topic which interests you in a country where the language is spoken (such as cinema, sport or fashion). You decide the priorities.

10. Point nine referred to **grammar**. Don't be afraid of it! It is simply the term for how we talk about the way a language works. Learn the grammar and revise it as you go along. There are boxes with grammar points throughout each of the units in this book, a grammar summary for each unit and a grammar overview for the whole book. You probably feel hesitant about grammatical terms such as 'direct object' or 'definite article' but they are useful labels and easily learned. If in doubt, refer to the Guide to grammatical terms.

11. In addition to listening-based work in class, you should regularly work in your own time on the accompanying audio material. In particular, try to reproduce the **pronunciation and intonation** (the 'music' of the language) of the recorded native speakers. It's easier if you work at this from the start and establish good habits than if you approximate to the sounds of the language and have to correct them later. It is important that you repeat and speak out loud rather than in your head. Why not work with a friend?

12. Always bear in mind that, in learning a foreign language, you can normally understand (listening and reading) more than you can express (speaking and writing). And understanding is essential for communication. Above all, relax when listening or reading: remember **you don't have to be sure of every word** to get the message. Above all, you don't need to translate into your native language as you go along.

13. To develop your ability to produce the language, work regularly with a partner on some of the exercises you have already done in class. Regular **practice** is the key. Remember fluency means speaking 'flowingly', not necessarily getting everything perfectly right. It is also a good idea to dip back into earlier units in the book to check you can still do your stuff.

14. To learn a language is to acquire something that can be used. Universities and colleges are increasingly international and you will almost certainly be able to make contact with **native speakers**. Try out your language, even at a basic level. Get them to correct your pronunciation, find out about their country and culture. And enjoy yourself!

15. In fact that's the way to approach your language-learning, as something special and **enjoyable**.

Tom Carty

1 Studenten

The focus of this unit is on information about yourself and others. You will learn to give such information and to ask basic questions in formal and informal situations. You will also learn how to understand information about individuals.

1 Zwei Studenten/Two students

a „Guten Tag. Ich heiße Anne Phillips. Ich komme aus Leeds. Ich lerne Deutsch."

Wie heißt du?	Ich heiße Anne.
Woher kommst du?	Ich komme aus Leeds.
Was lernst du?	Ich lerne Deutsch.

b „Hallo. Ich heiße Marc Berlande. Ich komme aus Marseille. Ich lerne Deutsch."

Heißt du Patrick?	Nein. Ich heiße Marc.
Kommst du aus Paris?	Nein. Ich komme aus Marseille.
Lernst du Spanisch?	Nein. Ich lerne Deutsch.

Grammatik

I	**ich heiße**	**ich komme**	**ich lerne**
you?	**heißt du?**	**kommst du?**	**lernst du?**

2 Und du?/And you?

With a partner, introduce yourselves and ask/answer questions.

3 Wo wohnst du?/Where do you live?

a „Ich heiße Anke Christiansen. Ich bin Deutsche. Ich komme aus Flensburg, aber ich wohne in Birmingham in England. Ich bin Studentin."

Grammatik

Gender (masculine/feminine):
Student/Studentin
Deutscher/Deutsche

Wie heißt du?	Ich heiße Anke.
Bist du Deutsche?	Ja.
Woher kommst du?	Ich komme aus Flensburg.
Wo wohnst du?	Ich wohne in Birmingham.

b „Ich heiße Peter Fiedler. Ich bin Österreicher. Ich komme aus Wien, aber ich wohne in New York. Ich bin Student."

Grammatik

Ich bin Student.
= I am *a* student.

Wie heißt du?	Ich heiße Peter.
Bist du Deutscher?	Nein. Ich bin Österreicher.
Woher kommst du?	Ich komme aus Wien.
Wo wohnst du?	Ich wohne in New York.

4 Rollenspiel/Role-play

With a partner, take on the roles of an interviewer and Anke or Peter, asking and answering as many questions as you can.

5 Welches Land?/Which country?

See if you can match up the nationalities with the countries.

Nationalitäten (m/f)

a Deutscher/Deutsche
b Österreicher/Österreicherin
c Engländer/Engländerin
d Grieche/Griechin
e Franzose/Französin
f Schotte/Schottin

g Belgier/Belgierin
h Ire/Irin
i Spanier/Spanierin
j Däne/Dänin
k Waliser/Waliserin
l Italiener/Italienerin

Länder					
Griechenland	Wales	Österreich	Schottland	Spanien	England
Dänemark	Frankreich	Irland	Deutschland	Italien	Belgien

6 Fünf Länder/Five countries

Listen carefully to the recording. You will hear five of the countries from exercise 5: write down which ones.

a _____ b _____ c _____

d _____ e _____

7 Marianne Möller

Without consulting the script below, listen to the interview. What do you notice about the questions? After looking at the script, compare it with exercise 3!

Wie heißen Sie? Ich heiße Marianne Möller.
Woher kommen Sie? Ich komme aus Hamburg. Ich bin Deutsche.
Wo wohnen Sie? Ich wohne in Manchester.
Sind Sie Studentin? Nein. Ich bin Lehrerin.

Grammatik

In all languages we speak differently according to the situation and the person we're talking to: a job interview is not like a chat with your best friend. German, like many other languages, has different words for 'you', familiar and formal. The questions in exercises 1 and 3 use **du**, the *familiar* word for 'you' and the questions in exercise 5 use **Sie**, the *formal* alternative.

Note the verb endings:

	familiar	*formal*
	kom<u>mst</u> du?	**komm<u>en</u> Sie?**
	wohn<u>st</u> du?	**wohn<u>en</u> Sie?**
The verb **sein** (to be) is *irregular*:	**bist du?**	**sind Sie?**

Students among themselves use the familiar **du**. You also use it with friends, family members and children. Otherwise the more formal **Sie** is used. Learn to use both.

8 Fragen/Questions

Fill in the table with the appropriate questions, then take turns with a partner to ask for the same information in familiar and then in formal mode.

Ask	*familiar*	*formal*
his/her name	a wie heißt	b *Wie heißen Sie?*
where she/he is from	c woher kommt sie	d woher kommen sie
where he/she lives	e wo wohnst die	f wo wohnen sie
whether she/he is English	g	h
whether he/she is a student	i *Bist du Student(in)?*	j

9 Kirsty und Tom

Read the remarks made by Kirsty and Tom, then fill in the gaps in the questions put to them in the interview. Finally, check what you have written by listening to the two interview extracts on the recording.

Ich bin Deutscher. Ich komme aus Berlin und wohne in London. Ich bin Lehrer.

Ich wohne in Frankfurt, aber ich komme aus Glasgow. Ich bin Schottin und lerne Deutsch.

a *From Tom's interview:*

i _____ Sie Engländer? Nein, ich bin Deutscher.

ii Wo _____ Sie? Ich wohne in London.

iii Kommen Sie _____ Frankfurt? Nein.

b *From Kirsty's interview:*

i _____ ? In Frankfurt.

ii _____ ? Nein, ich bin Schottin.

iii _____ ? Ja, ich bin Studentin.

10 Wer ist das?/Who is that?

a Das ist Marianne Möller. Sie ist Lehrerin.

Sie wohnt in Manchester, aber sie kommt aus Hamburg.

Sie ist Deutsche.

b Das ist Tom Paschke. Er ist Lehrer.

Er kommt aus Berlin und wohnt in London.

Er ist Deutscher.

c Das ist Marc Berlande. Er ist Student in Glasgow.

Er kommt aus Marseille. Er ist Franzose.

d Das ist Sue Edwards aus Birmingham.

Sie ist Studentin in Leipzig.

Sie ist Engländerin. Sie lernt Deutsch.

Grammatik

I	ich heiße	ich wohne	ich komme	ich bin
he	er heißt	er wohnt	er kommt	er ist
she	sie heißt	sie wohnt	sie kommt	sie ist

The first three verbs follow the *regular* pattern. Remember the last one, the verb **sein** (to be), is *irregular*.

11 Fragen

a
i Wer ist das?
ii Ist sie Sekretärin?
iii Wo wohnt sie?
iv Woher kommt sie?
v Ist sie Amerikanerin?

b
i Wie heißt er?
ii Ist er Polizist?
iii Wohnt er in Manchester?
iv Kommt er aus Köln?
v Ist er Deutscher?

c
i Heißt er Adham Sawfik?
ii Ist er Lehrer?
iii Wo wohnt er?
iv Woher kommt er?
v Ist er Schotte?

d
i Wer ist das?
ii Woher kommt sie?
iii Wo wohnt sie?
iv Lernt sie Spanisch?
v Ist sie Deutsche?

Grammatik

Don't confuse: **wer** = 'who' **wo** = 'where'!

12 Vier Studenten/Four students

a You should be able to work out what the missing verbs are in the following statements. Check your decisions by listening to the recording.

i Ich ___bin___ Deutsche. Ich ___wohne in___ (heiße) Silke und
___komme___ aus Stuttgart. Ich <u>studiere</u> Sport und Englisch.

ii Ich ___heiße___ Eva. Ich ___bin___ Spanierin, aber ich studiere in England. Ich studiere Literatur und ___lerne___ Englisch –
und Deutsch!

iii Ich ___heiße___ Michael. Ich ___komme___ aus Cork in Irland.
Ich ___bin___ Student in Birmingham. Ich studiere Biologie. Ich
___Lerne___ auch Deutsch.

iv Guten Tag. Ich ___heiße___ Yannis und ich ___komme___ aus
Griechenland. Ich ___bin___ Student hier in England. Ich
___wohne.___ in Brighton und studiere Psychologie.

b Now turn the students' statements beginning with **ich** (I) into statements beginning **er** (he) or **sie** (she) as appropriate.

Example: Ich heiße Karl → Er heißt Karl; Ich bin Studentin → Sie ist Studentin

13 Vorstellungen/Introductions

Introduce yourself to your classmates using exercise 12 as a model. Your tutor will then ask another member of the class to report what you said. (Check the academic subjects in the unit vocabulary on page 10: if yours is not there, use a dictionary or ask your tutor for help.)

14 Was sind Sie von Beruf?/What's your job?

Take on the role of a character from the first column, choosing an item from each of the other columns. Make sure the words for nationality and job are the correct gender for the person you are playing! Introduce yourself to a partner.

Example: *Guten Tag. Ich heiße Paul Dawson. Ich bin Engländer und ich komme aus Birmingham. Ich bin Automechaniker von Beruf.*

Name	aus ...	Land	Beruf
Paul Dawson	Paris	Deutsche(r)	Busfahrerin
Anne Doyle	Rom	Franzose/Französin	Student
Javed Siddiqi	München	Ire/Irin	Journalistin
Richard Barrow	Liverpool	Engländer(in)	Automechaniker
Petra Walters	Birmingham	Italiener(in)	Lehrerin
Colette Petit	Glasgow	Schotte/Schottin	Kellner
Paolo Zinetti	Galway		Polizist
Anke Herrmann	Sheffield		Sekretärin

 15 Wer ist das?

a Martin Heine ist Deutscher und kommt aus Leipzig. Er ist Student in Marburg. Er studiert Geschichte. Martins Freundin heißt Cristina. Sie kommt aus Rom und ist Sekretärin. Sie arbeitet in Frankfurt. Martin lernt Italienisch.

Fragen:
i	Woher kommt Martin?	**v**	Was ist sie von Beruf?
ii	Studiert er in Leipzig?	**vi**	Wo arbeitet sie?
iii	Wer ist Cristina?		
iv	Ist sie Deutsche?		

b Isabelle Bruneau ist Studentin in England und arbeitet als Kellnerin. Sie kommt aus Lyon in Frankreich. Sie lernt Englisch und Deutsch. Sie wohnt in London.

Fragen:
i Arbeitet Isabelle?
ii Ist sie Engländerin?
iii Wo ist Lyon?
iv Wo wohnt sie?

c „Hallo. Mein Name ist Bernd Voigt. Ich komme aus Bremen in Deutschland, aber ich wohne und arbeite in Salzburg in Österreich. Ich bin Journalist."

Fragen:
i Wie heißt er?
ii Wo ist Bremen?
iii Ist er Österreicher?
iv Was ist er von Beruf?

 16 Guten Tag, Herr Heine

One of you takes on the role of Martin from exercise 15, the other is an interviewer. The interviewer should ask him: what he's called, where he's from, what he is studying, where he is studying, where Cristina is from, where she works and what her job is. This is a formal interview, so use **Sie** for 'you'. (Remember it takes a different verb ending from **sie** 'she'!)

 17 Hallo, Silke!

Draft the text of an email introducing yourself to Silke. Ask her some questions as well, using the familiar **du**. (You will still often find it written with a capital D in letters, although the recent spelling reform has changed that.)

Am Ende der Stunde/At the end of the class

„Auf Wiedersehen!"/„Tschüss!"
„Bis nächste Woche!"

Extra!

18 Was macht er/sie?/What does he/she do?

Listen to the three speakers talking about themselves. You are not expected to understand everything they say but you ought to be able to note the information requested in the table and report back on it in German to the class/your partner.

Name	studiert?	aus?	wohnt in …?	arbeitet?
Annie	Literature	frank.	Dusseldorf	Bar
Jürgen	journalist	Birmingham	Austria	
Padma	Psychologie	Birmingham	Leeds	

19 Ursula ist Automechanikerin/Ursula is a car mechanic

Read this short article right through. Don't reach for your dictionary: you will probably not understand every word but you don't need to.

> Ursula Eggebrecht wohnt in Bremen. Die junge Amerikanerin (23 Jahre alt) kommt aus New York, aber sie studiert in Europa. Sie ist Psychologiestudentin an der Universität Bremen. Warum studiert sie nicht in New York oder Boston? „Mein Vater ist Deutscher und meine Mutter kommt aus Amsterdam", antwortet Ursula. „Ich bin Amerikanerin und Europäerin. Ich studiere hier in Deutschland und nächstes Jahr bin ich in Holland." Aber das kostet Geld und Ursula arbeitet auch. „Ja, ich habe einen interessanten Job – ich bin Automechanikerin!" Ursula repariert Autos.

a Once you've got the gist of the article, summarise it in English in two or three sentences.

b Now try to answer the questions in German.

 i Wo wohnt Ursula? _____

 ii Woher kommt sie? _____

 iii Was studiert sie? _____

 iv Studiert Ursula in Holland? _____

 v Arbeitet Ursula? _____

Grammatik

- **Nouns**

 - Always begin with a *capital letter*: **Lehrer**, **Studentin**.

 - Have a *gender*: so far you have met *masculine* nouns
 e.g. **Student**, **Engländer**, **Deutscher**, **Journalist**,
 and their *feminine* equivalents
 e.g. **Studentin**, **Engländerin**, **Deutsche**, **Journalistin**
 These nouns refer to people but, as you will see later, all German nouns have a gender.

 - No word for 'a' with professions and nationality:
 Ich bin Deutscher. I am <u>a</u> German.

- **Pronouns**

 So far you've met **ich** (I), **er** (he) and **sie** (she), as well as **du** (informal/familiar you) and **Sie** (formal you).

- **Verbs**

 - Regular verb pattern
 The infinitive (basic form) ends in **-en**: e.g. **wohnen** (to live).
 The **Sie**-form is the same as the infinitive.

ich wohn<u>e</u>	I live	**er/sie wohn<u>t</u>**	he/she lives
du wohn<u>st</u>	you live (informal)	**Sie wohn<u>en</u>**	you live (formal)

 Other regular verbs: **heißen***, **kommen**, **lernen**, **studieren**, **arbeiten***
 (* **heißen** has the form **du heißt**, with no extra **s**; **arbeiten** has the forms **du arbeit<u>est</u>** and **er/sie arbeit<u>et</u>**.)

 - Irregular verb **sein** to be

ich bin	I am	**er/sie ist**	he/she is
du bist	you are (informal)	**Sie sind**	you are (formal)

- **Forming questions**

 - Invert the subject-verb order used in statements:
 Statement: **Er wohnt in Berlin.** Question: **Wohnt er in Berlin?**
 subject – verb verb – subject

 - Note the 'W-words' introducing questions:

<u>Was</u> studieren Sie?	<u>Wer</u> ist das?	<u>Wie</u> heißt er?
<u>Wo</u> wohnst du?	<u>Woher</u> kommt sie?	<u>Warum</u> studierst du hier?

Grammatikübungen

1 Find nouns from the list to fill the gaps.

a Monika ist _____. Sie studiert Musik. Sie ist _____ – sie kommt aus Dresden.

b Martin ist _____ an der Universität. Er kommt aus Köln – er ist
_____.

c Eva kommt aus Madrid – sie ist _____. Sie arbeitet – sie ist
_____.

d Paolo kommt aus Rom – er ist _____. Er arbeitet – er ist
_____.

Journalist	Deutsche	Spanierin	Student
Italiener	Lehrerin	Studentin	Deutscher

2 Fill the gaps with a pronoun.

Peter ist Amerikaner. **a** _____ kommt aus New York. „Wohnen **b** _____ in New York, Peter?" – „Nein, **c** _____ wohne in Los Angeles und
d _____ arbeite in Hollywood."

Interessant, **e** _____ arbeitet in Hollywood! „Susi, arbeitest **f** _____ auch in Hollywood?" – „Nein. **g** _____ bin Studentin in San Francisco."

3 Complete the sentences with an appropriate form of a verb.

Der Lehrer **a** _____ Karl. Er **b** _____ in Hannover, er
c _____ aus Graz. „Woher **d** _____ Sie?" – „Ich
e _____ aus Graz." – „ **f** _____ das in Deutschland?" – „Nein,
in Österreich. Ich **g** _____ Österreicher." – „Sie **h** _____
Österreicher!"

4 Reconstruct the questions to which the following are the answers. (There could be more than one possibility.)

a Sie heißt Marianne.　　　**e** Ich komme aus München.
b Ich wohne in Liverpool.　　**f** Nein, ich bin Deutscher.
c Ja, ich bin Student.　　　**g** Er ist Kellner.
d Er arbeitet in Hamburg.　　**h** Sie lernt Deutsch.

5 W-Questions. Insert **was/wer/wie/wo/~~wohn~~** woher as appropriate.

„ **a** _____ ist das?" – „Das ist Martin." – „ **b** _____ wohnt er?" – „In Berlin." – „ **c** _____
heißt er? – „Braun. Martin Braun." – „ **d** _____ kommt er? – „Aus Berlin." – „ **e** _____ ist
er von Beruf?" – „Er ist Student." – „ **f** _____ studiert er?" – „Biologie."

Vokabeln

Exercise 1

Guten Tag	hello
ich	I
heißen	to be called
kommen (aus)	to come (from)
lernen	to learn
Deutsch	German (language)
wie heißt du?	what's your name?
du	you (informal)
wo(her)	where (from)
was	what
hallo	hello (informal)
nein	no

Exercise 3

ich bin	I am
Deutsche(r)	German (f/m)
aber	but
wohnen	to live
bist du?	are you?
ja	yes
Österreicher(in)	Austrian (m/f)
Wien	Vienna
Hannover	Hanover

Exercise 4

München	Munich

Exercise 5

Engländer(in)	Englishman/-woman
Grieche/Griechin	Greek (m/f)
Franzose/Französin	Frenchman/-woman
Schotte/Schottin	Scot (m/f)
Belgier(in)	Belgian (m/f)
Ire/Irin	Irishman/-woman
Spanier(in)	Spaniard (m/f)
Däne/Dänin	Dane (m/f)
Waliser(in)	Welshman/-woman
Italiener(in)	Italian (m/f)
Griechenland	Greece
Österreich	Austria
Schottland	Scotland
Spanien	Spain
Dänemark	Denmark
Frankreich	France
Irland	Ireland
Deutschland	Germany
Italien	Italian
Belgien	Belgium

Exercise 7

Sie	you (formal)
Lehrer(in)	teacher (m/f)

Exercise 10

wer	who
wer ist das?	who is that?
ist	is
er/sie	he/she

Exercise 11

Sekretärin	secretary (f)
Amerikaner(in)	American (m/f)
Polizist(in)	policeman/woman
Spanisch	Spanish (language)
Köln	Cologne

Exercise 12

studieren	to study
Sport	sport
Englisch	English (language)
Literatur	literature
hier	here
auch	also, as well
Biologie	biology
Psychologie	psychology

Exercise 14

Was sind Sie von Beruf?	What's your job?
Busfahrer(in)	bus driver (m/f)
Journalist(in)	journalist (m/f)
Automechaniker(in)	car mechanic (m/f)
Kellner(in)	waiter/waitress

Exercise 15

Geschichte	history
Freundin	(girl)friend
Freund	(boy)friend
arbeiten	to work
als	as
mein Name	my name

Extra/Grammatik/Weitere Übungen

warum	why
mit	with
und	and

Partnerarbeit

A

1 Vorstellungen/Introductions

Introduce yourself to your partner. After an initial greeting, tell him/her:

- your name
- the town or city you're from
- your nationality
- where you live

- that you're a student
- what you're studying
- that you work (if you do)
- … and what your job is

When you've got all the information across, your partner will check it back with you by making a series of statements about you e.g. **Sie heißen Martin** ('Your name is Martin'): tell her/him whether she/he is right and correct her/him where necessary (**Nein, ich heiße Mark!**).

richtig right, correct
falsch wrong
Können Sie das bitte wiederholen? Please could you repeat that?

2 Rollenspiel/Role-play

Your partner will take on up to four roles. Ask questions to obtain the information needed to fill in the form relating to each 'person' he/she plays. Their first names are Alex, Bernie, Chris and Sam. Use **du** or **Sie** but be consistent.

Name: _____ _____ _____ _____

Nationalität: _____ _____ _____ _____

Wohnort: _____ _____ _____ _____

Beruf: _____ _____ _____ _____

Arbeitet in: _____ _____ _____ _____

Partnerarbeit

1 Vorstellungen/Introductions

Greet your partner in German, then listen carefully to what he or she tells you, jotting down key words when it helps. You can ask for any information again but remember to stick to German!

When you are ready, check back on the information with your partner by making a series of statements. Use the formal **Sie** e.g. **Sie kommen aus Manchester**. He/She will then tell you whether or not you are correct.

richtig	right, correct
falsch	wrong
Können Sie das bitte wiederholen?	Please could you repeat that?

2 Rollenspiel/Role-play

Your partner has a form to fill in about the roles you are to play, which are outlined below. Answer her/his questions so that he or she can get the information right. The names have been chosen so that they can apply to a male or female but remember to use the correct gender for nationality and job. Speak only German!

Your name is Alex Andrews. You're English and you come from Liverpool but you live and work in New York as a journalist.

You are Chris Bradley. You're a teacher. You live and work in Denmark. You are Irish from Limerick.

You are Bernie Lyons. You are a bus driver in Glasgow. You live in Paisley and originally come from Motherwell.

Your name is Sam Humphreys. You work as a waiter/waitress and study literature. You come from Brighton and live in London, where you study and work.

2 Bibliothek oder Diskothek?

In this unit you will learn to talk about your daily routine.
You will also learn the numbers 1–99 and start using
the 24-hour clock.

1 Zahlen/Numbers

a Listen and repeat:

0	null	6	sechs	11	elf	16	sechzehn
1	eins	7	sieben	12	zwölf	17	siebzehn
2	zwei	8	acht	13	dreizehn	18	achtzehn
3	drei	9	neun	14	vierzehn	19	neunzehn
4	vier	10	zehn	15	fünfzehn		
5	fünf						

b Circle the numbers you hear.

3 5 6 9 12 14 17 18

c Write the numbers you hear (use figures).

_____ _____ _____ _____ _____ _____ _____ _____

d Write down a number and see if your partner can say it, then swap roles.

2 Zahlen

20	zwanzig	25	fünfu........
21	einundzwanzig	26	sechsundzwanzig
22	zweiundzwanzig	27	siebenundzwanzig
23	dreiundzwanzig	28	achtundzwanzig
24	vierundzwanzig	29	neunundzwanzig

3 Logik!/Logic!

See if you can work out the pattern for numbers from 30 to 99:

a Match the figures to the correct words.

73	einundachtzig
54	siebenundvierzig
66	dreiundsiebzig
47	achtunddreißig
95	vierundfünfzig
81	sechsundsechzig
38	fünfundneunzig

What is surprising about the word for 30?

b Write in the words.

30 _____
40 _____
50 _____
60 _____
70 _____
80 _____
90 _____

c Circle the five numbers you hear.

i 34/43 **ii** 45/54 **iii** 56/65 **iv** 78/87 **v** 89/98

d Say out loud:

92 44 79 31 63 57 85

4 Die Uhrzeit/The time

Once you are familiar with numbers you can start telling the time. The 24-hour clock is used more in German-speaking countries than it is in the English-speaking world.

9:00	9:10	9:15	9:25	9:30	9:45
9:59	21:05	21:20	21:35	21:50	

Grammatik

9 Uhr 9 o'clock **9.05 = neun Uhr fünf**

<u>um</u> **9.15 = um neun Uhr fünfzehn**
<u>at</u> nine fifteen

– Wie viel Uhr ist es?/Wie spät ist es?
What's the time?

– Es ist 9.45 (neun Uhr fünfundvierzig).

Grammatik

Definite article ('the'):
der (masculine)

der Morgen/der Vormittag morning	**am Morgen/am Vormittag** morgens/vormittags	
der Nachmittag afternoon	**am Nachmittag**	**nachmittags**
der Abend evening	**am Abend**	**abends**

 5 Am Morgen/In the morning

a Listen to Ralf talking about his morning routine, then fill in the times he gives. (Use figures.)

i

Ich stehe um
_____ auf.

ii

Ich frühstücke um
_____ .

iii

Ich gehe um
_____ an
die Universität.

iv

Die Vorlesung
beginnt um
_____ .

v

Ich trinke um
_____ Kaffee.

vi

Ich gehe um
_____ in die
Bibliothek.

Grammatik

Definite article ('the'):
die Vorlesung (feminine)

Grammatik

Aufstehen is a *separable verb*: its prefix
(**auf**) goes to the end of the sentence:
ich stehe früh auf I get up early

 b Fragen:

 i Steht Ralf um 8.00 auf?
 ii Wann frühstückt er?
 iii Um wie viel Uhr geht er an die Universität?
 iv Was beginnt um 9.00?
 v Trinkt er um 10.15 Cola?
 vi Wohin geht er um 11.00?

Grammatik

wann? when?
um wie viel Uhr? at what time?

6 Partnerübung/Partnerwork

Ask a partner the following three questions about his/her own morning routine using formal question forms with **Sie**. He/She then asks you the questions but this time using the informal **du** form.

Um wie viel Uhr … stehen Sie auf?/frühstücken Sie?/gehen Sie an die Uni?
 stehst du auf?/frühstückst du?/gehst du an die Uni?

7 Am Nachmittag/In the afternoon

„Was machen Sie nachmittags?"

„Ich gehe oft in die Bibliothek. Manchmal gehe ich in das Sportzentrum."

„Und heute?"

„Heute Nachmittag habe ich um 15 Uhr eine Vorlesung. Um 16 Uhr spiele ich Basketball."

Grammatik

Ich <u>gehe</u> oft in die Bibliothek. Oft <u>gehe</u> ich in die Bibliothek.
(See the item on word order in the unit Grammar section on page 20.)

Grammatik

Definite article ('the'):
das Sportzentrum (neuter)
Indefinite article ('a'):
<u>eine</u> Vorlesung (feminine)

Grammatik

Haben (to have) is *irregular*:
ich habe
du hast Sie haben
er/sie hat

8 Und was machen Sie nachmittags?

Describe your afternoons to the rest of the class.

| Ich gehe … | in die Bibliothek
in die Mensa/Kantine
in das Sportzentrum
in die Stadt
an die Universität
nach Hause
zur Arbeit
schwimmen | Ich spiele … | Basketball
Fußball
Tischtennis
Gitarre |
| | | Ich habe… | eine Vorlesung
ein Seminar
eine Deutschstunde |

Grammatik

Indefinite article ('a'): **<u>ein</u> Seminar** (neuter)

9 Heute Nachmittag/This afternoon

Describe what Tony is doing this afternoon:

13.30	library
14.30	into town
16.00	German class
17.10	sports centre: football
18.45	home

10 Was machen Sie abends?/What do you do in the evening?

Match the German verbs with their jumbled-up English equivalents.

Ich ...
1 bleibe zu Hause
2 gehe aus
3 sehe fern (*separable*)
4 höre Musik
5 lese ein Buch
6 schreibe E-Mails
7 tanze
8 trinke Bier

I ...
a listen to music
b drink beer
c stay at home
d dance
e go out
f watch TV
g read a book
h write emails

11 Abends

a Listen to the recording and see if you can complete the script by noting down what Bernd says.

b Then give the information in English: how often do the four students do the various things they mention?

Petra: „Abends gehe ich selten aus. Ich sehe oft fern oder höre Musik. Manchmal lese ich."

Ralf: „Ich bleibe nie zu Hause. Ich gehe in die Kneipe oder die Diskothek."

Jasmin: „Ich bleibe immer zu Hause. Ich schreibe E-Mails, aber ich sehe selten fern. Ich gehe um 23.00 ins Bett."

Bernd: „_Ich gehe oft aus. Ich trinke bie manchmal sbielch football._ _____ "

immer	oft	manchmal	selten	nie
always	often	sometimes	rarely	never

 12 Ihr Tagesablauf/Your daily routine

Fragen:

a Um wie viel Uhr stehen Sie auf?
b Gehen Sie abends aus?
c Wann frühstücken Sie?
d Was machen Sie abends zu Hause?
e Wann gehen Sie an die Universität?

f Wann gehen Sie ins Bett?
g Was machen Sie nachmittags?
h Um wie viel Uhr ist die Deutschstunde?
i Was machen Sie um 8.30, 11.00, 15.00, 21.00?

 13 Partnerübung/Partnerwork

Now ask a fellow student the questions from exercise 12, using the informal **du**-form.

 14 Annas Mahlzeiten/Anna's meals

Anna ist Studentin. Zum Frühstück isst sie Toast oder Joghurt. Sie trinkt eine Tasse Kaffee. Um 13.00 geht sie immer in die Mensa. Zum Mittagessen isst sie normalerweise ein Käsebrot oder ein Schinkenbrot und sie trinkt eine Cola. Das Abendessen ist um 18.00. Sie isst Nudeln mit Fisch oder Salat. Sie trinkt ein Glas Orangensaft. Sehr gesund!

das Frühstück	**zum Frühstück**	for breakfast
das Mittagessen	**zum Mittagessen**	for lunch
das Abendessen	**zum Abendessen**	for dinner

Fragen:

a Was trinkt Anna morgens?
b Geht sie oft in die Mensa?
c Wann isst sie ein Käsebrot?

d Trinkt sie abends eine Cola?
e Was isst sie zum Abendessen?
f Und was trinkt sie?

Grammatik

Learn the genders of nouns (see unit vocabulary page 22).

e.g.	*masculine*	*feminine*	*neuter*
'the'	**der Fisch**	**die Tasse**	**das Glas**
'a/an'	**ein**	**eine**	**ein**

Grammatik

Essen (to eat) is a *strong verb*: **ich esse**
(vowel change) **du isst** **Sie essen**
er/sie isst

 15 Rollenspiel/Role-play

With a partner, role-play a conversation with Anna. Ask her as many questions as possible, using the information in exercise 14. Use the informal **du**-form.

Extra!

16 Kontraste: zwei Studenten

Read the following timeplanners belonging to two students from Regensburg University and answer the questions below.

Vera

11.00:	aufstehen
12.30:	fernsehen („Heiße Liebe")
14.00:	Kaffee trinken mit Susanne (Café Bauer)
16.00:	Vorlesung (Literatur)
19.00:	Abendessen (Pizza und Cola)
20.30:	Kino (Film: Moulin Rouge)
23.00:	ausgehen und Wein trinken (Bar „Bei Joe")
1.00:	nach Hause gehen

Walter

7.00:	aufstehen
7.15:	Frühstück (Orangensaft und Müsli)
7.45:	schwimmen gehen
9.00:	Vorlesung (Chemie)
12.00:	Bibliothek
13.00:	Mittagessen (Mensa)
15.00:	Seminar (Politik)
19.00:	Abendessen (Salat) und Buch lesen

> **in die Bar** to the bar
> **ins Kino** to the cinema

Fragen:

a Trinkt Vera mit Paul Kaffee?
b Beginnt Veras Vorlesung um 14.00?
c Was macht sie am Abend?
d Wann geht Vera ins Kino?
e Um wie viel Uhr steht Walter auf?
f Was macht er am Vormittag?
g Wohin geht Walter um 12.00?
h Geht er abends aus?

17 Konversationen im Café

Listen to the two conversations at a cafe in Heidelberg. Although there will be some words you have not come across yet, you will be able to get the gist of the exchanges. See if you can tell when a conversation is formal and when it is more informal.

Collect as much information as you can about:
Annette Klaus Herr Wolf Frau Petri

Grammatik

- **Articles**

 - definite ('the'): **der** (masculine) **die** (feminine) **das** (neuter)
 - indefinite ('a'/'an'): **ein** **eine** **ein**
 - All nouns have a gender. To make sure you remember the gender of a noun, always learn it with its definite article:

 der Morgen **die Vorlesung** **das Frühstück**

- **Verbs**

 - The infinitive of *separable verbs* has a prefix:

 aufstehen, **ausgehen**, **fernsehen**.

 In the present tense, this prefix goes to the end of the sentence:

 Ich stehe um 8 Uhr auf. **Gehen Sie oft aus?**

 Separable verbs are formed by adding a prefix to an existing verb: the three above are formed from **stehen** (to stand), **gehen** (to go) and **sehen** (to see).

 - <u>Strong verbs</u> have a change of vowel-sound in the **du**-form and the **er/sie**-form:

lesen (to read)		**fernsehen** (to watch TV)	
ich lese	du l<u>ie</u>st	ich sehe fern	du s<u>ie</u>hst fern
Sie lesen	er/sie l<u>ie</u>st	Sie sehen fern	er/sie s<u>ie</u>ht fern

 (**Fernsehen** is separable and strong!)

 - **haben** (to have) is *irregular*:

 ich habe

 du hast Sie haben

 er/sie hat

- **Word order**

 - Adverbs come immediately after the verb: **Ich bleibe immer zu Hause.**

 Compare with: I *always* stay at home.

 - The verb has second place in the sentence:

 Take the statement **Sie geht um neun Uhr an die Uni(versität).**

 You can start with the time expression but, unlike in English, the subject (**sie**) is put after the verb, which keeps its position.

 Um neun Uhr geht sie an die Universität.

 - Note questions: **Gehst du heute in die Bibliothek?**

 Wann gehst du in die Bibliothek?

Grammatikübungen

1 Test yourself on the genders of the nouns you have met so far by putting them into masculine, feminine and neuter columns in your notebook.

Then check the answers on page 173 to see whether you were right.

Orangensaft	Kneipe
Diskothek	Lehrer
Bier	Kaffee
Tasse	E-Mail
Abend	Sportzentrum
Fisch	Glas
Toast	Studentin
Käsebrot	Deutschstunde

2 Complete the following sentences with an appropriate form of a verb from the list. Make sure you know which are irregular, separable and strong!

a Wann _____beginnt_____ die Vorlesung?
b Um 11.00 _____trinke_____ ich Kaffee.
c Er _____geht_____ nachmittags in die Bibliothek.
d Abends _____leist_____ sie ein Buch.
e Was _____essen_____ Sie zum Frühstück?
f Ich _____gehe_____ selten ~~aus~~. Ich _____bleibe_____ zu Hause.
g _____Hast_____ du heute ein Seminar?
h Um wie viel Uhr _____aufsteht_____ er _____ausgeht_____?

essen	aufstehen	bleiben	trinken	beginnen	gehen	ausgehen	haben	lesen	

3 Insert a time/frequency expression into each of the sentences **(i)** after the verb and **(ii)** at the start of the sentence. Make any necessary adjustments to the word order.

Example:

Sie geht an die Universität. (in the morning)

Sie geht <u>morgens</u> an die Universität. <u>Morgens</u> geht sie an die Universität.

a Eva geht in die Bibliothek. (in the afternoon)
b Ich esse Toast. (sometimes) ~~Manchmal~~ Ich esse tows' Ich esse manchmal tows.
c Er sieht fern. Ich sieht immer fern (always)
d Ich gehe nach Hause. (at 5 pm) Ich gehe punkt fünf nach Hause.
e Sie spielt Tischtennis. (often) Sie spielt oj Tischtennis
f Ich habe eine Deutschstunde. (today) Ich habe es Heute eine Deutschstd

21

2 Bibliothek oder Diskothek?

Vokabeln

Aufgabe 5

um	(before a time) at
aufstehen *sep*	to get up
frühstücken	to have breakfast
gehen	to go
an die Universität	to the university
die Vorlesung	lecture
beginnen	to begin
trinken	to drink
der Kaffee	coffee
in die Bibliothek	to the library
wann?	when?
um wie viel Uhr?	what time?
wohin?	where to?

Aufgabe 7

machen	to do
nachmittags	in the afternoon
oft	often
manchmal	sometimes
in das Sportzentrum	to the sports centre
heute	today
heute Nachmittag	this afternoon
spielen	to play
der Basketball	basketball

Aufgabe 8

die Mensa	canteen
die Kantine	canteen
die Stadt	town
nach Hause	(go) home
zur Arbeit	to work
schwimmen	to swim
Fußball	football
Tischtennis	table tennis
Gitarre	guitar
das Seminar	seminar
die Deutschstunde	German lesson

Aufgabe 10

bleiben	to stay, remain
zu Hause	at home
ausgehen *sep*	to go out
fernsehen* *sep*	to watch TV
Musik hören	to listen to music
lesen*	to read
das Buch	book

schreiben	to write
die E-Mail	email
tanzen	to dance
das Bier	beer

Aufgabe 11

abends	in the evening
oder	or
selten	seldom, rarely
nie	never
die Kneipe	pub
die Diskothek	discotheque
immer	always
ins Bett gehen	to go to bed
ins = in das	into

Aufgabe 14

die Mahlzeit	meal
Mahlzeiten	meals
das Frühstück	breakfast
zum Frühstück	for breakfast
essen*	to eat
isst	eats
der Toast	toast
der/das Joghurt	yoghurt
die Tasse	cup
eine Tasse Kaffee	a cup of coffee
das Mittagessen	lunch
zum Mittagessen	for lunch
normalerweise	normally
das Käsebrot	cheese sandwich
das Schinkenbrot	ham sandwich
die Cola	cola
das Abendessen	evening meal, dinner
zum Abendessen	for dinner
Nudeln *pl*	pasta
der Fisch	fish
der Salat	salad
das Glas	glass
der Orangensaft	orange juice
ein Glas Orangensaft	a glass of orange juice
sehr	very
gesund	healthy

* Verb strong in present tense

Partnerarbeit

A

1 Morgen/Tomorrow

A friend phones and wants to arrange a time when he/she can meet you. Greet your partner and tell him/her that

11:00 you have a lecture

13:00 you're going to the canteen for a cheese sandwich

14:30 you're going to the library

17:00 you have an Italian class

19:30 you play table-tennis

Remember to use the 24-hour clock!

Your partner will then ask some questions to make sure that he/she has got the correct information.

2 Wann?/When?

Ask your partner when he/she does things during the day and make a note of the information. Use the familiar **du**-form. Ask about ...

getting up	going into town
breakfast	playing football
lecture	watching television
drinking coffee	drinking beer

Do this exercise first using the informal, then using the formal 'you'.

Fahrräder auf dem Campus

Partnerarbeit

1 Morgen/Tomorrow

You phone a friend in order to arrange a time when the two of you can meet up. After the initial greeting, ask your friend what he or she is doing tomorrow. Form questions beginning **was** or **wann**. Use the familiar **du**-form.

… *am Morgen?* … *am Nachmittag?*
… *in die Mensa?* … *Tischtennis?*

2 Wann?/When?

Your partner asks you a number of questions about your activities in the course of a day. Answer the questions using the information below.

7.45	aufstehen	12.00	Stadt
8.00	Frühstück	15.15	Fußball spielen
10.00	Vorlesung	17.20	fernsehen
11.30	Kaffee	19.00	Bier

Fahrräder auf dem Campus

3 Familie

In this unit you will learn to talk about family and about everyday objects.

 1 Stephanies Fotoalbum

Listen to Stephanie talking about her family. Follow what she says by referring to the pictures below.

meine Eltern

meine Mutter
Martina (51)

mein Vater
Christian (53)

ich **Stephanie** (19)
(ledig)

mein Freund
Alex (21)

meine Schwester **Caroline** (25) (verheiratet),
ihr Mann **Heinz** (29), ihre Kinder **Jessica** (3),
Michael (2)

mein Bruder **Andreas** (22) (ledig),
seine Freundin **Tina** (23)

 2 Stephanies Familie

a Listen once more to Stephanie talking about her family.

Fragen:

i Wie alt ist Stephanie?	**v** Wo arbeitet ihr Vater?
ii Ist sie verheiratet?	**vi** Wie heißt Carolines Mann?
iii Was studiert Stephanie?	**vii** Hat Caroline Kinder?
iv Was ist ihre Mutter von Beruf?	**viii** Hat Andreas eine Freundin?

b Use the family album as a prompt to take on the role of Stephanie talking about her family.

Example: *Ich heiße Stephanie. Ich bin 19 Jahre alt. Meine Mutter heißt …*

3 Familie

Grammatik

Possessives

	'my'	'her'	'his'
masculine	**mein Bruder**	**ihr Bruder**	**sein Bruder**
feminine	**meine Schwester**	**ihre Schwester**	**seine Schwester**
neuter	**mein Auto**	**ihr Auto**	**sein Auto**
plural	**meine Eltern**	**ihre Eltern**	**seine Eltern**

3 Caroline und Andreas

Here are some details about Caroline and Andreas. Fill in the missing words: **sein(e)** or **ihr(e)**. Check your answers on the recording.

Das ist Caroline. Sie ist verheiratet und **a** _ihr_ Mann heißt Heinz. Er ist Bibliothekar von Beruf und er arbeitet in Gießen. Caroline hat zwei Kinder. **b** _ihre_ Kinder heißen Jessica und Michael. Sie sind drei und zwei Jahre alt. Die Kinder sind noch klein und Caroline arbeitet im Moment nicht. Sie hat ein Auto – **c** _sein_ Auto ist sehr alt. Caroline hat auch einen Bruder – Andreas. **d** _ihr_ Bruder ist nicht verheiratet.
e _ihr_ Schwester Stephanie studiert in Marburg. Sie ist neunzehn Jahre alt und ledig.
f _____ Freund heißt Alex. Carolines Eltern heißen Martina und Christian. **g** _____ Eltern wohnen in Frankfurt.

Das ist Andreas. Er ist nicht verheiratet, aber er hat eine Freundin. **h** _____ Freundin heißt Tina. Sie ist sehr nett. Andreas wohnt auch in Frankfurt und er studiert noch.
i _____ Eltern wohnen in der Beethovenstraße. Andreas hat ein Moped. **j** _____ Moped ist neu und fährt gut. **k** _____ Freund Ali studiert Biologie in Darmstadt. Nachmittags fahren Andreas und Ali oft zum Schwimmbad. Andreas hat viele Hobbys.
l _____ Hobbys sind Schwimmen, Musik und Filme.

4 Interviews

a Interview mit Andreas

Listen to the recording and fill in the gaps.

- Wie heißen Sie? – **i** _Mein_ Name ist Andreas.
- Wie alt sind Sie? – **ii** Ich bin _zwei_ Jahre alt.
- Sind Sie verheiratet? – **iii** Nein, ich bin _ledig_.
- Haben Sie eine Freundin? – Ja.
- Wie heißt Ihre Freundin? – **iv** _Mein_ Freundin heißt Tina.
- Haben Sie Geschwister? – **v** Ja. Ich habe _zwei_ Schwestern, aber keinen Bruder.
- Was ist Ihr Vater von Beruf? – **vi** Mein Vater ist _Ingenieur_ bei Siemens.
- Wie alt ist Ihre Mutter? – **vii** Meine Mutter ist _51_ Jahre alt.

b Interview mit Caroline

Work out what the questions below are, then check by listening to the recording.

i	_____?	– Ich bin 25.
ii	_____?	– Nein, ich bin verheiratet.
iii	_____?	– Mein Mann heißt Heinz.
iv	*Haben Sie Kinder?*	– Ich habe einen Sohn und eine Tochter.
v	_____?	– Meine Tochter ist 3 Jahre alt.
vi	_____?	– Ja, ich habe eine Schwester und einen Bruder.
vii	_____?	– Meine Mutter ist Architektin.

Grammatik

The indefinite article ('a')

ein Sohn (masculine), **eine** Tochter (feminine), **ein** Kind (neuter)

When a masculine noun is the object of a sentence **ein** becomes **einen**:

	masculine	*feminine*	*neuter*	*plural*
Sie hat ...	**einen Sohn**	**eine Tochter**	**ein Kind**	**Kinder**

NB: The feminine **eine** and neuter **ein** stay the same.

The negative of **ein** is **kein**. It follows the same pattern as **ein**.

Ich habe ...	**keinen Bruder**	**keine Schwester**	**kein Kind**	**keine Kinder**

Grammatik

Possessives

Ihr 'your' (formal) begins with a capital letter. This distinguishes it from **ihr** 'her'.
Like the other possessives, it follows the same pattern as **mein** and **ein**:

Ihr Sohn	**Ihre Tochter**	**Ihr Kind**	**Ihre Eltern**

5 Das ist meine Familie

Describe your family to a partner who sketches out your family tree on the basis of what you say. Check it afterwards, using only German to correct any errors. Reverse roles.

Example: *Ich habe einen Bruder und zwei Schwestern. Mein Bruder ist ...*

6 Und das ist seine/ihre Familie

Using the family tree drawn up in exercise 5, describe your partner's family to a third party/the class. Remember to use **er/sie** and the possessives **sein(e)/ihr(e)** as appropriate.

7 Großvaters Katze/Grandfather's cat

Herr Baumann ist Stephanies Großvater.

– Großvater, du hast kein Auto. – Nein. Ich habe ein Fahrrad.
– Hast du einen Fernseher? – Nein. Ich habe ein Radio.
– Hast du einen Computer? – Ich brauche keinen Computer!
– Und ein Handy? – Nein. Ich habe ein Telefon.
– Was hast du denn? – Eine Katze.

Make a list of what the grandfather does and doesn't own, using the correct form of **ein** or **kein**:

Stephanies Großvater hat ein(e/en): _____ , *er hat kein(e/en)* _____ etc.

8 Was hast du?/What have you got?

a Link the words below to the correct drawing.

b Note down the gender of the objects (*m*, *f* or *n*). If in doubt, use a dictionary.

c Take turns with your partner to ask and answer questions.
Choose either the informal or formal 'you' and be consistent.

| Hast du Haben Sie | einen eine ein | CD-Spieler *m* Brieftasche *f* Radio *n* Fernseher Handy Computer Kugelschreiber Handtasche Wörterbuch Kreditkarte Auto Fahrrad Katze | ? | Ja, ich habe | einen … eine … ein … |
| | | | | Nein, ich habe | keinen … keine … kein … |

 9 Was brauchst du?/What do you need?

With a partner, take turns to choose statements from the following list and say which objects from exercise 8 you need, using **mein**, **meine** or **meinen** as appropriate. In most cases, there is more than one possibility. Use your imagination!

Example: *Ich telefoniere oft ... Ich brauche mein Handy.*

Ich schreibe heute einen Test. Ich gehe abends in die Stadt.
Ich höre oft Musik. Heute kaufe ich ein.
Meine Eltern wohnen in Frankfurt. Ich telefoniere oft.
Ich bin Fußball-Fan.

Grammatik

Remember the possessives follow the pattern of the indefinite article **ein**, so there is a special masculine object form: **meinen** 'my' (similarly, **seinen** 'his', **ihren** 'her' etc.)

 10 Bleiben sie fit?/Do they keep fit?

Read the information about the Baumanns and the Schmidts and answer the true/false questions below. Correct any false statements.

Herr und Frau Baumann wohnen in Mannheim. Sie sind Rentner. Er ist 76 Jahre alt, sie ist 74. Sie bleiben fit und gesund. Sie essen viel Obst und Gemüse und gehen schwimmen. Sie fahren oft Rad und haben kein Auto. Sie lesen viel und hören Radio.
Herr Baumann sagt: Unser Hobby ist Fitnesstraining!

Herr und Frau Schmidt wohnen in München. Sie sind auch Rentner. Beide sind 80 Jahre alt. Sie rauchen viel und sehen immer fern. Sie haben ein Auto und sie essen oft Wurst und Pizza. Sie trinken auch manchmal Bier und gehen nie in das Sportzentrum. Ihr Hobby ist Fernsehen!

Richtig oder falsch?/True or false?

Familie Baumann		Familie Schmidt	
a Sie wohnen in München.	r/f	**f** Sie sind 79 und 80 Jahre alt.	r/f
b Sie arbeiten nicht.	r/f	**g** Sie haben kein Auto.	r/f
c Sie sind gesund.	r/f	**h** Sie essen oft Wurst.	r/f
d Sie essen Pizza.	r/f	**i** Sie trinken Bier.	r/f
e Sie haben ein Auto.	r/f	**j** Sie gehen oft ins Sportzentrum.	r/f

Grammatik

sie 'they': **sie wohnen** *regular verb.*
 sie sind 'they are' (from **sein** 'to be') *irregular verb.*
(Distinguish from **Sie** 'you' and **sie** 'she'.)

Possessives: **unser** (our), **ihr** (their)

11 Wir essen gesund .../We eat healthily ...

Listen to the interviews with Herr Baumann and Frau Schmidt. The following summaries each contain one inaccurate point: which is it?

a He is 76. They are healthy. They eat lots of fruit and vegetables. They go swimming and cycling. They often watch TV. They listen to the radio.

b She is 80. They often eat pizza. They drink beer.
They sometimes drink wine. They never cycle.

Grammatik

wir 'we': **wir wohnen** *regular verb*
 wir sind 'we are' (from **sein** 'to be') *irregular verb*

12 Partnerübung

Q Hast du/Haben Sie ... einen Freund/eine Freundin?
 einen Bruder/eine Schwester?
 Kinder/einen Sohn/eine Tochter?
 einen Hund/eine Katze?

A Ja/Nein, ich habe einen/keinen Bruder/zwei Brüder *etc.*

Plurals: **Brüder**, **Schwestern**, **Söhne**, **Töchter**, **Hunde**, **Katzen**

Q Wie heißt dein(e)/Ihr(e) ... Freund(in)?
 Mutter/Vater/Schwester/Bruder/Tochter/Sohn?
 Katze/Hund?
A Mein(e) Vater/Mutter heißt ...

Q Wie heißen deine/Ihre ... Eltern/Kinder/Geschwister?
A Meine Eltern heißen ...

Q Wie alt ist dein/Ihr Freund?
 deine/Ihre Freundin? etc.

Grammatik

Possessive: **dein** 'your' (informal):
dein Vater (m) **deine Mutter** (f) **dein Kind** (n) **deine Eltern** (pl)

Extra!

13 Familie, Freunde und Hobbys

a You will hear three people talking about their respective families, friends and hobbies. Draw up a grid like the one below. Jot down in it in German keywords as much relevant information as possible.

Name	Familie	Freunde	Hobbys
Annelie			
Markus			
Hanna			

b With the help of your notes, write a summary in German. Use whole sentences.

14 Statistik

Was haben junge Frauen/Rentnerinnen und was haben junge Männer/Rentner?

Sie haben …	Frauen (20)	Frauen (65)	Männer (20)	Männer (65)
Computer	67%	21%	76%	17%
Fernseher	88%	92%	90%	93%
Auto	54%	43%	66%	72%
Handy	75%	26%	78%	22%
Hund	18%	51%	12%	54%
Kreditkarte	83%	16%	87%	21%

Make up sentences using the statistical information above and the adverbs from Unit 2: **immer/oft/manchmal/selten/nie**.
The word **fast** 'almost' helps in some cases.

Example: *Junge Frauen haben fast nie einen Hund.*
Rentner haben selten eine Kreditkarte.

Grammatik

- **Indefinite article ('a'/'an')**

 ein Computer **eine Kreditkarte** **ein Auto**
 (masculine) (feminine) (neuter)

 – When a masculine noun is the object of a sentence, the indefinite article is **einen**.
 The feminine and neuter indefinite articles remain unchanged.

Ein Computer	**kostet**	**1600 Euro.**	**Peter**	**braucht**	**einen Computer.**
— Subject —	verb		Subj	verb	—— object ——

 Peter braucht eine Kreditkarte/ein Auto.

 – **Kein** is the negative of **ein** and follows the same pattern:

 Kein Computer kostet 50 Euro! **Peter braucht keinen Computer.**
 No computer costs 50 euro! Peter doesn't need a computer
 (literally *Peter needs no computer.*)

 – This special form of the indefinite article or **kein** is called the *accusative*.

- **Pronouns and verbs**

 Wir (we) and **sie** (they) are followed by a verb form which is the same as the infinitive:
 Wir wohnen in Mannheim. Sie bleiben fit.
 Exception: *irregular verb* **sein** (to be): **wir/sie sind** (we/they are)

- **Possessives**

	masculine	*feminine*	*neuter*	*plural*
my	**mein**	**meine**	**mein**	**meine**
your (informal)	**dein**	**deine**	**dein**	**deine**
your (formal)	**Ihr**	**Ihre**	**Ihr**	**Ihre**
his/its	**sein**	**seine**	**sein**	**seine**
her/its	**ihr**	**ihre**	**ihr**	**ihre**
our	**unser**	**unsere**	**unser**	**unsere**
their	**ihr**	**ihre**	**ihr**	**ihre**

 – **Ihr** (your) is capitalised in the same way **Sie** (you) is capitalised.
 ihr (her/their) corresponds to **sie** (she/they).

 – **Mein** and the other possessives follow the pattern of the indefinite article **ein**:
 mein Computer, meine Kreditkarte, mein Auto.
 Ich brauche meinen Computer. **Er braucht seinen Computer.**
 Brauchen Sie Ihren Computer? **Wir brauchen unseren Computer.**

Grammatikübungen

1 Give the correct form of **ein** or **kein**. Remember to check the genders of nouns!

 a Ich kaufe heute e_ine_ Brieftasche. _wallet_

 b Er trinkt abends e_in_ Bier und liest e_in_ Buch.

 c Sie hat e_inen_ Computer, aber k_ein_ Handy.

 d Ich habe e_inen_ Hund und e_ine_ Katze.

 e Morgens esse ich e_in_ Käsebrot.

 f Er hat e_ine_ Tochter und e_inen_ Sohn.

 g Ich habe k_eine_ Geschwister.

2 Give the correct form of an appropriate verb.

 Wir **a** _____ Studenten und **b** _____ in Heidelberg. Wir **c** _____ Fahrräder und **d** _____ fit. Wir **e** _____ viel Obst, aber wir **f** _____ manchmal viel Bier!

3 Karin or Claus? You will hear two people talking about themselves, a man and a woman. Listen to the recording and answer the questions. Note that they are mixed up, some refer to him and some to her!

 a Was ist ihre Mutter von Beruf?

 b Wie heißt sein Bruder?

 c Wo wohnt seine Freundin?

 d Wie heißt ihre Katze?

 e Was ist seine Mutter von Beruf?

 f Wie alt ist ihre Schwester?

 g Wie heißt ihre beste Freundin?

 h Wie heißt sein Hund?

 i Was ist sein Vater von Beruf?

 j Wie alt ist ihre Mutter?

4 Match the statements below with the sentences on the right and add the missing endings (if any!).

 1 Ich telefoniere oft.

 2 Er schreibt E-Mails.

 3 Sie lernt Deutsch.

 4 Er besucht seine Großeltern in Mannheim.

 5 Ich höre abends Musik.

 6 Sie kauft heute Nachmittag ein.

 a Ich brauche mein__ Radio.

 b Sie braucht ihr__ Kreditkarte.

 c Er braucht sein__ Auto.

 d Er braucht sein__ Computer.

 e Sie braucht ihr__ Wörterbuch.

 f Ich brauche mein__ Telefon.

Vokabeln

Aufgabe 1

Eltern *pl*	parents
Kinder *pl*	children
Jahre alt	years old
ledig	single
die Mathematik	mathematics
die Informatik	computer science
die Mutter	mother
der/die Architekt(in)	architect (m/f)
der Vater	father
der/die Ingenieur(in)	engineer (m/f)
bei	at, for
die Schwester	sister
verheiratet	married
der Mann	husband; man
noch	still
klein	small
der Bruder	brother

Aufgabe 2

wie alt?	how old?
das Auto	car

Aufgabe 3

der/die Bibliothekar(in)	librarian (m/f)
im Moment	at the moment
nicht	not
alt	old
nett	nice
das Moped	moped
neu	new
fahren*	to go/drive
das Schwimmbad	swimming pool
viele	many
Hobbys *pl*	hobbies
das Schwimmen	swimming
Filme *pl*	films

Aufgabe 4

die Geschwister *pl*	brothers and sisters
der Sohn	son
die Tochter	daughter

Aufgabe 7

der Großvater	grandfather
das Fahrrad	bicycle
der Fernseher	TV set
das Radio	radio
der Computer	computer
brauchen	to need

das Handy	mobile phone
Was hast du denn?	What have you got, then?
die Katze	cat

Aufgabe 8

der CD-Spieler	CD-player
die Brieftasche	wallet
der Kugelschreiber	ballpoint pen
die Handtasche	handbag
das Wörterbuch	dictionary
die Kreditkarte	credit card

Aufgabe 9

einkaufen *sep*	to shop
der Test	test
telefonieren	to telephone
der Fan	fan

Aufgabe 10

der/die Rentner(in)	pensioner (m/f)
viel	a lot
das Obst	fruit
das Gemüse	vegetable(s)
Rad fahren*	to cycle
das Fitnesstraining	fitness training
beide	both
rauchen	to smoke
die Wurst	sausage

Aufgabe 11

dann	then
der Hund	dog

Possessives

mein	my
dein	your *informal*
Ihr	your *formal*
sein	his
ihr	her/their
unser	our

Extra/Grammatikübungen/Partnerarbeit/ Weitere Übungen

jung	young
fast	almost
kaufen	to buy
die Großeltern *pl*	grandparents
der Stammbaum	family tree
besuchen	to visit

For guidance on plurals, see the Grammar Reference section at the end of the book.

*Verb strong in present tense

Partnerarbeit

1 Stammbaum/Family tree

Describe the family presented in the family tree below to Partner B. He/She will draw up a diagram with the information you provide and then check the details by asking questions about individual family members. Start with Ulrike ...

Hannelore (75) und **Gregor** (79) – ihre Großeltern

Gisela (50)		**Herbert** (53)
ihre Mutter	ihre Eltern	ihr Vater

ihr Bruder **Manfred** (21)	**Ulrike** (18)	ihr Bruder **Walter** (25)
seine Freundin **Vera** (20)	ihr Freund **Thomas** (21)	seine Frau **Sabine** (26)
sein Hund **Gomez**	ihre Katze **Mikesch**	ihre Kinder **Hanna** (2)
		Benno (1)

2 Du brauchst ...

Your partner will tell you what he/she is doing. You tell him/her what he/she needs for each activity, choosing <u>two</u> items from the following list. He/She then responds by telling you whether he/she has those items or not. Use your imagination!

Check any genders you are not sure of.

Sie brauchen *ein(e/en)* ...
Du brauchst ...

Handy	Kugelschreiber	Auto
Fernseher	Kreditkarte	Computer
Fahrrad	Katze	Bibliothek
Wörterbuch	Freund(in)	
Videorekorder	CD-Spieler	
Radio	Bier	

Partnerarbeit

B

1 **Stammbaum**/Family tree

Your partner will describe Ulrike's family in some detail, providing you with information on their names, ages and relation to Ulrike. Complete the diagram below and then check if your information is correct by asking your partner questions about each family member.

Hannelore (__) und _____ (__) – ihre _____

_____ (__) _____ (53)
_____ Mutter _____ _____

ihr _____ (__) **Ulrike** (__) _____ **Walter** (__)
seine Freundin ____ (__) ihr _____ (__) seine _____ (__)
_____ **Gomez** ____ Katze _____ ____ Kinder _____ (__)
 _____ (1)

2 **Was brauche ich?**

Tell your partner what you're doing (the activities are listed below).
For each one, he/she will suggest what you need. You then respond by telling him/her whether you have what he/she suggests. Use your imagination!

Ich lerne Deutsch. Ich telefoniere viel.

Ich fahre in die Stadt. Ich tanze oft.

Ich kaufe ein Moped. Ich höre abends Musik.

Ich habe ein(e/en) ...
Ich habe kein(e/en) ...

4 Am Wochenende

In this unit you will learn how to talk about your leisure time, to express likes and preferences, to make suggestions and issue invitations. You will also learn the days of the week and the other way to tell the time.

 1 Was machst du gern?/What do you like doing?

Listen to Silvia, Felix and Anna, saying what they like doing and fill in the gap in each of the sentences below.

a __Felix__ kocht gern.

b Sylvia _____ gern spazieren.

c _____ kauft gern Kleider.

d Felix _____ gern.

e Sylvia liest _____ Krimis.

f Anna fährt gern _____ .

Grammatik	Grammatik
Lesen 'to read' (**er/sie liest**) and **fahren** 'to drive/go' (**er/sie fährt**) are *strong verbs*.	**ich koche** <u>gern</u> 'I like cooking' **er/sie kocht** <u>gern</u> 'he/she likes cooking'

 2 Und du? Was machst du gern?

Example: Ich *gehe gern ins Kino* etc.

spazieren gehen · rauchen · lesen · Auto fahren · Kleider kaufen · kochen · schwimmen · in die Kneipe gehen · fernsehen · Musik hören · tanzen · ins Kino gehen · Fußball spielen

3 Umfrage/Survey

You will know most of the food and drink vocabulary in this exercise. Check the rest in the unit vocabulary. Take it in turns to ask the class. One student keeps count of the responses and gives the results at the end.

Wer trinkt gern …
Kaffee/Tee/Mineralwasser/Cola/Orangensaft/Bier/Wein?

Wer isst gern …
Pizza/Pommes frites/Obst/Gemüse/Salat/Fleisch/Fisch?

Wer geht gern …
ins Kino/in die Diskothek/ins Sportzentrum/einkaufen/
schwimmen/spazieren?

Example: 15 *Personen trinken gern Kaffee, 17 trinken gern Tee … usw.*

4 Richtig oder falsch?

Listen as Thomas and Karin are asked about their preferences. Which statements are true and which false?

a Thomas never drinks milk. t/f
b Thomas doesn't like beer. t/f
c Karin doesn't like wine. t/f

d Karin doesn't drink mineral water. t/f
e Karin prefers tea to cola. t/f

Grammatik

gern/lieber/am liebsten
Das ist Thomas. Was macht er gern? …

Thomas trinkt *gern* Kaffee.
Er trinkt *lieber* Apfelsaft.
Er trinkt *am liebsten* Weißwein.
Er trinkt *nicht gern* Milch.

5 Sie trinkt gern Tee

Look at the following list of food and drink items. Make up sentences indicating the likes and dislikes of Gudrun, Frank und Gabi.

	Cola	Tee	Bier	Wein	Salat	Pizza	Käse	Fisch	
Gudrun	👍👍	👍	👎	👍👍👍	👍👍	👎	👍	👍👍👍	
Frank	👎	👍👍	👍👍👍	👍	👍	👍👍👍	👍👍	👎	
Gabi	👍	👍👍👍	👎		👍👍	👎	👍	👍👍👍	👍👍

6 Und was isst/trinkst du gern?

Get together with a partner and find out what he/she likes or does not like to eat and drink. Tell the class about your partner's likes and dislikes. (Use a dictionary where necessary.)

 7 Was machst du am Wochenende?/What are you doing at the weekend?

Listen to the conversation on the phone between Astrid and Christoph and note down in English what they like (or don't like) doing at the weekend.

8 **Die Uhrzeit**/The time

In addition to the 24-hour clock, which you have already met, there is another way of telling the time in German which is used in most everyday conversations just as in English.

 a Listen to the times.

Viertel <u>nach</u> zehn **halb elf** **Viertel <u>vor</u> elf**

Note that **halb elf** means 10.30 not 11.30!

fünf (Minuten) **zwanzig (Minuten)** **zwanzig (Minuten)**
<u>nach</u> zehn **<u>nach</u> zehn** **<u>vor</u> elf**

zwölf Uhr/Mittag **zwölf Uhr/Mitternacht**

 b Using the 12-hour clock, write down (in figures) the times you hear:

 i _____ **ii** _____ **iii** _____ **iv** _____ **v** _____

 c Say these times:
Example: *Viertel nach acht*
8.15 8.30 8.45 8.05 8.20 8.40 4.10 7.25 2.35 5.45 9.50 11.55

 9 Die Tage der Woche/The days of the week

Repeat the days of the week and learn them!

Montag Dienstag Mittwoch Donnerstag Freitag Samstag/Sonnabend Sonntag
(**Samstag** heißt **Sonnabend** in Norddeutschland)

> **Samstag + Sonntag = das Wochenende**
> **<u>am</u> Montag**: 'on Monday' **montags**: '(on) Mondays' (regularly)

10 Einladung/Invitation

a Without reading the script, listen to the recording of Petra and Thomas: what do they agree to do? When you have answered that question, read the script:

Petra: Hallo, Thomas. *Wie geht's?* ~how are you?~

Thomas: Gut, danke. Petra, was machst du denn heute Abend?

Petra: Ich muss für mein Examen arbeiten. Warum?

Thomas: Ich will essen gehen. *Kommst du mit?* ~Are you coming along.~

Petra: Heute kann ich *leider* nicht ausgehen, *tut mir Leid.* ~I'm sorry.~

Thomas: Oh, aber *vielleicht* können wir am Mittwoch ins Restaurant gehen?

Petra: Am Mittwoch … Ich gehe um halb acht mit Martin ins Kino.

Thomas: *Schade.* Kannst du am Freitag ausgehen?

Petra: Ja, *das geht.* Um wie viel Uhr?

Thomas: Gegen neun Uhr, *ist das in Ordnung?* ~what about~

Petra: Ja, das ist okay. Wohin gehen wir?

Thomas: Vielleicht ins „Buena Vista", das ist sehr gut. Isst du gern spanisch?

Petra: Spanisch … ja, aber ich esse lieber italienisch.

Thomas: Dann müssen wir ins „Bella Italia" gehen. Die Pizza ist dort fantastisch.

Petra: Prima. *Wo treffen wir uns?* ← ~where shall we meet~

Thomas: Um Viertel vor neun am Stadttheater. Ich muss jetzt gehen – meine Gitarrenstunde *fängt um drei Uhr an.* ~start~

Petra: Tschüss Thomas, *bis Freitag.* ~See you on Friday.~
~Bye~

b Which of the words or phrases in italics is the equivalent of:

i (That's a) pity **ii** Is that all right? **iii** I'm sorry **iv** Are you coming along?
v That's fine **vi** perhaps **vii** See you on Friday **viii** How are you? **ix** 'Bye
x Where shall we meet? **xi** starts/begins **xii** unfortunately

Grammatik

Können 'to be able to', 'can', **müssen** 'to have to', 'must', **wollen** 'to want to' are known as *modal verbs*. They are usually followed by a second verb in the *infinitive* form which comes at the end of the sentence. Modal verbs have a distinctive pattern:

können:	ich kann	du kannst	er/sie kann	wir/Sie/sie können
müssen:	ich muss	du musst	er/sie muss	wir/Sie/sie müssen
wollen:	ich will	du willst	er/sie will	wir/Sie/sie wollen

Example: **Ich muss in die Bibliothek gehen – ich kann heute nicht ausgehen.**
I have to go to the library – I can't go out today.

Note: **Er muss nicht gehen** means 'He doesn't have to go', not 'He must not go'.

c Now go back to the dialogue script and find the modal verb forms and the infinitives which follow them.

11 Ich habe keine Zeit/I've no time

Fragen:

a Warum hat Stefan morgen keine Zeit?

b Was will Anna machen?

c Hat Stefan am Mittwoch Zeit?

d Wann trifft Anna ihre Freundinnen?

e Wann können sie Tennis spielen?

f Warum muss Stefan zu Hause sein?

12 Was kann man machen?/What can you do?

a When there is a clear context, you can often understand written information including words you have not met before. Read the information without referring to the vocabulary list. Find in it the German for the English phrases listed below:

PIZZERIA „NAPOLI"
Italienische Küche
Täglich von 17 Uhr bis 23 Uhr.

Altdeutsche Bierstube
Biergarten Mittagstisch Weinkarte
kinderfreundlich
Öffnungszeiten: Mo-Fr 12.00-21.00
Sa 11.30-23.00 So 12.00-14.30

Stadttheater. „*Cyrano de Bergerac*"
von Edmond de Rostand
Samstag 20 Uhr Eintritt 5 Euro.

Charly's Diskothek. Samstag ab 23 Uhr
Große Tanznacht mit DJ Benny Ahrens

Kino am Bahnhofsplatz. „**Herr der Ringe**" ab 12 Jahren
Mo-Fr 19.30 Sa/So 15.30, 19.30
Mo-Do €6,50 (Kinder 3,50) Fr-So 7,50 (Kinder 4,00).

i opening times

ii admission/entrance

iii Italian cuisine

iv from 11 pm

v daily

vi wine list

vii children welcome

Grammatik

Was kann man am Wochenende machen? – <u>Man kann</u> ins Restaurant gehen.
The handy pronoun **man** means 'one', 'you'. It is followed by the **er/sie** form of the verb.
Man kann *in die Kneipe/ins Theater/in die Diskothek/ins Kino* gehen.
(**ins** = **in das**)

b Referring to the information in the advertisements, answer the following questions:

i Was kann man am Samstagnachmittag machen?

ii Was kann man samstags um 23 Uhr machen?

iii Was kann man am Sonntagabend machen?

iv Wann kann man am Sonntag ins Kino gehen?

v Wann kann man ins Restaurant gehen?

vi Wann kann man ins Theater gehen?

 13 Im Restaurant

Petra:	Haben Sie einen Tisch für zwei Personen?
Kellner:	Ja, dort drüben am Fenster.
Thomas:	Gut, wir nehmen den Tisch.
Petra:	Wir möchten gern die Speisekarte.
Kellner:	Einen Moment bitte … Hier ist die Speisekarte.
Petra:	Vielen Dank. (*nach 5 Minuten …*)
Kellner:	Was möchten Sie, bitte?
Petra:	Ich nehme die Pizza Spezial. Kann ich auch einen Salat haben?
Kellner:	Ja natürlich … Tomatensalat oder Cäsarsalat?
Petra:	Ich nehme den Tomatensalat.
Kellner:	Einmal Pizza Spezial und Tomatensalat …Und für Sie?
Thomas:	Ich bekomme die Tomatensuppe und das Huhn mit Sahnesauce.
Kellner:	Und was möchten Sie trinken?
Thomas:	Kann ich die Weinkarte sehen, bitte? … Wir nehmen den Weißwein Nummer 12, bitte.
Kellner:	Einmal den Chardonnay, in Ordnung. Sonst noch etwas?
Petra:	Danke, das ist alles.

Ich nehme/bekomme/möchte … einen Salat/**eine** Pizza/**ein** Eis

den Tomatensalat/**die** Pizza Spezial/**das** Vanilleeis

Grammatik

Definite article ('the'):
der Salat (masculine), **die** Pizza (feminine), **das** Eis (neuter).

Accusative form: When a masculine noun is the object of a sentence, **der** becomes **den**, while the feminine and neuter definite articles remain unchanged:
Ich nehme … den Salat **die** Pizza **das** Eis

 Using the menu below, role-play a dialogue along the lines of the one at the top of this page.

SPEISEKARTE

Tomatensuppe	€5,50
Gemüsesuppe	€6,00
Pizza Romano	€9,60
Pizza Salami	€10,00
Weißwein/Rotwein	€3,00
Mineralwasser	€1,70
Vanille-/Schokoladeneis	€3,80

Extra!

14 Manfreds Woche

A market research company is doing a survey about student lifestyles and Manfred is being asked about his activities during one particular week. Listen carefully to the interview and note down in German what he is doing on the days given. Use the 24-hour clock.

NB: There is information about the whole week – make sure you select what he says about the days in question.

 Montag **Donnerstag** **Samstag**

15 Zusammen oder allein?/Together or alone?

Read below an account of what Sabine and Rolf like (and dislike!) as far as leisure activities and food are concerned. What can they do together? Find as many activities as possible that they can share, and also those they cannot share.

Sabine

> Ich bin sehr sportlich und gehe oft ins Sportzentrum. Am liebsten spiele ich Tennis, aber ich mache auch gern Aerobic und manchmal gehe ich schwimmen. Fußball spiele ich nicht gern. Samstags gehe ich immer ins Kino - am liebsten sehe ich amerikanische und britische Filme. Ich gehe gern in die Kneipe, aber ich trinke nie Bier. Ich trinke lieber Wein oder Apfelwein. Ins Restaurant gehe ich nicht oft, denn das kostet viel Geld. Ich koche lieber mit Freunden zu Hause und wir essen zusammen. Spaghetti mit Sauce esse ich besonders gern! Ich höre gern Musik und gehe auch manchmal in die Diskothek, aber ich tanze lieber auf Partys. Das macht mehr Spaß. Am Wochenende gehe ich manchmal spazieren, aber am liebsten bleibe ich sonntags im Bett!

Rolf

> Abends bleibe ich gern zu Hause und lese. Ich sehe auch gern fern und höre Musik - am liebsten höre ich Jazz und Soul. Freitags gehe ich oft in die Disko, denn ich tanze sehr gern. Ich fahre gern Auto und oft fahre ich nach München und gehe dort ins Kino. Ich sehe gern alte amerikanische Filme, aber am liebsten sehe ich Science-fiction Filme. In München kann man auch gut italienisch essen! Ich gehe fast nie in die Kneipe, denn ich rauche nicht und trinke nicht gern Bier. Am liebsten trinke ich im Sommer Apfelwein im Gartencafé. Ich gehe oft schwimmen und spiele manchmal Fußball mit Freunden, aber ins Sportzentrum gehe ich nie. Das ist langweilig. Am Wochenende besuche ich manchmal meine Eltern, aber ich gehe lieber mit meinen Freunden aus.

Example: *Sabine und Rolf können zusammen Musik hören.*
 Sie können nicht zusammen Bier trinken.

Grammatik

- **Liking and preference**

 - The adverb **gern** indicates a liking. It comes directly after the verb:
 Ich trinke <u>gern</u> Tee. I like drinking tea.
 Ich gehe <u>gern</u> ins Kino. I like going to the cinema.

 - **Lieber** indicates preference:
 Ich gehe gern ins Kino, ich gehe <u>lieber</u> ins Theater.
 I like going to the cinema but I prefer (going to) the theatre.

 - **Am liebsten** expresses what you like most of all:
 Ich trinke <u>am liebsten</u> Rotwein. Ich gehe <u>am liebsten</u> ins Restaurant.

- **Modal verbs**

 - **können** 'to be able to'/'can'
 ich kann du kannst er/sie kann
 wir/Sie/sie können

 - **müssen** 'to have to', 'must'
 ich muss du musst er/sie muss
 wir/Sie/sie müssen

 - **wollen** 'to want to'
 ich will du willst er/sie will
 wir/Sie/sie wollen

 - These *irregular* verbs all follow the same distinctive pattern and are usually followed by a second verb in the infinitive form at the end of the sentence.

 Ich <u>will</u> am Montag ins Restaurant <u>gehen</u>. I want to go to the restaurant on Monday.
 1 2

- *man*

 This useful pronoun is used much more often than its English equivalent, 'one':
 Am Wochenende kann <u>man</u> spät aufstehen.
 At the weekend one/you can get up late.

- **Definite article: the accusative form**

 In Unit 3 you saw the *accusative* form of the indefinite article before masculine nouns, used when the noun is the object of the sentence: **Er kauft ein<u>en</u> Computer.**

 The definite article, too, has an accusative form: before masculine nouns it changes from **der** to **den** when the noun is the object of the sentence. The feminine (**die**), neuter (**das**) and plural (**die**) definite articles remain unchanged.

 Der Rotwein kostet 3 Euro. **Ich nehme <u>den</u> Rotwein.**
 — subject — verb verb — object —

Grammatikübungen

1 Express (1) liking/ (2) preference/ (3) 'like most of all'/ (4) 'don't like' for the following:

	1	2	3	4
a Ich trinke …	Mineralwasser	Cola	Orangensaft	Bier
b Er isst …	Pasta	Pizza	Pommes frites	Salat
c Ich …	lese	höre Musik	spiele Gitarre	gehe spazieren
d Sie gehen …	ins Kino	in die Stadt	ins Sportzentrum	in die Diskothek

2 Complete each sentence by choosing the correct form of an appropriate modal verb and an infinitive from the two sets of verbs below.

„**a** _____ du heute Abend ins Restaurant **b** _____?" „Es tut mir Leid, ich **c** _____ heute nicht **d** _____. Ich **e** _____ zu Hause **f** _____ ."
„Was **g** _____ Sie **h** _____?" „ **i** _____ wir bitte die Weinkarte **j** _____?"

Modals:	Infinitives:
können willst wollen kann muss	**bleiben ausgehen sehen gehen trinken**

3 Explain to a German-speaking friend what you can do in Stoke-on-Trent, where she/he will be an exchange student. Use the pronoun **man**.

Stoke-on-Trent, Staffordshire (240,000 inhabitants) has two local universities. Student social life is lively. There are many clubs and discos, good traditional pubs and two multi-screen cinemas. If eating out, try one of the excellent Balti restaurants. The New Victoria Theatre in neighbouring Newcastle-under-Lyme has a national reputation. The large Potteries Shopping Centre and the shopping and leisure complex at Festival Park cater for your retail needs. The beauty of the Peak District is a short drive away.

4 Max and Sabine have shared a flat but are now moving on. They have agreed to divide up their belongings by choosing one item at a time. Write out what happens, turn by turn.

Sabine nimmt den/die/das …,
Max nimmt den/die/das … etc.

Fernseher Radio Videorekorder
CD-Spieler Handy Katze
Hund Wörterbuch CDs
Moped Computer

Vokabeln

See Appendix p. 190 for more vocabulary in exercise 14 and Extra!

Days of the week (see Aufgabe 9)

Montag	Monday
Dienstag	Tuesday
Mittwoch	Wednesday
Donnerstag	Thursday
Freitag	Friday
Samstag	Saturday
Sonnabend	Saturday (N. Germany)
Sonntag	Sunday
Norddeutschland	North Germany
das Wochenende	weekend
am Montag	on Monday
montags	on Mondays (regularly)

Aufgabe 1

gern	(see grammar)
die Kleider *pl*	clothes
spazieren gehen	to go for a walk
Krimis *pl*	detective stories
kochen	to cook
Auto fahren*	to drive a car
– er/sie fährt	

Aufgabe 2

das Kino	cinema

Aufgabe 3

der Tee	tea
der Wein	wine
das Mineralwasser	mineral water
die Pommes frites *pl*	chips
das Fleisch	meat

Aufgabe 4

die Milch	milk

Aufgabe 8

Viertel	quarter
vor	before
nach	after
halb	half (to the next hour)

Aufgabe 10

die Einladung	invitation
wie geht's?	how are you?
gut, danke	fine, thanks
denn	(here =) then
für	for
das Examen	exam

mitkommen *sep*	to come along/come too
leider	unfortunately
(es) tut mir Leid	I'm sorry
vielleicht	perhaps
schade	(that's a) pity
das geht	that's OK
gegen	(here =) about
in Ordnung	all right, OK
gut	good
die Pizza	pizza
dort	there
fantastisch	fantastic
prima!	great!
treffen*	to meet
– er/sie trifft	
wo treffen wir uns?	where shall we meet?
am Stadttheater	at the Stadttheater
jetzt	now
anfangen* *sep*	to begin, start
– er/sie fängt ... an	

Aufgabe 11

die Zeit	time

Aufgabe 13

italienische Küche	Italian cuisine
täglich	daily
von ... bis ...	from ... until ...
„Die Altdeutsche Bierstube"	name of pub
der Biergarten	beer garden
der Mittagstisch	lunchtime menu
die Weinkarte	wine-list
kinderfreundlich	welcoming to children
Öffnungszeiten *pl*	opening hours
der Eintritt	entrance, admission
ab	from
große Tanznacht	big dance night

Aufgabe 14

der Tisch	table
Personen *pl*	persons
dort drüben	over there
am Fenster	by the window
möchte(n) *irreg*	would like
die Speisekarte	menu
vielen Dank	many thanks
nehmen*	to take (here = to have)
– er/sie nimmt	
bitte	please
natürlich	of course
einmal	once (here = one)

* Verb strong in present tense

Partnerarbeit

1 Suche Partner .../Lonely Hearts

a Partner B wants to put a Lonely Hearts ad in the local paper. Find out if he/she likes the following activities by asking the appropriate questions.

cinema swimming reading music pub shopping

sports centre French cuisine watching TV writing emails

 ♀

22, blond und schlank, sucht netten Mann für gemeinsame Aktivitäten: sie ist sportlich und schwimmt gern, geht oft ins Kino u. Restaurant, Interesse für klassische Musik, aber geht auch gern in die Disko; am liebsten trinkt sie ein gutes Glas Wein mit Freunden ...

 ♂

Er ist 24 und groß (1,98m), Nichtraucher, aber trinkt gern Rotwein; Architekt; möchte gern zusammen mit einer interessanten jungen Frau Köln kennen lernen. Er interessiert sich für Theater, Kino und gutes Essen. Er kocht gut und gern, aber noch lieber geht er chinesisch essen. Wer möchte ihm Köln zeigen?

b On the basis of what emerged in exercise **a**, help Partner B to draft an ad describing himself/herself and his/her ideal partner. The two examples above will give you some ideas.

2 Einladung

Invite your partner to join you in a variety of activities. Unfortunately, he/she seems to be reluctant to do so and comes up with a string of excuses. You know that he/she cannot resist the temptation of pizza, though ... Keep your trump card until last!

The following vocabulary will come in handy:

Willst du ... Kannst du ...	heute Abend Samstagnachmittag morgen Abend	einkaufen/schwimmen gehen in die Kneipe gehen tanzen gehen ins Konzert gehen spazieren gehen Fußball spielen italienisch essen gehen

Partnerarbeit

1 Suche Partner .../Lonely Hearts

a You want to put a Lonely Hearts ad in the local paper. Partner A will ask questions about your likes and dislikes in order to compile your profile. Answer the questions using the information below. If you do not like an activity ☹, tell your partner what you prefer.

cinema ☺

swimming ☹
(tennis ☺)

reading ☺

pub ☹
(restaurant ☺)

shopping ☹
(going for a walk ☺)

music ☺

watching TV ☺

sports centre ☺

French cuisine ☹
(Italian ☺)

writing emails ☹
(telephoning ☺)

b On the basis of what emerged in exercise a, Partner A will help you to draft an ad describing you and your ideal partner. The two examples below will give you some ideas.

♀	♂
22, blond und schlank, sucht netten Mann für gemeinsame Aktivitäten: sie ist sportlich und schwimmt gern, geht oft ins Kino u. Restaurant, Interesse für klassische Musik, aber geht auch gern in die Disko; am liebsten trinkt sie ein gutes Glas Wein mit Freunden …	Er ist 24 und groß (1,98m), Nichtraucher, aber trinkt gern Rotwein; Architekt; möchte gern zusammen mit einer interessanten jungen Frau Köln kennen lernen. Er interessiert sich für Theater, Kino und gutes Essen. Er kocht gut und gern, aber noch lieber geht er chinesisch essen. Wer möchte ihm Köln zeigen?

2 Einladung

Your partner invites you to join him/her in a variety of activities. You are a bit reluctant as you are not too keen on his/her company, so you think up a number of excuses. However, there is one proposition you cannot resist – a pizza washed down with a glass of red wine in your favourite Italian restaurant ….

The following vocabulary will come in handy:

Tut mir Leid, ich kann	heute Abend morgen Abend Samstagnachmittag	leider nicht	einkaufen gehen, tanzen gehen, etc.
Ich muss	arbeiten/meine Mutter besuchen/kochen/E-Mails schreiben/einkaufen gehen etc.		

Oh ja, sehr gern! Yes, with pleasure.

5 Zu Hause

In this unit, you will learn to talk about where you and others live.

 1 Handygespräche/Conversations on a mobile

a *Astrid calls Ute:*

- Hallo?
- … Oh … Hallo, Tom … Ist Ute da?
- Ich glaube, sie ist noch im Bett … Moment …
 Nein, sie ist gerade unter der Dusche – sie sagt, sie ist in zwanzig Minuten fertig.
- Tom, ich bin jetzt im Unterricht! Ich rufe später an, um etwa Viertel nach zehn.
- OK. Tschüss.
- Tschüss.

b *Markus calls Silvia:*

- Hallo.
- Hallo, ich bin's … Was machst du?
- Ich arbeite.
- In der Bibliothek?
- Nein – in meinem Zimmer. Ich sitze am Computer …
- Schade … ich bin mit Anna und Jens im Eiscafé. Wann bist du fertig?
- Ich weiß nicht – ich hab' noch viel zu tun.
- OK, ich rufe später an. Tschüss.
- Tschüss.

 Fragen:

i Ist Ute noch im Bett?	**iii** Was macht Silvia?	**v** Wo ist Markus?
ii Wo ist Astrid?	**iv** Wo ist sie?	**vi** Was macht er später?

Grammatik

in: Up to now, you have met this preposition in contexts where it is telling us 'where to' (**wohin**), involving a change of place:
Er geht in den Supermarkt/in die Diskothek/ins (= in das) Sportzentrum.
It is followed by an *accusative* form.

When it tells us simply 'where' (**wo**), it is followed by the *dative* form of the article:
masculine and neuter **dem/einem**, feminine **der/einer**:
Sie ist im Unterricht. Ich arbeite in der Bibliothek. Wir sind im Eiscafé.
 (masculine) (feminine) (neuter)

 (**im = in dem**)

Possessives follow the pattern of the indefinite article **ein**:
Ich arbeite in meinem Zimmer.

As you will see later, certain other prepositions are followed by the accusative or the dative depending on the context.

 2 Wo seid ihr?/Where are you?

Yasmin and Dieter want to meet up with their friends Paul and Ursula. Yasmin phones Paul.

a Listen to the recording and fill in the missing locations.

– Hallo, Paul. Wir sind im **i** _____ . Wo seid ihr?

– In der **ii** _____ .

– Wann ist eure Deutschstunde?

– Um drei Uhr. Wir sind um fünf fertig. Wie lange bleibt ihr im

 iii _____ ?

– Bis halb fünf – dann gehen wir nach Hause.

– Geht ihr heute Abend aus?

– Vielleicht … Was wollt ihr machen?

– Wir sind ab neun Uhr in der **iv** _____ .

– Ja, OK … bis neun Uhr!

– Tschüss!

 b Role-play the dialogue with a partner, changing the locations. Remember the gender of the noun determines whether it is preceded by **im** or **in der**.

> ### Grammatik
>
> The plural of **du**, the familiar 'you', is **ihr**. The verb ends in **-t**:
> **ihr bleibt, ihr geht, ihr wollt**. Irregular verb **sein** 'to be': **ihr seid**.
> The corresponding possessive 'your' is **euer** (masculine and neuter),
> **eure** (feminine and plural) – **eure Deutschstunde**.

 3 Ein Haus

Label the picture of a house using the word-list. Try to work out what the German words mean before checking them in the unit vocabulary!

das Wohnzimmer
die Küche
das Schlafzimmer
das Badezimmer
die Garage
der Balkon
das Esszimmer

4 Das ist unsere Wohnung/This is our flat

Bernd writes to Gavin about his new flat.

> Das erste Zimmer links ist das Esszimmer. Es ist ziemlich klein: Es gibt nur einen Tisch und vier Stühle. Das zweite Zimmer links ist das Wohnzimmer. Es gibt ein Sofa, zwei Sessel, ein Bücherregal und einen Fernseher. In der Ecke steht eine Lampe. Rechts von dem Wohnzimmer ist die kleine Küche. Wir haben einen Elektroherd, einen Kühlschrank, eine Waschmaschine und eine Mikrowelle. Es gibt auch einige Schränke.
> Rechts von der Küche ist unser Schlafzimmer. Es gibt natürlich ein Bett und zwei Nachttische, auch einen Kleiderschrank und einen Stuhl. Das letzte Zimmer ist das Badezimmer/WC. Es ist sehr modern. Es gibt eine Dusche und eine Badewanne.
> Es gibt keinen Garten.

Grammatik

es gibt ('there is'/'there are'): when this construction is followed by a masculine noun in the singular, the distinctive accusative form must be used, that is, **den/einen** rather than **der/ein**: **Es gibt <u>einen</u> Tisch**.

Remember, feminine and neuter articles do not have a distinctive accusative form and remain unchanged (**die/eine**, **das/ein**): **Es gibt eine Dusche, ein Bett** etc.

a Label the rooms on this plan of the flat.

b Without looking at the vocabulary, try to find in the text the German for these words. Then check to see whether you got them right!

lamp, wardrobe, electric cooker, bookshelves (singular in German!), washing machine, bed, bath, cupboards, sofa, fridge, bedside tables, armchairs, microwave, shower.

5 Möbel/Furniture

Write down what furniture there is in the hand-drawn living room directly below, before listening to the description on the recording. Then describe the other rooms.

6 Meine Wohnung oder mein Haus

Give information about where you live or your parents' house.

Fragen:

a Was gibt es in dem Wohnzimmer?

b Gibt es einen Fernseher im Schlafzimmer?

c Was gibt es in der Küche?

d Wo sitzen Sie abends?

e Wie viele Schlafzimmer gibt es?

f Essen Sie in der Küche?

g Gibt es eine Garage?

 7 Peters Zimmer/Peter's room

> Peters Zimmer ist klein und dunkel. Auf dem Fußboden liegen CDs und Kleider. Es gibt Bücher und Papiere auf dem Stuhl, Tassen und Teller auf dem Schreibtisch. Zwei Gläser stehen auf seinem Computer. Unter dem Bett gibt es Bierflaschen. Peter putzt nicht, er kocht nicht, er räumt nie auf, er will nicht einkaufen oder abwaschen.

 a Fragen:

 i Wo sind die Bierflaschen?

 ii Was gibt es auf dem Stuhl?

 iii Wo sind die Gläser?

 iv Was gibt es auf dem Schreibtisch?

 b Cover up the text and describe Peter's room to your partner, using the picture.

Grammatik

<u>Prepositions</u>

Like **in**, the prepositions **auf**, and **unter** are followed by the *dative* when they describe *location*, where something is: **CDs liegen auf <u>dem</u> Fußboden**.
Contrast with **legen** 'to lay, put down': **Er legt das Buch auf <u>den</u> Stuhl.** (There's a change of place, so *accusative*.)

 8 Einladung

a In the text on the next page there are a number of adjectives. See if you can find the German equivalents of those listed here. Go for the more obvious ones first and then use your powers of deduction and a process of elimination to work out the rest.

1 bright/light	**7** comfortable	**13** new
2 cosy	**8** small	**14** kitschy
3 modern	**9** compact	**15** old-fashioned
4 wonderful	**10** big	**16** exclusive
5 dark	**11** great	**17** dear/expensive
6 cold	**12** warm	**18** delicious

b In the text, the German equivalents of the adjectives from 10 to 18 have an ending (**-en**, **-e** or **-es**), those 1 to 9 have none. From the text, can you work out in which circumstances an adjective has an ending and when it doesn't? Check your answer against the Grammar box on the next page.

Stefan and Monika have a new flat. They've invited their friends, Andreas and Verena, for coffee, and they're showing them round …

M Das ist unser Wohnzimmer … Es ist schön und hell, und es gibt einen großen Balkon. Wir haben noch keinen Fernseher, aber wir kaufen nächste Woche einen.

A Das ist wirklich gemütlich. Ihr habt tolle Sessel! Und der Balkon ist besonders praktisch. Im Sommer kann man auf dem Balkon grillen und Partys feiern.

S Hoffentlich gibt es einen warmen Sommer!

M … So, das ist unser Esszimmer. Die Stühle habe ich vom Sperrmüll.

V Wirklich? Die sind ja ganz modern. Habt ihr auch die Kissen vom Sperrmüll?

S Nein, Monika kann sehr gut nähen …

V Die Kissen sind wunderbar … Und das ist euer Schlafzimmer?

M Ja, es ist ein bisschen dunkel und kalt, aber das ist okay. Wir haben ein neues Bett, von Ikea. Es ist sehr bequem.

A Das ist ein großes Zimmer … Ihr braucht noch eine Lampe für das Bett!

S Ja, das stimmt. Monika hat eine kitschige, altmodische Lampe, aber …

M Moment mal! Das ist eine ganz exklusive, teure Lampe von meinem Ex-Freund …

S Und das ist die Küche … sehr klein, aber kompakt und gemütlich. Und hier gibt es jetzt Kaffee und Kuchen!

V Wo kauft ihr die Kuchen?

S Monika backt köstliche Kuchen – wir kaufen sehr selten beim Bäcker.

V Nächste Woche kommt ihr in die Felsingstraße, und ich backe einen Schokoladenkuchen – in Ordnung?

S Das ist eine fantastische Idee!

Grammatik

Note the endings on adjectives after the indefinite article in the accusative singular, and with no article in the accusative plural:

einen groß<u>en</u> Balkon **eine kitschig<u>e</u> Lampe** **ein neu<u>es</u> Bett** **köstlich<u>e</u> Kuchen**
masculine feminine neuter plural

If the adjective is not before the noun, there is no ending: **Das Bett ist sehr bequem.**

The prepositions **von**, **zu** and **bei** (and some others) are always followed by a dative form: <u>zum</u> **Kaffeetrinken**, <u>von</u> **mein<u>em</u> Ex-Freund**, <u>beim</u> **Bäcker**.
(**zum = zu dem, beim = bei dem**)

9 Was haben Monika und Stefan?

a On the basis of the conversation above, make up sentences about the couple's flat. Include an adjective with an appropriate ending.
 Example: Sie haben einen großen Balkon.

b Do the same for your own accommodation: Ich habe / Wir haben …

Extra!

10 Mein Haus

a You will hear three people talking about themselves and their accommodation. Listen carefully to Volker, Silvia and Oliver describing where they live and note down the relevant information using the headings below, and German key words. Don't worry if you don't understand everything – just note down as much as you can.

Name	Wohnort	Zimmer	Möbel
Volker			
Silvia			
Oliver			

b Using the information collected above, write a short description in German of where these three people live. Use whole sentences.

11 Die Partneruniversität/Partner university

An exchange student from a German university writes a letter home to her friend.

> Hallo Andrea!
>
> Wie geht es dir? Ich bin schon acht Wochen in Exeter und will heute endlich einen Brief schreiben ... Die Universität ist sehr schön und groß und es gibt einen Park und viele Studenten auf dem Campus. Ich wohne mit zwei englischen Studentinnen zusammen, Ann und Kathy.
>
> Mein Zimmer ist sehr klein: Es gibt ein Bett, einen Schreibtisch, einen Stuhl und ein Bücherregal - das ist fast alles! *'almost everything'* Außerdem habe ich natürlich meinen CD-Spieler, Poster und viele Fotos von zu Hause. In der Wohnung gibt es noch vier andere Zimmer: zwei Zimmer für Ann und Kathy, ein Wohnzimmer und ein Esszimmer. Das Wohnzimmer ist groß und gemütlich. Am Abend sehen wir oft zusammen fern oder gehen in die Studentenbar, und mein Englisch ist jetzt schon viel besser. In der Küche gibt es einen Gasherd und einen Kühlschrank, aber keine Mikrowelle. Ich koche hier nicht gern, denn ich kann nicht gut mit Gas kochen. Die Würstchen sind immer schwarz!
>
> Tschüss und bis bald,
> Deine Uschi.
>
> PS: Es gibt keine Dusche - nur eine Badewanne!!

Fragen:

i Wie lange ist Uschi schon in Exeter?

ii Was gibt es auf dem Campus?

iii Wohnt sie allein?

iv Wie viele Zimmer gibt es?

v Was macht Uschi abends?

vi Was gibt es in der Küche?

Grammatik

- **Articles and possessives**

 – The basic form is used when the noun is the *subject* of a sentence. It is called the *nominative*.
 The *definite article* shows number and gender:
 singular: masculine **der**, feminine **die**, neuter **das**; plural: **die**
 The *indefinite article* has a simpler pattern:
 masculine and neuter **ein**, feminine **eine**. There is no plural.
 The *possessives* and **kein** follow a pattern based on **ein/eine**:
 masculine and neuter **mein dein sein ihr unser Ihr euer kein**
 feminine and plural **meine deine seine ihre unsere Ihre eure keine**

 – You have seen earlier that when a masculine singular noun is the *object* of a sentence, the article preceding it changes from **der/ein/mein** etc. to **den/einen/meinen** etc. The feminine, neuter and plural forms remain as in the nominative: **Ich kaufe einen Tisch, eine Lampe und ein Sofa. Am Wochenende besuche ich meine Eltern.**

 This form is called the *accusative*. As you've seen, the accusative is different from the nominative <u>only</u> in front of masculine nouns. The accusative is also used after **in** (and certain other prepositions) when they tell us 'where to' (**wohin**). It is also used after **es gibt** (there is/are): **Er geht oft in den Garten. Es gibt einen Balkon.**

 – As you have seen in this unit, when **in** (and certain other prepositions such as **auf** and **unter**) tell us 'where' (**wo**), they are followed by a *dative* form:
 masculine/neuter: **dem/einem/meinem** feminine: **der/einer/meiner**:
 Arbeitest du in deinem Zimmer? Helga ist in der Küche.
 The dative must always be used after certain other prepositions, e.g. **bei**, **mit**, **von**, **zu**.

- **Adjectival endings**

 When adjectives occur before a noun, they have an ending. In this unit, you are introduced to the pattern <u>indefinite article + adjective + noun</u> in the *accusative*:
 Masculine: **Es gibt einen großen Balkon.**
 Feminine: **Sie hat eine altmodische Lampe.**
 Neuter: **Wir haben ein neues Bett.**
 and to the pattern <u>adjective + plural noun</u>: **Ihr habt tolle Sessel!**

- **Informal 'you'**
 The plural of **du** is **ihr**, verb ending **-t**: **Ihr habt eine schöne Wohnung!**

Grammatikübungen

1 Complete ten sentences using in each case the correct (accusative) form of the indefinite article after **es gibt**. A tip: you will need to be sure of the gender of each noun!

In meinem Zimmer gibt *es einen/eine/ein* … Radio … Computer … Lampe
 … Fernseher … Schreibtisch

In unserer Küche gibt es *einen/eine/ein* … Kühlschrank … Elektroherd … Tisch
 … Waschmaschine … Mikrowelle

2 Accusative or dative? Which of the bracketed forms is correct?

 a Nachmittags arbeiten wir in (*die/der*) Bibliothek.
 b Geht ihr oft (*ins/im*) Kino?
 c Sie steht im Moment unter (*die/der*) Dusche.
 d Ich sitze an (*meinen/meinem*) Schreibtisch.
 e Er geht (*ins/im*) Zimmer und arbeitet.
 f Abends sehe ich (*ins/im*) Wohnzimmer fern.

3 Using the dative. Complete with the correct entry from the list at the end of the exercise.

 a Wir kaufen selten _____ Bäcker – Monika backt gern. Sie ist immer _____ Küche!
 b Ich habe die Lampe _____ Freund.
 c Die Lampe ist jetzt _____ Tisch _____ Schlafzimmer.
 d Er wohnt _____ Freundin zusammen.
 e Sie laden uns _____ Kaffeetrinken ein.

auf einem	in der	zum	mit seiner	beim	von einem	im

4 Add an ending to the adjective *where appropriate*.

 a Ihr habt eine schön___ Küche!
 b Meine neu___ Wohnung ist sehr modern___ .
 c Es gibt ein klein___ Esszimmer.
 d Unsere Sessel sind elegant___ und bequem___ .
 e Er hat einen klein___ Balkon, aber keinen Garten.
 f Ich kaufe morgen eine teur___ Lampe für mein Schlafzimmer.

5 How do you say …

 a Do you live here in Rostock? (To a middle-aged couple you have just met.)
 b You bake delicious cakes. (To your boyfriend/girlfriend.)
 c Do you have a flat with a garage? (To an estate agent.)
 d Do you have a shower or a bath? (To fellow students who have moved in together.)

Vokabeln

See Appendix p. 190 for more vocabulary from Aufgabe 8, Extra!, Grammatikübungen and Partnerarbeit

Aufgabe 1

glauben	to think, believe
im Bett	in bed
gerade	just
unter	under
die Dusche	shower
sagen	to say
fertig	finished
im Unterricht	in a class
anrufen *sep*	to phone
später	later
etwa	about, roughly
ich bin's	it's me
das Zimmer	room
sitzen	to sit
das Eiscafé	ice-cream parlour
ich weiß nicht	I don't know
viel zu tun	a lot to do

Aufgabe 3

ihr seid	you are (pl, informal)
euer/eure etc.	your (pl, informal)
wie lange?	how long? (time)
das Wohnzimmer	living room
die Küche	kitchen
das Schlafzimmer	bedroom
das Badezimmer	bathroom
die Garage	garage
der Balkon	balcony
das Esszimmer	dining room

Aufgabe 4

der/die/das erste, zweite	the first, second
links	(on the) left
ziemlich	fairly
Stühle *pl*	chairs
der Stuhl	chair
das Sofa	couch
Sessel *pl*	armchairs
das Bücherregal	bookcase
die Ecke	corner
stehen	to stand
die Lampe	lamp
rechts von	to the right of

der Elektroherd	electric cooker
der Kühlschrank	refrigerator
die Waschmaschine	washing machine
die Mikrowelle	microwave
einige	some
Schränke *pl*	cupboards
Nachttische *pl*	bedside tables
der Kleiderschrank	wardrobe
die Badewanne	bath
der Garten	garden

Aufgabe 7

dunkel	dark
auf	on
der Fußboden	floor
liegen	to lie
Bücher *pl*	books
Papiere *pl*	papers
Tassen *pl*	cups
Teller *pl*	plates
der Schreibtisch	desk
Gläser *pl*	glasses
Bierflaschen *pl*	beer bottles
putzen	to clean
aufräumen *sep*	to tidy up
abwaschen* *sep*	to wash up

Aufgabe 8

schön	beautiful
hell	bright
groß	big
nächste Woche	next week
wirklich	really
gemütlich	cosy
toll	great
besonders	especially
praktisch	practical
der Sommer	summer
grillen	to barbecue
Partys feiern	have parties
hoffentlich	hopefully
warm	hot, warm
ganz	quite
modern	modern
Kissen *pl*	cushions
der Sperrmüll	bulky refuse
(often picked up by bargain-hunters)	
nähen	to sew
wunderbar	wonderful
ein bisschen	a bit
bequem	comfortable

*Verb strong in present tense

Partnerarbeit

1 Wohnungsplan

Swap information with your partner in order to complete the plan of a flat below. Ask questions to find out about the rooms that are still blank on your plan. You will also tell him/her how the living room is furnished (couch, armchair, bookcase, two lamps, TV set).

He/She will then tell you about the furniture/equipment in one room. Sketch it in on the plan.

Compare notes afterwards.

Example: **A** Wo ist das Badezimmer? **B** Links/Rechts vom/von der …
A Im Wohnzimmer gibt es …

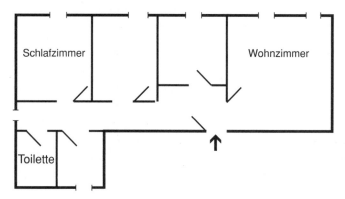

2 Wo ist Stefan?

Tell your partner what these men are doing at home. He/She responds by indicating which room the man is in. Use the pictures below, then try to think of other activities.

Example: **A** Stefan hört Musik. **B** Er ist im Wohnzimmer.

1 Stefan's listening to music

2 Felix 3 Carsten 4 Ralf

3 Ulrike ist im Kino

Your partner tells you about Ulrike's leisure activities, and you respond by indicating where Ulrike pursues this activity.

Example: **B** Ulrike sieht einen Film. **A** Sie ist im Kino.

Partnerarbeit

B

1 Wohnungsplan

Swap information with your partner in order to complete the plan of a flat below. Ask questions to find out about the rooms that are still blank on your plan. She/He will also give you details of the furniture in one room. Sketch it in on the plan.

You then tell her/him what there is in the kitchen (electric cooker, microwave, fridge, washing machine).

Compare notes afterwards.

Example: **B** *Wo ist die Toilette?* **A** *Links/Rechts vom/von der …*
B *In der Küche gibt es …*

2 Stefan ist im Wohnzimmer

Your partner says what the men are doing, and you tell him/her which room each man is in.

Example: **A** *Stefan hört Musik.* **B** *Er ist im Wohnzimmer.*

3 Was macht Ulrike?

You tell your partner about Ulrike's leisure activities, and he/she tells you where Ulrike is. Try to think of as many possibilities as you can.

Example: **B** *Ulrike isst eine Pizza.* **A** *Sie ist im Restaurant.*

1 She's eating a pizza.

2 3 4

6 In der Stadt

In this unit you will learn how to ask for and understand directions and talk about locations in a town. You will also learn how to express likes and dislikes, particularly in relation to clothes.

1 Kennst du die Felsingstraße?/Do you know Felsingstraße?

– Kennst du die Felsingstraße?
– Das ist *nicht weit von dem Krankenhaus*, oder …?
– Genau – *wir sind um die Ecke*. Nimmst du den Bus?
– Ja, die Linie fünf.
– Es gibt eine Haltestelle in der Humboldtstraße. *Geh über die Straße* und dann rechts. *Die nächste Straße links* ist die Sankt-Johann-Straße. Es gibt eine Kirche *an der Ecke. Geh am Krankenhaus vorbei* und nimm die zweite Straße rechts: das ist die Felsingstraße. Die Nummer 72 ist *auf der linken Seite* – wir sind *im ersten Stock*.
– Gibt es nicht eine Schule dort *in der Nähe*?
– Ja, wir sind *direkt gegenüber der Schule*.

a Among the phrases in italics, find the German equivalents of:

i	on the left-hand side	**vi**	the next street on the left
ii	cross the street	**vii**	directly opposite the school
iii	go past the hospital	**viii**	not far from the hospital
iv	we are round the corner	**ix**	nearby
v	on the corner	**x**	on the first floor

Grammatik

The *imperative* is the form of the verb used for giving instructions:
Geh **über die Straße. **Nimm** die zweite Straße rechts.**
For the informal imperative singular, take the **du**-form of the verb and simply remove the -st ending: **geh(st)** → **geh**, **nimm(st)** → **nimm**.

Über, an and **auf** belong to the category of prepositions followed by the accusative or the dative. Here **über** indicates change of place ('where to') rather than location, so the article is in the accusative: **über die Straße. An** and **auf** indicate location in this text, so the articles following them are in the dative: **an der Ecke, auf der linken Seite.**

b On the basis of the instructions, draw a sketch-map showing how to get to the flat from the bus stop. Include all the locations mentioned. Compare your sketch with a partner's.

 2 Es ist nicht weit/It's not far …

Referring to your sketch but not the text, describe how you get to the flat in **1**. Use the **ich-**form: *Ich gehe über die Straße …*

die Ampel

die Kreuzung

 3 Wie komme ich zum Goethehaus?/How do I get to the Goethehaus?

a Rafael lives in Berlin and is visiting Frankfurt am Main for the first time. Listen to the recording and fill in the missing items in the conversations between Rafael and two passers-by. The street names are in italics.

An der U-Bahn-Station Willy-Brandt-Platz
- Entschuldigen Sie bitte, wie komme ich zum Goethehaus?
- Ah, das ist nicht **a** _____. Gehen Sie hier die *Friedensstraße* geradeaus und nehmen Sie dann die erste Straße **b** _____. Das ist die *Bethmannstraße*. Gehen Sie am **c** _____ vorbei bis zur Kreuzung und dann links in die *Berliner Straße*. Nach etwa fünf Minuten gehen Sie halblinks in den *Großen Hirschgraben*. Das Goethehaus ist dann gleich auf der linken **d** _____.
- Vielen Dank für Ihre Hilfe. Auf Wiedersehen.
- Auf Wiedersehen!

Vor dem Goethehaus
- Entschuldigung, wie komme ich am besten zur Paulskirche?
- Da müssen Sie hier über die Straße gehen und dann die **e** _____ rechts rein – in die *Weißadlergasse*. Nehmen Sie dann die zweite Straße **f** _____ und gehen Sie **g** _____ bis zur Ampel. Dort gehen Sie **h** _____ die *Berliner Straße* und dann sehen Sie die Paulskirche schon.
- Vielen Dank!

Grammatik

Gehen Sie! (Go!) **Nehmen Sie!** (Take!)
Imperative (formal): reverse the normal order. **Sie nehmen → nehmen Sie!**
For the *informal plural*, use the **ihr-**form without the pronoun: **Geht! Nehmt!**

b Now look at the map and try to follow the directions given on the previous page. Do you get to the right places?

Frankfurt am Main, Innenstadt

Entschuldigen Sie, wie komme ich **zum** …	Paulsplatz? **zur** … Dom Goethehaus Rathaus Museum	Post? Markthalle U-Bahn-Station

Gehen Sie geradeaus/links/rechts … bis zum/zur … am/an der … vorbei
Nehmen Sie die erste/zweite/dritte/vierte Straße rechts/links.
Der/Die/Das … ist … auf der rechten/linken Seite.

4 Entschuldigen Sie ...

Refer to the map of Frankfurt. Here are the answers, what were the questions? When you have decided, check by listening to the recording.

a *Sie sind an der U-Bahn-Station Willy-Brandt-Platz.*
„Es ist in der Berliner Straße. Gehen Sie hier geradeaus, an der Paulskirche vorbei. Es ist auf der rechten Seite, an der Ecke zur Domstraße."

b *Sie sind vor dem Goethehaus*
„Gehen Sie hier links in die Berliner Straße. Nehmen Sie dann die zweite Straße rechts, so kommen Sie zum Römerberg. Gehen Sie links, an der U-Bahn-Station vorbei, und es ist auf der linken Seite, vor dem Dom."

5 Wohin?

Working with a partner and referring to the map and question/answer guidelines on the previous page, role-play asking for and giving directions to locations in Frankfurt city centre. Remember to agree where you are starting from!

6 Die Innenstadt/The town centre

Match up the German words with their English equivalents. Check your decisions in the unit vocabulary page 72.

1	die Bank	**a**	railway station
2	der Buchladen/die Buchhandlung	**b**	Karstadt department store
3	der Bahnhof	**c**	florist's
4	die Kirche	**d**	bank
5	der Supermarkt	**e**	petrol station
6	die Post	**f**	pharmacy
7	die U-Bahn-Station	**g**	bookshop
8	die Apotheke	**h**	baker's
9	das Kaufhaus „Karstadt"	**i**	chemist's, drug store
10	die Tankstelle	**j**	church
11	das Blumengeschäft	**k**	underground station
12	die Bäckerei	**l**	post office
13	die Drogerie	**m**	supermarket

7 In der Nähe/Nearby

Listen and fill in the gaps.

a *Sie sind am Bahnhof*
– Entschuldigen Sie, gibt es hier in der Nähe eine Apotheke?
– Eine Apotheke? … Ja. Gehen Sie hier **a** _____ und nehmen Sie die **b** _____ Straße links. Sie kommen dann zur Rheinstraße – gehen Sie rechts an der **c** _____ . Die Apotheke ist auf der linken Seite **d** _____ Karstadt.
– Danke.
– Bitte.

b *Im Goetheweg, auf dem Campus*
– Entschuldigen Sie, gibt es eine Bank in der Nähe?
– Ja, … gehen Sie hier rechts in den Goetheweg, **e** _____ um die Ecke und dann **f** _____ . An der Ampel gehen Sie wieder rechts: Die Bank ist auf der **g** _____ Seite.
– Vielen Dank.

danke thanks **vielen Dank** thanks a lot **bitte** it's my pleasure/no problem (also means 'please'.)

Now check the directions against the street plan below!

 8 Gibt es ...?

With a partner, role-play asking if there is one of the following nearby and giving directions. Use the street plan. Remember **es gibt** is followed by the accusative!

Sie sind vor dem Bahnhof
ein Buchladen, ein Parkhaus, ein Restaurant

Sie sind im Goetheweg
eine Bäckerei, ein Supermarkt

9 Fragezeichen/Question marks

 a You will hear a set of three directions given by passers-by. Trace these directions on the map on page 65 to find out which mystery locations they lead to. The locations are marked with letters in circles on the map. The point of departure in all cases is the exit from the station.

 b There are no directions to the fourth mystery location. Once you have identified it, tell your partner how to get there.

10 Neben der Bank/Next to the bank

 a Read this short text, referring to the street plan on page 65:

> Hier ist die Innenstadt.
> Die Post ist **gegenüber** einer Bäckerei und **neben** einer Drogerie.
> Die Bäckerei ist **zwischen** einem Buchladen und einem Kaufhaus.
> Das Krankenhaus ist **hinter** einer Apotheke.
> Das Museum ist **vor** der Bibliothek.

b Fill in the gaps
 i Der Supermarkt ist _____ e_____ Tankstelle und e____ Blumengeschäft.
 ii Die Tankstelle ist neben e_____ _____ .
 iii Das Rathaus ist gegenüber d_____ Bahnhof.
 iv Das Blumengeschäft ist _____ e_____ _____ und e_____ _____ .
 v Der Supermarkt ist vor d_____ _____ .

c Describe the locations of:
 i die Bar **ii** das Kino **iii** die Schule **iv** die Bibliothek **v** der Park

11 In unserer Stadt/In our town

With a partner, agree on how you would give a German speaker directions for how to get between two locations in your town or a city you both know.

12 Im Kaufhaus/In the department store

Monika and Claudia are in Karstadt, a department store. Claudia wants to buy a dress as she's going to a wedding soon.

In der Abteilung „Damenbekleidung"/In the ladieswear department
(A = shop assistant)

C: Schau mal, Monika, dieses Kleid – ist das nicht toll?

M: Mmmhh, ich weiß nicht … Die Farbe gefällt mir nicht. … Aber wie findest du dieses?

C: Ja doch, hübsch. Welche Größe ist es? … 38, das ist richtig.
Ich probiere das Kleid mal an … (*tries it on*)
Nein, dieses Kleid gefällt mir nicht – es ist zu lang. Vielleicht nehme ich diesen Rock hier … eine neue schwarze Bluse habe ich zu Hause. Wie gefällt dir dieser Rock?

M: Sehr schick … und sexy! Hm … ist der Rock nicht zu kurz?

C: Nein, das ist in Ordnung … Du, dieser Rock gefällt mir! Und das ist auch die richtige Größe.

M: Prima … wie teuer?

C: 45 Euro, das ist okay.

A: Kann ich Ihnen helfen? Gefällt Ihnen dieser Rock?

C: Ja danke, ich nehme den Rock …
Ich muss noch etwas für Michael kaufen, er braucht ein neues Hemd. Er hat eine schicke Hose, eine neue Jacke, aber kein Hemd – nur alte T-Shirts … Furchtbar! Er trägt nie einen Anzug …

M: Komm, da müssen wir in die Herrenabteilung. …
Schau mal, diese Krawatte *musst* du für Michael kaufen …

C: Krawatte mit Micky Maus … ich weiß ja nicht, ein bisschen bunt!

Fragen:
a Warum kauft Claudia das Kleid nicht?
b Was kauft sie?
c Was will sie für Michael kaufen?

Grammatik

Ich kaufe *diesen* Rock.	D*ieser* Rock <u>gefällt</u> mir.
Ich kaufe *diese* Bluse.	D*iese* Bluse <u>gefällt</u> mir.
Ich kaufe *dieses* Kleid.	D*ieses* Kleid <u>gefällt</u> mir.
Ich kaufe *diese* T-Shirts.	D*iese* T-Shirts <u>gefallen</u> mir.

die Jeans (*pl*)

der Pullover

die Weste

das Jackett

die Schuhe (*pl*)

der Mantel

die Trainingsschuhe

die Socken (*pl*)

 13 Das gefällt mir nicht

Your friend is in a negative mood and does not like any of the things you want to buy. One of you asks, the other replies.

Example: *Wie findest du diesen Rock? Dieser Rock gefällt mir nicht.*

a Wie findest du …

i dieses T-Shirt?	**iv** diesen Pullover?	**vii** dieses Kleid?
ii diese Jacke?	**v** diese Socken?	**viii** dieses Jackett?
iii dieses Hemd?	**vi** diesen Rock?	**ix** diese Schuhe?

b Swap roles and take the conversation one step further: from the items below choose reasons for not liking particular items of clothing.

zu lang	zu kurz	zu teuer	zu klein	zu groß
zu modern	zu altmodisch	zu langweilig	zu bunt	

Example: *Wie findest du diese Jacke? Die Jacke gefällt mir nicht. Sie ist zu altmodisch.*
 Und dieser Rock? Er ist zu lang.

Grammatik

Demonstrative adjective
Dieser follows the pattern of the definite article **der**, **die**, **das** etc.
nominative: **dieser Rock**, **diese Jacke**, **dieses Hemd**.
accusative: **Ich nehme diesen Pullover.**

(Reminder: Feminine and neuter accusative remain as in the nominative.)

Pronouns
'it' = **er** for masculine nouns, **sie** for feminine, **es** for neuter

14 Was trägst du?/What are you wearing?

a Get together with a partner and describe the clothes he/she is wearing. Swap roles.

b Now each partner takes it in turns to describe what another student in the class is wearing. See if your partner can guess who you are talking about. To help you to be more specific, here is a list of colours. You ought to be able to work out what most of them are …

blau	**rot**	**grün**	**gelb** (yellow)	**braun**	**weiß**	**schwarz** (black)	**beige**

Examples: *Sie trägt einen blauen Pullover (m.)*
 Sie trägt eine grüne Jacke. (f.)
 Er trägt ein rotes Hemd. (n.)
 Er trägt schwarze Schuhe. (pl)

Extra!

Berlin Stadtmitte

Berlin ist die Hauptstadt von Deutschland. Es gibt viele wichtige und interessante Sehenswürdigkeiten in Berlin, zum Beispiel den *Reichstag* und das *Brandenburger Tor*. Hier ist ein Plan von der Stadtmitte.

KEY		
1 Reichstag	6 St. Hedwigs-Kathedrale	U = Underground
2 Brandenburger Tor	7 Staatsoper	S = Railway Station
3 Russische Botschaft	8 Humboldt-Universität	
4 Staatsbibliothek	9 Neue Wache	
5 Königliche Bibliothek	10 Deutsches Historisches Museum	
	11 Berliner Dom	

15 Wohin will der Tourist gehen?

A visitor to Berlin arrives at the *Bahnhof Friedrichstraße* and asks for directions to three tourist attractions in the town centre. Listen to the recording and follow the directions on the map above. Where does the tourist want to get to?

a _Brandenburger Tor_ b _Berliner Dom_ c _Brandenburger_

16 Stadttour

You are on a city centre sightseeing tour during a visit to Berlin. Listen to the tour guide's commentary as the bus drives through the streets shown above. Give three of the various places mentioned, plus an item of information about each of them. Remember you are not expected to understand everything!

Museum
Berliner Dom

Reichstag - british architect Norman foster
Deutschlands Parlament

Unter den Linden - biggest road in Berlin
Union 1st Unt Karl Marx Haus.

Grammatik

- **The imperative**

 The imperative is used to give instructions.

 - When addressing one or more people with whom you are on *formal* terms, reverse the order of the pronoun **Sie** and the verb: **Sie gehen** → **Gehen Sie!**

 - When talking to someone with whom you are on *informal* terms, the imperative form is based on the **du**-form of the verb. Delete the **-st** ending: **du gehst** → **geh! du arbeitest** → **arbeite!**

 - If you are speaking *informally* to more than one person, you use the **ihr**-form of the verb but without the pronoun: **ihr geht** → **geht!**

- **D*ieser* (this), *jeder* (each, every), *welcher*? (which?) follow the pattern of the definite article:**

masculine (nominative)	*feminine*	*neuter*	*plural*
der	**die**	**das**	**die**
dieser, jeder, welcher	**diese** etc.	**dieses** etc.	**diese** etc.

 Dieser Rock/Diese Jacke/Dieses Kleid ist schön. Diese Schuhe sind teuer.

 - As with the article, the accusative form is the same as the nominative, except for the masculine: **den/diesen**. Example: **Ich kaufe diesen Pullover.**

- *gefallen*

 - This verb expresses liking for objects. (Use **gern** after the verb to express liking for activities: **Ich spiele gern Basketball.**) Because **gefallen** means literally 'to please', you have to be careful: **Die Jacke gefällt mir** 'I like the jacket' (literally 'The jacket pleases me'.)

 - **Gefallen** is always followed by a dative object. The dative pronoun corresponding to **ich** is **mir** (me), **du** → **dir** (you, informal singular), **Sie** → **Ihnen** (you, formal).
 „Gefällt dir dieses Kleid?" – „Ja, es gefällt mir sehr."
 "Gefallen dir diese Schuhe?" – „Nein, sie gefallen mir nicht."

- **Prepositions**
 - The prepositions you have met so far are mostly followed by the dative. Some always (such as **zu**, **von**, **mit**, **gegenüber**), some when they tell us 'where' (**wo**) (such as **in**, **auf**, **an**, **über**).

 - There are prepositions which are always followed by the accusative. Examples you have met are **für**, **um**, **durch** and **entlang**:
 durch den Park (through the park), **um die Ecke** (round the corner),
 die Straße entlang (along the street).
 Note that **entlang** normally comes after the noun.

Grammatikübungen

1 Complete the sentences with an appropriate verb in the imperative from the list at the end. You are talking to (**a**) a stranger in the street; (**b**) a fellow-student; (**c**) friends of yours, a young couple. Note: there are two surplus verbs in the list!

i _Trink_ nicht so viel Bier! (b)
ii _Kommen Sie_ hier über die Straße. (a)
iii _Kommt_ nächsten Montag. (c)

iv _Bring_ eine Flasche Wein. (b)
v _Geht_ am Kino vorbei. (c)
vi _Arbeite_ in der Bibliothek. (b)

kommt	kommen Sie	~~bring~~	bringt
~~trink~~	~~geht~~	gehen Sie	~~arbeite~~

2 Complete each question with (**a**) the appropriate form of **gefallen**, and (**b**) the correct form of the demonstrative adjective, then (**c**) complete the reply. You must be sure of genders!

i Gefällt/Gefallen dir dies___ Kleid? Ja, *es* gef_____ mir sehr.
ii _____ dies___ Jacke? Nein, *sie* gef_____ mir nicht.
iii _____ dies___ Rock? Ja, _____
iv _____ dies___ Krawatte? Nein, _____
v _____ dies___ Schuhe? Nein, _____
vi _____ dies___ Pullover? Ja, _____

3 Match up the correct halves of the sentences.

1 Die Bank ist hier an ...
2 Ich gehe morgens durch ...
3 Die Apotheke ist in ...
4 An der Ampel gehen Sie über ...
5 Er wohnt mit ...
6 Die Kinder spielen Fußball in ...
7 Unsere Wohnung ist um ...
8 Gehen Sie ... entlang.

a ... dem Park.
b ... die Ecke, in der Bahnhofstraße.
c ... die Adenauerstraße.
d ... der Brandtstraße.
e ... den Park.
f ... der Ecke.
g ... seiner Freundin zusammen.
h ... die Straße.

Frankfurt-am-Main Kaiserstraße.

6 In der Stadt

Vokabeln

See Appendix p. 190 for more vocabulary from exercises 12, 13 and 14.

Aufgabe 1

kennen	to know (be familiar with)
nicht weit von	not far from
das Krankenhaus	hospital
oder?	(here =) isn't it?
genau	exactly
um	round
der Bus	bus
die Linie	route
die Haltestelle	stop
über	over, across
die Straße	street
der/die/das nächste …	the next (also: nearest)
die Kirche	church
an der Ecke	on the corner
vorbeigehen *sep*	to go past
auf der linken Seite	on the left-hand side
im ersten Stock	on the first floor
die Schule	school
in der Nähe	nearby
(direkt) gegenüber	(directly) opposite

Aufgabe 3

das Goethehaus	Goethe's birthplace
entschuldigen Sie	excuse me
wie komme ich zu …	how do I get to …
geradeaus	straight on
das Parkhaus	multi-storey car park
die Kreuzung	crossroads
halblinks	fork left
gleich	immediately
die Hilfe	help
… rein	into …
bis zu	as far as
die Ampel	traffic lights
sehen*	to see
der Paulsplatz	square in Frankfurt
der Dom	cathedral
das Rathaus	town hall
das Museum	museum
die Post	post office
die Markthalle	market hall
die U-Bahn	underground
die Station	station (on underground)

Aufgabe 4

vor	in front of, before

Aufgabe 6

die Bank	bank
der Buchladen	bookshop
der Bahnhof	railway station
der Supermarkt	supermarket
die Apotheke	pharmacy
das Kaufhaus	department store
die Tankstelle	petrol station
das Blumengeschäft	flower shop
die Bäckerei	baker's/bakery
die Drogerie	chemist's, drug store

Aufgabe 7

wieder	again

Aufgabe 9

der Kreisverkehr	roundabout
durch	through

Aufgabe 10

die Innenstadt	the town centre
neben	next to
zwischen	between
hinter	behind

Aufgabe 12

schau mal	look!
das Kleid	dress
die Farbe	colour
gefallen*	lit. to please (but see Grammar)
finden	to find, think of
hübsch	pretty
welche(r/s)	which
die Größe	size
richtig	right, correct
anprobieren *sep*	to try on
(zu) lang	(too) long
der Rock	skirt
schwarz	black
die Bluse	blouse
schick	elegant, chic
kurz	short
helfen*	to help
etwas	something
das Hemd	shirt
die Hose	trousers
die Jacke	jacket
das T-Shirt	T-shirt
furchtbar	terrible

*Verb strong in present tense

Partnerarbeit

1 Was trägt Sophie?

Your partner describes what Sophie is wearing and you decide which of the three drawings below corresponds to this description. When you think you know, show your partner the drawing you think she/he is describing.

2 Lars trägt ...

Now you describe Lars' clothes in the drawing below. Your partner will show you which of the three pictures on the Partner B page he/she thinks you are describing. Tell him/her whether it's right (**richtig**).

Er trägt ...

3 Kleider

Once you've found which picture of Sophie was being described, look at all three pictures with your partner and discuss the differences. Do the same with the pictures of Lars.

Hier trägt er/sie (k)ein(e/en) ...

Partnerarbeit

B

1 Sophie trägt …

Describe what Sophie is wearing in the picture below. Your partner will show you which one of the three drawings on the Partner A page he/she thinks you have described.

Tell him/her whether it's right (**richtig**).

Sie trägt …

2 Was trägt Lars?

Now you have to decide which picture of Lars your partner is describing. When you think you know, show him/her.

3 Kleider

Once you've found which picture of Lars was being described, look at all three pictures with your partner and discuss the differences. Do the same with the pictures of Sophie.

Hier trägt er/sie (k)ein/e/n …

7 Fahren

In this unit you will learn to talk about dates, travel and accommodation, make travel enquiries and buy tickets.

1 Die Monate

Repeat the months and learn them.

Januar	April	Juli	Oktober
Februar	Mai	August	November
März	Juni	September	Dezember

im März, am neunzehnten März

19 März

2 Wann bist du frei?/When are you free?

Ute wants to fix a date for a visit to her parents in Berlin. Her boyfriend, Hans, is very busy in March.

- Du weißt, dass ich im März keine Zeit habe …
- Aber bist du am neunzehnten frei?
- Nein, ich verbringe zwei Tage bei meinen Freunden in Dresden.
- Wann kommst du zurück?
- Am einundzwanzigsten – am Abend.
- Du bist also am zweiundzwanzigsten frei?
- Ich habe einen Termin beim Zahnarzt … und ab dem dreiundzwanzigsten arbeite ich, um Geld für die Sommerferien zu verdienen.
- Ich gebe auf!

Grammatik

Word order
- **Dass** introduces a subordinate clause and sends the verb to the end.
 Du weißt, dass ich diese Woche keine Zeit habe.
- The construction **um … zu** (**um Geld zu verdienen** 'in order to earn money') also has the verb at the end (in the infinitive form).

Dative plural: possessive **-en** ending, noun **-n** ending: **bei meinen Freunden**.

3 Wann?

To give a date, you have to combine the month (see exercise 1) with an ordinal number ('first', 'twenty-fifth' etc.). You met some of these in Unit 6:
im ersten Stock, die dritte Straße rechts.

These two examples are irregular: the regular pattern is easy to learn:

der zweite, der fünfte, der neunzehnte; der zwanzigste, der einunddreißigste

See the fuller list on the grammar page, p. 82.

> **Wann ist dein/Ihr Geburtstag?**
> **Mein Geburtstag ist <u>der</u> zwöl<u>fte</u> (12.) Februar** ('the 12th of February').
> **Wann hast du/haben Sie Geburtstag?**
> **Ich habe <u>am</u> 12. (zwölf<u>ten</u>) Februar Geburtstag** ('on the 12th of February').

a Complete the sentences:
 i Heute ist der _____ .
 ii Mein Geburtstag ist der _____ .
 iii Ich habe am _____ Geburtstag.

b Give the dates: **i** 24/1 **ii** 15/4 **iii** 9/6 **iv** 3/10 **v** 10/12

c Listen to the recording and write down (in figures) the five dates you hear:
 i _____ **ii** _____ **iii** _____
 iv _____ **v** _____

d Find out the birthdays of five classmates.

4 Ein Sprachkurs in Deutschland/A language course in Germany

Read the text and decide how Vijay would answer the questions below, then check the interview on the recording to see what he says.

> Seit sechs Monaten lernt Vijay Basran Deutsch. Das macht Spaß und er bekommt sehr gute Noten. Um sein Deutsch zu verbessern, macht Vijay einen intensiven Sprachkurs. Der Kurs findet zu Ostern in Bonn statt und dauert 10 Tage. Vijay lernt Deutsch, weil er nach dem Studium im Ausland arbeiten möchte.

a Wie lange lernen Sie Deutsch? **d** Wie lange dauert der Kurs?
b Was machen Sie zu Ostern? **e** Warum lernen Sie Deutsch?
c Warum machen Sie diesen Kurs?

Grammatik

<u>Word order</u>
Um sein Deutsch zu verbessern, <u>macht</u> Vijay einen Sprachkurs.
◄—————————————►,
When a subordinate clause comes first, the main verb follows immediately, after a comma.
Weil (like **dass**) is a *subordinating conjunction* and sends the verb to the end.
Er lernt Deutsch, weil er im Ausland <u>arbeitet</u>..

Seit 6 Monaten/Seit Oktober lernt Vijay Deutsch.
Vijay has been learning German for 6 months/since October.
Note the present tense in German.

 5 Bestätigungsschreiben/Letter of confirmation

Vijay receives this letter from the administrator of his Easter German course in Bonn. Summarise in English the information it contains.

Bonn, 3. Februar 2003

Sehr geehrter Herr Basran,

wir bestätigen hiermit die folgende Zimmerreservierung im Studentenwohnheim Ferdinandstraße:

Unterkunft: 1 Einzelzimmer mit Bad und Dusche
Fernseher, Video und Telefon auf dem Zimmer
Verpflegung: Gemeinschaftsküche (für kleine Mahlzeiten)
Mensa (Öffnungszeiten: 11.30 – 14.15 Uhr)
Daten: vom 31. März bis 9. April
Preis: 16,50 Euro pro Nacht (ohne Frühstück)

Das *Studentenwohnheim* liegt sehr zentral (Straßenbahnhaltestelle ca. 5 Minuten).
Freizeitmöglichkeiten: Sportzentrum (auf dem Campus)
Kino und Theater (Innenstadt)
Hallenbad und Fitness-Studio
Fahrradvermietung für Touren am Rhein

Mit freundlichen Grüßen

E. von Kummerfeld

 6 Am Fahrkartenschalter/At the ticket window

a Vijay fliegt nach Düsseldorf und fährt dann mit dem Zug nach Bonn. Am Flughafen Düsseldorf gibt es einen Bahnhof und Vijay kauft eine Fahrkarte.

Vijay:

Wann fährt der nächste Zug nach Bonn?
Muss ich umsteigen?
Wann kommt der Zug in Bonn an?
Was kostet eine Rückfahrkarte?
Okay, ich nehme den Zug um 11.54.
Einmal Bonn, hin und zurück, bitte.

The ticket clerk:
Bitte?
Um 11.54.
Nein, er fährt direkt nach Bonn.
Um 12.46.
Mit dem Intercityzug, 32 Euro.

b Listen to the recording and complete the dialogue by filling in the gaps.

Bitte schön?

Wann fährt der nächste Zug nach **a** _____? Um **b** _____.
Muss ich umsteigen? Ja, Sie müssen in Hamburg umsteigen.
Wann bin ich in Hamburg? Um **c** _____.
Und wann fährt der Zug nach Kiel ab? Um 14.35, von Gleis **d** _____.
Was kostet eine einfache Fahrt? **e** _____.
Gut, zweimal einfach nach Kiel, bitte.

c Find the German equivalents to these phrases in the two dialogues above.

i Do I have to change?
ii When does the train arrive?
iii How much is a return ticket?
iv One return to Bonn

v Two singles to Kiel
vi The next train
vii When does the train to Kiel depart?
viii From platform 3

d With a partner, role-play the dialogues outlined below.

i Bremen? 8.14
Umsteigen? Nein
Ankommen? 9.17
Einfach? 27 Euro
1 × einfach

Auf Gleis neun – bitte einsteigen! Der Zug nach Bonn fährt ab ...

ii Leipzig? 13.08
Umsteigen? In Berlin
Berlin ankommen? 13.46
Berlin abfahren? 13.55, Gleis 9
Leipzig ankommen? 14.58
Rückfahrkarte? 41 Euro
2 × hin/zurück

Grammatik

<u>Verb families:</u> **umsteigen**, **einsteigen**: what do you think **aussteigen** means?

7 **An der Rezeption**/At reception

– Guten Morgen, ich heiße Vijay Basran. Ich komme aus England und ich mache den Sprachkurs hier.
– Herzlich willkommen! Wie kann ich Ihnen helfen?
– Ich habe ein Zimmer hier im Studentenheim *vom 31. März bis zum 9. April*. Wo bekomme ich den Schlüssel für das Zimmer?
– Ich habe den Schlüssel hier ... Einen Moment, ja, *Zimmer Nummer 34, im dritten Stock*. Leider gibt es keinen Fahrstuhl, aber da ist *Fritz*, unser Pförtner. Geben Sie ihm den Koffer! Er zeigt Ihnen gern das Zimmer.
– Das ist schon in Ordnung, der Koffer ist nicht schwer.
– Ah, hier ist *Anna Schubert*, Ihre Teamleiterin. Sie organisiert *das Freizeitprogramm*. Sagen Sie ihr, wenn Sie Probleme haben.
– Freut mich, Sie kennen zu lernen.

a Listen carefully to the recording of Frau Hilfiger and Vijay Basran at the reception of the **Studentenwohnheim**. The transcript on the previous page is largely the same as the recording but there are some inaccurate details (in *italics*). What are they?

b Working with a partner, summarise the scene in English.

Grammatik

Dative pronouns
Four verbs in the above dialogue are followed by a pronoun in the dative.

geben – to give (to so.)	**Geben Sie <u>ihm</u> den Koffer.**
	Give him the suitcase.
sagen – to say (to so.)	**Sagen Sie <u>ihr</u>, wenn Sie Probleme haben.**
	Tell her if you have problems.
helfen – to give help (to so.)	**Wie kann ich <u>Ihnen</u> helfen?** How can I help you?
zeigen – to show (to so.)	**Er zeigt <u>Ihnen</u> gern das Zimmer.**
	He'll be glad to show you the room.

The following dative pronouns occur in the dialogue above:
mir (to me) **ihm/ihr** (to him/her) **Ihnen** (to you – formal)

These pronouns are also used after prepositions taking the dative. Can you find the example in the dialogue?

8 **Am Hotel**/At the hotel

James, one of Vijay's university friends, is visiting him in Bonn during the German course. Vijay is booking a hotel room for him and his girlfriend.

- Guten Tag, ich möchte ein Zimmer reservieren, bitte.
- Ja, ... wann brauchen Sie das Zimmer?
- Vom 5. April bis zum 8. April.
- Also, drei Nächte. ... Möchten Sie ein Einzelzimmer oder ein Doppelzimmer?
- Ein Doppelzimmer, bitte.
- Wir haben Zimmer mit Bad und Dusche und Zimmer mit Dusche.
- Was kosten die Zimmer?
- Mit Bad und Dusche, 72 Euro pro Nacht, einschließlich Frühstück. Mit Dusche, 59 Euro.
- Ich nehme ein Zimmer mit Bad und Dusche.
- Ein Doppelzimmer mit Bad und Dusche, Anreise am 5. April, Abreise am 8. April. ... Wie heißen Sie, bitte?
- Das Zimmer ist für einen Freund von mir, Herrn White, und seine Freundin. Ich gebe Ihnen seine Adresse und seine Telefonnummer.
- Danke.

Grammatik

Ich gebe <u>Ihnen</u> seine Adresse I'll give <u>you</u> his address
This sentence has an *indirect* object (**Ihnen**) as well as a direct object (**seine Adresse**).
What I'm giving is the address, I'm giving it <u>to</u> you (dative in German).
– Which of the four sentences in the previous grammar box have both sorts of object?

7 Fahren

 Using the previous dialogue as a model, role-play a similar scene with a partner. The differences are:

You want a single room; with a shower; from 29 June to 2 July; i.e. four nights; the room is for you, so give your name when asked.

9 An der Straßenbahnhaltestelle/At the tram stop

To get about most towns, you have to be able to use an automatic ticket machine. Can you follow the instructions? The questions will help you to focus on the key information.

2 Zielwahl
Wenn Sie ein anderes Ziel erreichen wollen, suchen Sie es im alphabetischen Verzeichnis. Hier finden Sie die Zielnummer.

3 Fahrpreisinformation
– Drücken Sie eine Schnellwahltaste oder tippen Sie die Zielnummer.
– Wählen Sie die gewünschte Fahrkarte (Erwachsene, Kinder, Tageskarte).
Der Automat gibt Ihnen den Fahrpreis.

4 Zahlung
Sie können mit Münzen oder Geldscheinen zahlen. Restgeld erhalten Sie zurück.

1 Schnellwahl
Für Fahrtziele in der Innenstadt drücken Sie die entsprechende Taste.

Read the information about the ticket machine and answer the questions in English:

a What is the rapid choice option for? What do you have to do?
b What must you do if your destination is not included in the rapid choice menu?
c How do you get information on fares (two ways are mentioned)?
d What are the three sorts of ticket named?
e What are we told about payment?

Extra!

10 Sprachkurs

Listen to two students talking about their advanced German summer course in Munich. Draw up a grid like the one below and fill it in in English, incorporating as much information as you can gather from the conversation.

	Personal details	Course information	Homework/ duties	Friends on course
Paloma				
Jean-Paul				

11 Hotel-Info

HEIDELBERG

Hotel Winter – ab €69*
– Autobahn 1,5 km, Bahnhof 1,5 km, Flughafen 90 km
Preise inklusive Frühstück, Wellness-Bereich und Parkplatz

– Alle Zimmer mit Dusche und WC
– Alle Zimmer mit Kabelfernsehen, Telefon und Mini-Bar
– Parkplatz
– Ruhige Lage in einer Seitenstraße
– Seminarräume
– Terrasse und Biergarten
– Wellness-Bereich mit Fitnessgeräten, Solarium und Sauna
– Restaurant (gastronomisches Menü und regionale Spezialitäten)
– gemütliche Bar

Wir sind direkt am Neckarufer mit schöner Aussicht von der Terrasse. Innerhalb von wenigen Minuten erreichen Sie die weltberühmten Sehenswürdigkeiten Alt-Heidelbergs.

You and a friend are going by car to Heidelberg for a short break. Your friend favours staying in a student hostel, but you'd prefer to stay in this hotel. Draft an email in English in which you persuasively summarise what the hotel offers.

See how much you understand before referring to the vocabulary at the back of the book. Compare notes with a classmate.

Grammatik

- **Subordinate clauses**

 - These clauses are introduced by *subordinating conjunctions* (see the Guide to Grammatical Terms and the Grammar Summary for more details) such as **wenn**, **weil** and **dass**. There must be a comma before the subordinating conjunction.

 - The verb in the clause goes to the end: **Du weißt, dass ich keine Zeit <u>habe</u>.**
 This puts it after any infinitive which would be at the end anyway:
 Er lernt Deutsch, weil er im Ausland arbeiten <u>möchte</u>.

 - Note the construction **um ... zu** with an infinitive, expressing 'in order to':
 Ich mache den Kurs, <u>um</u> mein Deutsch <u>zu</u> verbessern. The infinitive goes to the end.

 - When a subordinate clause begins a sentence, it is treated as the first item in the sentence and so is followed by the verb of the main clause. A comma marks the end of the subordinate clause:
 Wenn Sie ein anderes Ziel erreichen wollen, suchen Sie im Verzeichnis.
 subordinate clause main clause

- ***seit***

 Ich lerne Deutsch seit September. **Ich lerne Deutsch seit sechs Monaten.**
 I've been learning German <u>since</u> September. ... <u>for</u> six months.

 This preposition does the work of two English equivalents. Note that in German the present tense is used (because the situation is still going on).
 Seit is followed by the dative: **Seit ein<u>em</u> Jahr.**

- **Dative plural**

 Articles, possessives, adjectives and nouns all end in **-n**. Add the ending to the noun if its plural form does not already end in an **-n**. Exception: nouns with a plural ending in **-s**.
 Sie können mit Münzen oder Geldschein<u>en</u> zahlen.
 Ich helfe dir mit <u>den</u> schwer<u>en</u> Koffer<u>n</u>.

- **Dative pronouns**

 mir dir ihm/ihr uns Ihnen ihnen euch
 See also pages 148, 149 and 152 for the *Indirect Object*.

- **Ordinal numbers**

der	erste	zwanzig<u>ste</u>	Am ...	ers<u>ten</u>
	zwei<u>te</u>	einundzwanzig<u>ste</u>		zwei<u>ten</u>
	dritte			zwanzig<u>sten</u>
	vier<u>te</u>	dreiß<u>igste</u>		
	fünf<u>te</u>	vierzig<u>ste</u>		

 (NB: 7 der sie**bte**)

Grammatikübungen

1 Put the two sentences together, turning the underlined one into a subordinate clause. Use each of **dass**, **weil**, **wenn**. One of them has to be used twice. Be careful to get the word order right!

a Sie kann leider nicht kommen. <u>Sie schreibt am vierzehnten einen Test.</u>

b Ich weiß. <u>Er bekommt sehr gute Noten.</u>

c Wir haben keine Zeit. <u>Wir arbeiten jeden Abend.</u>

d <u>Das Wetter ist schlecht.</u> Ich komme schon am neunzehnten zurück.

In the following, use **um ... zu** to put the English into German:

e Sie fahren nach Deutschland *in order to do a German course*.

f Ich habe einen Job *in order to earn money for the summer holidays*.

2 Translate the words in brackets into German: You'll need **seit**, and a noun in the dative.

a (*For three years*) wohnt Dieter mit (*his friends*) Uwe und Hans zusammen.

b (*Since November*) hilft er (*his parents*) im Büro.

3 Translate the following sentences into German. Take care to use the correct pronoun:

a Klaus gives him a letter.

b Markus goes with her to the cinema.

c I can show you (formal) a good café.

d Tell me if you (formal) have problems!

e How are you (informal, singular)?

f Ali shows them his new car.

4 a Write the dates in words:
Example: der erste März

 i 1.3 (nach London fahren/ich)

 ii 26.6 (Geburtstag haben/sie sing.)

 iii 3.10 (zum Zahnarzt gehen/er)

 iv 15.5 (umziehen/wir)

 v 30.1 (einen Test schreiben/ich)

 vi 7.8 (zum Sprachkurs fahren/wir)

 vii 11.11 (anfangen/der Sprachkurs)

 viii 27.2 (essen gehen/wir)

b Make sentences using the outlines given. Make sure you use the correct form of the verb and date. Also check your word order!
Example: <u>Am ersten März fahre ich nach London.</u>

Vokabeln

See Appendix p. 190 for vocabulary for exercise 9

Aufgabe 2

du weißt	you know
frei	free
verbringen	to spend (time)
zurückkommen *sep*	to come back
also	so, therefore
der Termin	appointment
der Zahnarzt	dentist
das Geld	money
die Sommerferien *pl*	summer holidays
verdienen	to earn
aufgeben* *sep*	to give up

Aufgabe 3

der Geburtstag	birthday

Aufgabe 4

seit	since, for (time) – see Grammar
Monate *pl*	months
Spaß machen	to be fun
Noten *pl*	grades
verbessern	to improve
intensiv	intensive
der Sprachkurs	language course
stattfinden *sep*	to take place
zu Ostern	at Easter
dauern	to last
Tage *pl*	days
weil	because
das Studium	study
im Ausland	abroad

Aufgabe 5

bestätigen	to confirm
hiermit	herewith
folgend	following
die Zimmerreservierung	room booking
das Studentenwohnheim	hall of residence
die Unterkunft	accommodation
das Einzelzimmer	single room
die Verpflegung	catering
die Gemeinschaftsküche	communal kitchen
pro Tag/Nacht	per day/night
ohne	without
liegen	to lie, be situated

die Straßenbahn	tram
ca. = circa = zirka	about
Freizeitmöglichkeiten *pl*	leisure opportunities
das Theater	theatre
das Hallenbad	indoor swimming pool
das Fitness-Studio	keep-fit centre
die Fahrradvermietung	bicycle hire
Touren *pl*	tours
der Rhein	River Rhine

Aufgabe 6

fliegen	to fly
der Flughafen	airport
die Fahrkarte	ticket (for travel)
Bitte?	How can I help you?
der (nächste) Zug	the (next) train
umsteigen *sep*	to change (trains/ buses)
ankommen *sep*	to arrive
kosten	to cost
die Rückfahrkarte	return ticket
mit dem Intercity(zug)	by Intercity
hin und zurück	return
abfahren* *sep*	to depart
Gleis x	Platform x
einfach	(here) single
einsteigen *sep*	to get on, board

Aufgabe 7

Herzlich willkommen!	Welcome!
Wie kann ich Ihnen helfen?	How can I help you?
der Schlüssel	key
der Fahrstuhl	lift
der Pförtner	porter
geben	to give
ihm	to him
der Koffer	suitcase
schwer	heavy
die Teamleiterin	team leader *f*
ihr	to her
(Es) freut mich, Sie kennen zu lernen	Pleased to meet you

Aufgabe 8

reservieren	to reserve, book
Nächte *pl*	nights
das Doppelzimmer	double room
einschließlich	including
die Anreise/Abreise	arrival/departure
die Adresse	address
die Telefonnummer	phone number

*Verb strong in present tense

Partnerarbeit

A

1 Zuginformation

You are making arrangements for a trip in Germany. Your partner is a friend who you have asked to get some train information. He/She will give only information you specifically ask for.

You speak first.

- Tell your partner you want to go from Cologne to Darmstadt. Say you want to go between 9.00 and 10.00 in the morning. Ask if there is a train at that time.
- Find out if you have to change and where.
- When do(es) the train(s) get into Darmstadt?
- Check the details with your partner by summarising the information you have been given.
- Tell him/her which train you will get.

2 Wann fahren wir nach Spanien?

You discuss on the phone with your partner when you will be going to Spain together but there are a few problems …

Play your part in the conversation, using the prompts below. German is the only language you have in common.

You speak first:

Hi, (name), when can we go to Spain?

„ … "

July is fine. Have you got time after the 15/7?

„ … "

On the 22nd? But my lectures start on the 1st of September.

„ … "

That is great. Do we take the train in Germany?

„ … "

How much does a return ticket cost?

„ … "

Oh! Can we fly from Düsseldorf?

„ … "

That is okay. Do we reserve a room in a hotel?

„ … "

Good idea. Is the hall of residence central?

„ … "

Thank you. I'll buy the train tickets to Düsseldorf.

Partnerarbeit

1 Zuginformation

Your partner is a friend making arrangements for a trip in Germany and has asked you to get some information about trains.

He/She will speak first. Give only information you are asked for!

Cologne	(Change in	Arr	Dep)	Arrives Darmstadt
9.29	Frankfurt	11.17	11.32	11.59
9.46	Mainz	11.31	12.09	12.32
10.22	Frankfurt	11.44	12.05	12.49

At the end of your conversation, your partner will give you back the information you have given him/her, so you can check he/she has understood correctly. He/She will also tell you which train he/she will get.

2 Wann fahren wir nach Spanien?

You are Partner A's friend. You discuss on the phone when you will be going to Spain together – but there are a few problems … . Play your part in the conversation, using the prompts below. German is the only language you have in common.

Partner A speaks first.

„ … "

Mmmhh, it is already June now… perhaps in July?

„ … "

I'm sorry, no – the 15th is my birthday! … And a week later?

„ … "

Perhaps we can go on the 2nd of July?

„ … "

No, that is too expensive.

„ … "

Hmmm, just a moment … about 180 euro.

„ … "

Yes, that is no problem. But we have to go to Düsseldorf by train and change.

„ … "

Perhaps in a student hall of residence. One can have single rooms or double rooms in Madrid.

„ … "

Yes, only 10 minutes by bus to the city centre. I can reserve a room because I have the phone number.

„ … "

'Bye!

8 Gestern

In this unit you will learn to talk about events in the past. You will also learn how to describe states of mind and emotions.

1 **Was hast du gestern gemacht?**/What did you do yesterday?

a Listen to the recording and see if you can fill in the missing question and answer at the end of the conversation.

- Hallo, Horst ... Wie geht's?
- Danke gut, Sabine. Und dir? Was *hast* du denn gestern *gemacht*?
- Gestern ... ach ja, ich *habe* am Nachmittag bei Aldi für ein italienisches Essen *eingekauft*: Nudeln, Tomaten, Salat, Rotwein, Parmesan. Abends *habe* ich für Manfred und Vera *gekocht*, und dann *haben* wir zusammen Musik *gehört* und ein bisschen *getanzt*. Später – sehr spät, so gegen Mitternacht – *haben* wir noch Karten *gespielt* ...
- Ein toller Abend!
- _____?
- _____.

b Fragen:
 i Wo hat Sabine eingekauft?
 ii Was hat sie gekauft?
 iii Was haben die Freunde nach dem Essen gemacht?
 iv Und was haben sie sehr spät gemacht?

Grammatik

<u>The perfect tense</u>
To talk about events in the past, you normally use the *perfect tense* in German.
Regular (weak) verbs form the perfect tense as follows:
the appropriate form of the verb **haben** plus the *past participle*.

ich	habe <u>gekocht</u>	wir	haben <u>gekocht</u>
du	hast <u>gekocht</u>	Sie	haben <u>gekocht</u>
er, sie, es	hat <u>gekocht</u>	sie	haben <u>gekocht</u>
		ihr	habt <u>gekocht</u>

NB: *Separable verbs*: **Sabine hat ein<u>ge</u>kauft.**

<u>Word order</u>: Note the position of the the past participle:
Was hast du gestern <u>gemacht</u>?

2 Ein Tag in den Semesterferien/A day in the vacation

Listen to the recording and note the differences with the text below. The verbs (in *italics*) remain the same but the details are different. Write out the corrected text.

> Um halb elf *hat* Verena gestern zwei Brötchen mit Marmelade *gegessen*, und dazu *hat* sie eine Tasse Kaffee mit Milch *getrunken*. Nach dem Frühstück *hat* sie einige E-Mails an ihre Freunde im Ausland *geschrieben*: an Markus in Australien, Inge in Israel und Rolf in Spanien. Sie *hat* lange Zeitung *gelesen* und dann nachmittags im Café Bauer ihre Mutter *getroffen*. Sie *haben* beide eine heiße Schokolade mit Sahne *getrunken* und viel geredet. Am Abend *hat* Verena ihre Freundin Susi *angerufen*, um sie ins Kino einzuladen. Leider hatte Susi keine Zeit, weil sie babysitten musste. Das war schade – der Film war spannend.

Grammatik

Strong verbs:

Note how the past participle is formed:

essen	**gegessen**	**lesen**	**gelesen**
trinken	**getrunken**	**treffen**	**getroffen**
schreiben	**geschrieben**	**anrufen**	**angerufen**

There is often a change of vowel in the past participle (see Grammar page 94).

NB: The verbs **haben**, **sein** and all *modal* verbs are usually used in the *simple past* or *imperfect tense* – **sie hatte**, ... **war**, ... **musste**, ... **konnte**.

3 E-Mail an Andreas

```
Hallo Andreas
Heute habe ich endlich Zeit! Ich hatte in den letzten zwei Wochen schrecklich viel
zu tun, und deshalb konnte ich dir nicht schreiben.
Gestern war kein schöner Tag für mich. Ich bin zu spät aufgestanden und hatte keine
Zeit zum Frühstücken. Ich bin mit dem Bus zur Uni gefahren, denn es hat geregnet.
Mein Professor war krank - also keine Vorlesung! Ich bin den ganzen Nachmittag in
der Bibliothek geblieben und habe ein wichtiges Buch für meine Dissertation gesucht,
aber leider nicht gefunden. Zum Glück ist mein Freund Julius gekommen, und wir sind
ins „Café Chaos" gegangen. Das war interessant, denn er hat mir von seiner neuen
Arbeit erzählt. Um halb acht war ich wieder zu Hause und habe den ganzen Abend
ferngesehen … langweilig!
Ich muss jetzt gehen, denn ich treffe Marina um Viertel nach acht.
Harald
```

Grammatik

Some verbs form the perfect tense with the appropriate form of **sein** instead of **haben**.

 a Read the text and find the past participles with **sein** (e.g: **ich <u>bin</u> aufgestanden**). There are four, in addition to the example given. What are the infinitives of those verbs (e.g. the infinitive of **aufgestanden** is **aufstehen**)?

 b Harald did not think much of yesterday: summarise in English what happened.

 c Without referring to the text, tell the story of Harald's day using the outline below. Use the **er**-form of the perfect tense. Remember to use **haben** or **sein** with the correct past participle (weak or strong) and remember the word order rules!

Harald ist …
spät aufstehen – Bus Uni fahren – regnen – Professor krank – Bibliothek bleiben – Buch suchen – nicht finden – Freund kommen – Café gehen – Abend fernsehen.

 4 Was hat Carima gestern gemacht?/What did Carima do yesterday?

a Look at the pictures below and write a caption for each picture. Remember to use the perfect tense to talk about past events. Make sure you use the correct form of the verb. If in doubt, consult the grammar page 94.

b Compare your version with the recording.

 5 Im Café

Listen to the recording of two conversations in a café in Bielefeld. Answer the questions below.

a *Frau Huber und Frau Malzahn*
 i Warum hat Frau Huber letzte Woche nicht gearbeitet?
 ii Was hat sie in der Stadt gemacht?
 iii Wer war auch im Café?
 iv Was hat Herr Schulz gemacht?

b *Uschi und Horst*
 i Warum ist Horst in Bielefeld?
 ii Wo hat er Monika das erste Mal gesehen?
 iii Was haben Horst und Monika dann gemacht?
 iv Wie lange ist Uschi schon mit ihrem Freund zusammen?

 6 Hallo, Anna …

Write an email to your friend in Berlin telling her what you have been doing in the last couple of weeks. The verbs given below (in the infinitive) might give you some ideas.

> ausgehen nach (London) fahren ins Konzert gehen viel arbeiten
> neuen Freund treffen Aufsatz schreiben ins Sportzentrum gehen …

 7 Gestern Abend/Last night

Katrin is angry with Dieter.

– Hallo.
– *Schweigen*
– Was ist los?
– Dieter, wo warst du gestern Abend?
– Ich habe dir gesagt … ich war in der Bibliothek.
– Bis wann?
– Ich habe bis etwa 10 Uhr gearbeitet. Dann bin ich nach Hause gegangen. Ich war müde.
– Bist du direkt nach Hause gegangen?
– Fast … . Ich habe unterwegs ein Bier getrunken. … Mit Mario.
– Wo?
– In der Campus-Bar.
– Genau! Silvia hat dich dort gesehen. Du hast die ganze Zeit mit Antje gesprochen. Und du hast sie geküsst!
– Nein! Antje hat mich geküsst. Ich war total überrascht. Und wir waren nicht allein – Mario war da.
– Wirklich? Silvia hat ihn nicht gesehen …

Grammatik

Accusative pronouns: these are used for the *direct object* of a verb.
Sie hat <u>mich</u> geküsst ('She kissed <u>me</u>') **Silvia hat <u>dich</u> gesehen** ('Silvia saw <u>you</u>')
Sie hat <u>ihn</u> nicht gesehen. ('She didn't see <u>him</u>')
Du hast <u>sie</u> geküsst ('You kissed <u>her</u>')

a Fragen:
 i Wo war Dieter bis 10 Uhr?
 ii Warum ist er nach Hause gegangen?
 iii Er ist nicht direkt nach Hause gegangen – Wohin ist er gegangen?
 iv Was hat er gemacht? (Silvias Version!)

b Working with a partner and without looking at the text, take on the role of Dieter and say what happened yesterday evening using the following prompts:

 Bibliothek arbeiten – 10 Uhr nach Hause – Bier trinken – Antje sprechen – mich küssen – überrascht

The partner takes the role of Silvia and insists on her version of what she saw!

8 **Was machst du jetzt?**/What are you going to do now?

Mario und Dieter are discussing the situation.
– Also … Man hat euch in der Bar gesehen?
– Noch schlimmer, Silvia hat uns gesehen! Sie hat Katrin alles erzählt.
– Was machst du jetzt?
– Ich sage die Wahrheit. Vielleicht ist sie nicht mehr so böse … Sie liebt mich!
– Hm …

Grammatik

Accusative pronouns:
Man hat <u>euch</u> gesehen ('you' plural, informal) **Silvia hat <u>uns</u> gesehen** ('us')

a In the short passage above, find the German equivalents of:
 i even worse **ii** told **iii** the truth **iv** angry **v** loves

b Without reference to the text, role-play the scene with a partner, using these prompts:
 Mario: – Bar gesehen? Dieter: – Silvia! – Katrin erzählt
 – Jetzt? – Wahrheit – böse – liebt!

c With a partner, script and role-play the resulting conversation between Dieter and Katrin. Act it out!

9 Wie geht's heute?/How are things today?

a Try to match up the adjectives with their English equivalents. Two of them occur earlier in this unit! Check your decisions by referring to the unit vocabulary.

1	krank	**a**	sad
2	optimistisch	**b**	in love
3	(un)glücklich	**c**	bored
4	hungrig	**d**	pleased
5	verliebt	**e**	(un)happy
6	gestresst	**f**	tired
7	ängstlich	**g**	optimistic
8	überrascht	**h**	disappointed
9	müde	**i**	ill
10	froh	**j**	anxious
11	enttäuscht	**k**	stressed
12	erkältet	**l**	hungry
13	traurig	**m**	suffering from a cold
14	gelangweilt	**n**	surprised

b Complete each sentence with an appropriate adjective.

i Pauls Mannschaft, Bayern München, hat 2:0 gewonnen. Er ist …

ii Sabine hat heute Morgen gearbeitet. Am Nachmittag muss sie das Haus putzen und die Kinder von der Schule abholen. Sie ist …

iii Matthias hat den Arzt gesehen und muss drei Tage im Bett bleiben. Er ist …

iv Herr Christiansen will Cannelloni nach Italien exportieren. Er ist …

v Karin will Karl wieder sehen. Sie ist …

vi Ich habe im Sommer eine Prüfung. Ich bin …

c And how do you feel at the moment? Tell your partner and explain why.

Frankfurter Römer

Extra!

10 Der Sprachkurs

Listen to Paloma and Jean-Paul (whom you have already met in Unit 7) talking about what they did during their time in Munich, where they attended different advanced German summer courses.

Fragen:

a Wie lange ist Paloma in München geblieben?

b Wann hat der Unterricht angefangen?

c Was hat Paloma in ihrer Freizeit gemacht?

d Wer ist Paola?

e Hat Jean-Paul der Sprachkurs gefallen?

f Was sagt er über den Sprachkurs?

g Was hat er in seiner Freizeit gemacht?

h Wer ist Nathalie?

11 Mein Wochenende

> ### Karin
>
> Mein Wochenende? Das war schrecklich! Am Samstag habe ich zu lange geschlafen und ich bin erst um halb elf aufgestanden. Dann bin ich in die Stadt gegangen. Ich habe eine schicke Boutique gesucht, weil ich ein neues Kleid kaufen wollte. Ich habe zwölf Kleider anprobiert, aber ich habe nichts gefunden: zu klein, zu lang, zu teuer, zu langweilig … Dann war ich frustriert, es war kalt und es hat geregnet. Ich bin mit dem Bus nach Hause gefahren, aber das war auch schwierig. Der Fahrkartenautomat war kaputt, ich hatte kein Kleingeld und der Busfahrer konnte den Zehn-Euro-Schein nicht wechseln. Um halb sieben hat mein Freund angerufen und gesagt, dass er nicht mit mir ins Kino gehen kann – so eine Enttäuschung! Ich war traurig, habe eine Flasche Wein aufgemacht und den Fernseher angeschaltet …

> ### Kurt
>
> Mein Wochenende war ganz fantastisch. Ich bin um halb zehn aufgestanden, und meine Freundin hat Frühstück geholt – Croissants und Ei. Wir haben einen schönen Ausflug in die Berge gemacht und dann haben wir in einem kleinen Restaurant gegessen. Das Essen war köstlich und das Wetter gut. Am Nachmittag haben wir zu Hause ein bisschen im Garten gesessen und ein Glas Wein getrunken. Um acht Uhr sind wir zu einer Party gegangen, denn mein Freund Holger hatte Geburtstag. Er hat draußen im Garten gefeiert, weil es so warm war. Die Würstchen haben gut geschmeckt, die Musik war wunderbar und wir haben viel getanzt. Ich habe einige alte Freunde getroffen und viel Spaß gehabt. Um Mitternacht sind Nadine und ich nach Hause gegangen – das war ein toller Tag!

a Summarise the two contrasting weekends in English.

b Write an account of your own weekend in German.

Grammatik

- **Perfect tense**

 - To talk about events that happened in the past, German-speakers tend to use the *perfect tense*. It has two elements:
 an *auxiliary verb* (in the normal second position in the sentence)
 and a *past participle* (at the very end of the sentence)

 - The *auxiliary* is a present tense form of either:
 haben ich habe, du hast, er/sie/es hat or **sein** ich bin, du bist, er/sie/es ist
 wir/Sie/sie haben, ihr habt wir/Sie/sie sind, ihr seid

 - The *past participle* follows one of two patterns: either:

 <u>1 weak</u> **ge...t** or <u>2 strong</u> **ge...en**
 kaufen → gekauft **kommen → gekommen**
 einkaufen → eingekauft **ankommen → angekommen**
 e.g. **Wir <u>haben</u> ein neues Auto <u>gekauft</u>.**
 Er <u>hat</u> ein Bier <u>getrunken</u>.
 Ich <u>bin</u> in die Stadt <u>gegangen</u>.

 - While weak past participles are totally predictable, you have to learn the individual strong past participles as many have a vowel change compared to the infinitive (**nehmen → genommen, trinken → getrunken**). There is a list of strong verbs on page 158 which also indicates which of them have **sein** as auxiliary.

 - All the verbs which are strong in the present tense (**du-** and **er/sie-** forms) follow the strong pattern for their past participle (e.g. **fahren** – present: **du fährst**, **er/sie fährt**; past participle: **gefahren**).

 - Some verbs which are not strong in the present tense follow the strong pattern for the past participle (e.g. **kommen** – present: **du kommst**, **er/sie kommt**; past participle: **gekommen**).

- **Accusative pronouns**

 Accusative pronouns indicate the direct object in a sentence:
 Sie hat <u>ihn</u> in der Campus-Bar gesehen. She saw <u>him</u> in the campus bar.
 (She did the seeing, so she is the subject: she saw him, so he is the direct object.)

mich	**dich**	**ihn**	**sie**	**es**	**uns**	**Sie**	**sie**	**euch**
me	you (inf, sing)	he/it (m)	she/it (f)	it (n)	us	you (formal)	them	you (inf, pl)

 Remember the accusative is also used after certain prepositions: always (e.g. **für**, **um**, **durch**) or sometimes (e.g. **in**, **auf**, **an**).

Grammatikübungen

1 Complete these perfect tense sentences with the past participle of the appropriate verb from the list and the correct form of the auxiliary.

a Hans und Heide _haben_ in New York ~~gefahren~~ _gewohnt_ .

b Wir _haben_ gestern einen neuen Computer _gekauft_ .

hat **c** Antje ~~habe~~ mich _geküsst_ – ich war total überrascht! _totally surprised_

d „ _hast_ du gut _geschlafen_ ?" – „Ja, ich war sehr müde."

e „ _Haben_ Sie den Brief _geschrieben_ ?" – „Nein, noch nicht."

f Ich _habe_ heute Vormittag nicht _gefrühstückt_

g Wir _haben_ mit dem Bus _gefahren_ .

h „Wohin ~~hast seid~~ ihr _gegangen_ ?" – „In die Stadt."

i Peter ~~hat ist~~ nicht zu unserer Party _gekommen_ , er ~~hat~~ _ist_ zu Hause _geblieben_ .

j Anna ~~hat~~ _ist_ sehr früh _aufgestanden_

Directional preposition

fahren	schlafen	küssen	schreiben	aufstehen (sep)	
kaufen	frühstücken	gehen	kommen	bleiben	wohnen

2 a Insert the correct accusative pronoun.

i Julia hat _____ in der Stadt gesehen. (*her*)

ii Er hat _____ geküsst. (*us*)

iii Wir haben es für _____ gemacht. (*you, informal sing.*)

iv Ich habe _____ gekauft. (*it, masc*)

v Sie hat _____ in der Bar gesehen. (*you, informal plural*)

vi „Wo sind die Brötchen?" – „Ich habe _____ alle gegessen!" (*them*)

b Put in the correct pronoun in the sentences below. Remember the difference between direct (accusative) and indirect (dative) objects, and bear in mind which form follows the prepositions.

i Hast du (*ihn/ihm*) in der Vorlesung gesehen?

ii Ich bin gestern mit (*sie/ihr*) ins Kino gegangen.

iii Klaus hat (*ihn/ihm*) das Buch schon gegeben.

iv Verena hat (*mich/mir*) gestern angerufen.

v Diese Flasche Wein ist für (*dich/dir*).

vi Er trifft (*sie/ihnen*) um halb neun vor dem Kino.

vii Kannst du (*mich/mir*) helfen?

viii Wir haben (*sie/ihnen*) getroffen.

Vokabeln

Aufgabe 1

Und dir?	And how are you?
gemacht	past participle of machen
das Essen	meal
eingekauft	pp of einkaufen
Tomaten *pl*	tomatoes
gekocht	pp of kochen
gehört	pp of hören
getanzt	pp of tanzen
gegen	around
gespielt	pp of spielen
Karten *pl*	cards

Aufgabe 2

Brötchen *pl*	rolls
die Marmelade	jam
gegessen	pp of essen
getrunken	pp of trinken
Australien	Australia
lange	a long time
die Zeitung	newspaper
heiß	hot
die Schokolade	chocolate
die Sahne	cream
geredet	pp of reden
reden	to talk
angerufen	pp of anrufen
babysitten	to babysit
spannend	exciting

Aufgabe 3

endlich	at last
in den letzten 2 Wochen	in the last 2 weeks
schrecklich	terribly
deshalb	therefore
aufgestanden	pp of aufstehen
zur Uni	to university
gefahren	pp of fahren*
geregnet	pp of regnen
krank	ill
den ganzen Nachmittag	all afternoon
geblieben	pp of bleiben
gesucht	pp of suchen
gefunden	pp of finden
zum Glück	luckily

gekommen	pp of kommen
gegangen	pp of gehen
erzählt	pp of erzählen
erzählen	to tell
ferngesehen	pp of fernsehen*

Aufgabe 5

allen Kollegen	to all the colleagues

Aufgabe 6

der Aufsatz	essay

Aufgabe 7

Was ist los?	What's the matter?
bis wann?	until when?
müde	tired
unterwegs	on the way
gesprochen	pp of sprechen*
sprechen*	to speak
geküsst	pp of küssen
küssen	to kiss
überrascht	surprised

Aufgabe 8

noch schlimmer	even worse
alles	everything
die Wahrheit	truth
böse	angry
lieben	to love

Aufgabe 9

optimistisch	optimistic
(un)glücklich	(un)happy, (un)lucky
hungrig	hungry
verliebt	in love
gestresst	stressed
ängstlich	anxious, afraid
froh	glad, pleased
enttäuscht	disappointed
erkältet	suffering from a cold
traurig	sad
gelangweilt	bored
die Mannschaft	team
gewonnen	pp of gewinnen
gewinnen	to win
abholen *sep*	to collect (someone)
die Prüfung	exam

*Verb strong in present tense

Partnerarbeit

1 Was hat Karen gemacht?

Fill in the blanks in Karen's diary by asking questions about what she did then. Answer your partner's questions to help him/her fill the diary too.

Example: *Was hat Karen am Donnerstagnachmittag gemacht?*
 Sie hat/ist …

	Donnerstag	Freitag	Samstag
Vormittag	10 Uhr Vorlesung (Mathe)		Frühstück mit Sabine (10.30)
Nachmittag		nach Frankfurt fahren (Museum)	
Abend	Tischtennis spielen mit Markus (7.30)		mit Klaus ins Kino gehen (8 Uhr)

2 Und was hast du gemacht?

Now ask your partner what he/she did on certain days and complete the diary below, using the information you are given.

	Mittwoch	Samstag
Vormittag		
Nachmittag		
Abend		

3 Adjektive

a From this list of adjectives denoting physical condition, states of mind, feelings and emotions, your partner will mime five. You must work out which they are.

froh, erkältet, unglücklich, gestresst, hungrig, müde, fit, enttäuscht, optimistisch.

b Now it's your turn. Mime the following five adjectives:

ängstlich krank verliebt gelangweilt traurig

Partnerarbeit

1 Was hat Karen gemacht?

Fill in the blanks in Karen's diary by asking questions about what she did then. Answer your partner's questions to help him/her fill the diary too.

Example: *Was hat Karen am Donnerstagnachmittag gemacht?*
 Sie hat/ist …

	Donnerstag	Freitag	Samstag
Vormittag		einkaufen (Aldi)	
Nachmittag	treffen im Café 1.30 - Eva		Ausflug nach Heidelberg/Eltern
Abend		arbeiten (Studentenbar)	

2 Und was hast du gemacht?

Now ask your partner what he/she did on certain days and complete the diary below, using the information you are given.

	Mittwoch	Samstag
Vormittag		
Nachmittag		
Abend		

3 Adjektive

a Mime the following adjectives so that your partner can work out what they are:

müde froh gestresst erkältet hungrig

b Now your partner will mime five adjectives from the following list denoting physical condition, state of mind, feelings and emotions. You must work out which they are.

unglücklich, gelangweilt, optimistisch, krank, enttäuscht, verliebt, traurig, ängstlich, fit.

9 Lebensläufe

In this unit you will continue learning to use the perfect tense in talking about the past, this time in the context of your life, experience and education and those of others. You will also learn how to apply for a job.

1 In welchem Jahr?/In which year?

a ... ist Königin Victoria gestorben?
b ... hat der Zweite Weltkrieg geendet?
c ... sind die Amerikaner auf dem Mond gelandet?
d ... ist die Berliner Mauer gefallen?
e ... hat Brasilien die Fußballweltmeisterschaft in Südkorea und Japan gewonnen?

> 1945 2002 1989
> 1901 1969

In the gaps below, **(i)** fill in the missing year from the five given above, and **(ii)** write out the current year:

neunzehnhundertfünfundvierzig
neunzehnhunderteins

zweitausendzwei
neunzehnhundertneunundsechzig

i _____ ii _____

2 Wer bin ich?

1
> Ich bin im Jahre 1756 in Salzburg, Österreich geboren. Ich habe Opern, Symphonien, Violinkonzerte und Klavierkonzerte komponiert.

2
> Ich bin 1918 in Südafrika geboren. Ich habe 26 Jahre im Gefängnis verbracht, aber später bin ich Präsident geworden.

3
> Ich bin 1943 in New York geboren und bin Filmschauspieler. Ich habe zweimal einen Oscar erhalten: 1975 für meine Rolle als Don Corleone im Mafia-Film *Der Pate* II und 1981 für die Rolle vom Boxer Jake La Motta in *Wie ein wilder Stier*.

4
> Ich bin im Jahre 1940 in Liverpool geboren. Ich war Sänger und Songschreiber und habe das Lied *Imagine* geschrieben.

a Identify the four people! – *Das ist* ...

b Work out how to say the years of their birth on the basis of the examples in exercise 1.

c Then check your answers to **a** and **b** by listening to the recording.

d Write a similar description of a famous person, a woman this time. Your partner tries to work out who it is. Then he/she tries out a mini-biography on you.

Perfect tense
- Verbs with an infinitive ending in **-ieren** are weak but do not have the prefix **ge-** in their past participle: **komponieren** ('to compose') → **ich habe komponiert**.
- Verbs with the prefixes **ver-**, **be-**, **ent-** and **er-** (these are the commonest, there are others) also do without the **ge-** prefix in their past participle: **verbringen** ('to spend time'): **ich habe verbracht**. These are called *inseparable* prefixes.
- Mixed verbs: **verbringen** has features of both *strong* (it changes its vowel sound **i → a**) and *weak* (its past participle ends in **-t**) verbs. **Bringen** and all the verbs based on it follow this *mixed* pattern. Another mixed verb is **denken** ('to think') → **ich habe gedacht**.

3 Marias Leben/Maria's life

A
Sie haben es gar nicht verstanden. Mein Bruder und meine Schwester haben studiert und ich habe immer gute Noten bekommen, aber das Studium hat mich einfach nicht interessiert.

B
Ich habe mit 19 die Schule verlassen. Ich wollte nicht weiter studieren, ich wollte arbeiten, Geld verdienen, leben! Ich habe eine Stelle als Bankangestellte gefunden, habe ein bisschen Geld verdient und bin oft ausgegangen!

C
Ich bin im Jahre 1955 in Berlin geboren, aber meine Eltern sind bald danach umgezogen. Ich bin also in Hamburg aufgewachsen.

D
Wir haben drei Kinder. Ich habe 1985 meine Stelle bei der Bank aufgegeben, weil ich mehr Zeit mit den Kindern verbringen wollte. Ich arbeite nicht mehr – ich bin jetzt Großmutter und habe viel zu tun!

E
Meinen Mann habe ich im Sportverein kennen gelernt. Ich habe 1978 geheiratet und wir haben eine kleine Wohnung gefunden. Wir waren sehr glücklich, obwohl wir kein Geld hatten!

a The above extracts from an interview are not in the correct order. Re-arrange them, then check your version by listening to the recording. To guide you, here are the questions the interviewer asked:
- Sind Sie Hamburgerin?
- Haben Sie studiert?
- Wie haben Ihre Eltern reagiert?
- Wann haben Sie geheiratet?
- Haben Sie Kinder?

b In the interview, find the German equivalents of:

i I found a job	**vi** I got to know my husband
ii I got married	**vii** My parents moved house
iii I grew up in Hamburg	**viii** I was born
iv I gave up my job	**ix** I always got good grades
v I left school	

c Fragen:

i Ist Maria in Berlin aufgewachsen?	**iv** Was hat sie im Jahre 1978 gemacht?
ii Was haben ihre Eltern gemacht?	**v** Warum hat sie die Stelle aufgegeben?
iii Warum hat sie nicht studiert?	**vi** Was ist sie jetzt von Beruf?

4 In Berlin geboren

Retell Maria's life story without reference to the text of exercise 3. Use the perfect tense.

Maria ist in Berlin geboren, aber ...

umziehen – in Hamburg aufwachsen – gute Noten bekommen – Schule verlassen – Stelle finden – Mann kennen lernen – heiraten – drei Kinder: Stelle aufgeben

5 Der Lebenslauf von Beate Winkler/Beate Winkler's CV

Geburtsdatum:	8.11.1980
Geburtsort:	Reutlingen
Staatsangehörigkeit:	deutsch
Familienstand:	ledig

Schule
Aug. 87 – Juni 91	Grundschule Reutlingen
Aug. 91 – Juni 99	Gymnasium Tübingen
	Abitur (Durchschnittsnote 2,4)

Universität
Okt. 99 – April 03	Ruprecht-Karls-Universität Heidelberg
	Studium: Anglistik und Computerlinguistik
	Studienabschluss: Magister

Berufserfahrung
April 00– Sept. 00	Assistentin Computerfirma NETwork
April 01 – Aug. 01	Übersetzungsbüro „Lingua-Service"

Ferienjobs
00/01	Barpersonal in der Studentenbar „Odysseus"
02/03	Kellnerin im Restaurant „Akropolis"

Sprachkenntnisse
Englisch fließend, Französisch und Italienisch.

Using Beate's CV as a model, draft your own German **Lebenslauf**.

6 Auf dem Arbeitsamt/At the job centre

Beate has finished her course at university and is now looking for a job. Fill in the gaps using the vocabulary below, then check by listening to the recording.

„ **a** _____ August 1991 bis Juni 1999 habe ich das Ludwigsgymnasium in Tübingen besucht und mein **b** _____ mit der Durchschnittsnote 2,4 gemacht. Ich habe gleich **c** _____ dem Abitur mit dem Studium in Heidelberg **d** _____ – meine Studienfächer waren Anglistik und Computerlinguistik. Dieses Jahr im **e** _____ habe ich meine Magisterprüfung gemacht. Ich suche jetzt eine Stelle, und ich würde gern meine Sprachkenntnisse nutzen, denn ich **f** _____ fließend Englisch, ziemlich gut Französisch und ein **g** _____ Spanisch. In den Semesterferien habe ich in einer **h** _____ und in einem Übersetzungsbüro gearbeitet, das heißt, ich habe etwas Erfahrung in der Arbeitswelt gesammelt. Im Semester habe ich manchmal **i** _____ in einer Kneipe und in einem Restaurant **j** _____, weil das Studentenleben ziemlich teuer ist. Ich interessiere mich für Fremdsprachen, und natürlich auch für **k** _____. Ich möchte gern mit Menschen zusammenarbeiten, **l** _____ ich am liebsten in einem Team arbeite …"

spreche	Computer	April	angefangen	bisschen	von
Computerfirma	abends	Abitur	gearbeitet	nach	weil

ich würde gern … /ich möchte gern …

To express plans, wishes or hopes, you can use one of these constructions:

ich/er, sie, es	würde/möchte	Sie/wir/sie	würden/möchten
du	würdest/möchtest	ihr	würdet/möchtet

Ich würde gern/möchte gern in einer Computerfirma <u>arbeiten</u>.

7 Hanna und Jens

a Hanna und Jens bump into one another in a bar and catch up on their education, holiday jobs and plans for the future. Fill in the grid below with the relevant information.

	Schule/Universität	Ferienjobs	Berufliche Pläne
Hanna			
Jens			

b Write a brief account for each person, using the information you have collected.
Example: *Hanna hat die Viktoriaschule besucht …*

8 Und Sie?

a **Was haben Sie gemacht?** Work together with a partner and tell one another about your education and any work experience you have. Use the glossary and a dictionary if necessary.

b **Was würden Sie gern beruflich machen?** Now tell one another what you would like to do when you finish university. These can be realistic plans, but you can also use your imagination!

9 Referenz/Reference

On an employment agency evaluation form, applicants are rated on a set of characteristics, some of which are listed below.

a Can you work out what most of them mean? Check in the unit vocabulary list page 108.

motiviert	freundlich	gute Sprachkenntnisse
enthusiastisch	kommunikativ	Fähigkeit MS Office
selbständig	pünktlich	mobil
teamorientiert	zuverlässig	fleißig
flexibel	organisiert	

b Which of the above characteristics do you think would be required of someone thought suitable for the post advertised here? Explain why in German.

> **SPEZIALIST FÜR FLUGREISEN – EUROPAWEIT!**
> – Kundenberatung in unseren Läden in vier Ländern, am Telefon und im Internet.
> – Sind Sie motiviert und flexibel, besitzen Sie Teamgeist?
> – Wir bieten Ihnen ein interessantes Arbeitsfeld in unserem jungen Reservierungsteam.

c Which of the characteristics listed do you possess?

10 Ich bewerbe mich um .../I am applying for ...

> # Übersetzer/in ins Englische
>
> *Wir* sind ein Übersetzungsbüro in Erlangen.
> *Wir* spezialisieren uns auf technische Übersetzungen.
> *Wir* suchen eine/n Übersetzer/in ins Englische.
> *Wir* bieten ein gutes Gehalt und eine gute Arbeitsatmosphäre.
>
> *Sie* haben ausgezeichnete Englisch- und Computerkenntnisse.
> *Sie* sind zuverlässig und pünktlich.
> *Sie* können selbständig arbeiten, aber Sie arbeiten auch gern im Team.
> *Sie* sind flexibel.
>
> *Bewerbungen an:* Frau Marion Hoffman, Übersetzungsbüro Urban, Kantstr. 5, Erlangen.

a Beate is interested in the job advertised on the previous page. Read the advertisement and her letter of application.

b Then draft Uwe's similar letter applying for the job advertised below, using the CV details given.

Beate Winkler
Gervinusstr. 35
45527 Heidelberg

Frau Hoffmann
Übersetzungsbüro Urban
Kantstr. 5
99096 Erlangen

Sehr geehrte Frau Hoffmann,
ich habe Ihre Stellenanzeige mit Interesse gelesen und möchte mich um die Stelle als Übersetzerin bewerben. Ich habe das Studium der Anglistik und Computerlinguistik in Heidelberg im April mit der Magisterprüfung abgeschlossen. Ich spreche fließend Englisch und habe sehr gute Computerkenntnisse.
Von April bis August 2001 habe ich in einem Übersetzungsbüro gearbeitet. Dort habe ich in einem Team von vier Kollegen gearbeitet. Ich musste flexibel sein, denn wir hatten viele wichtige Termine. Ich würde gern bei Ihnen arbeiten.

Mit freundlichen Grüßen,

Beate Winkler

Wir suchen …

Zuverlässiges Personal für unser Internationales Konferenzzentrum in Berlin.

Kellner/in für Cafeteria

Der/die Bewerber/in muss

- pünktlich und fleißig sein
- Englisch und Französisch sprechen
- teamorientiert und flexibel sein
- auch im Stress arbeiten können!
- Erfahrung im Restaurantmetier haben
- nachmittags/abends arbeiten können

Uwe Heimann

geb.:	Feb. 1981
Mai 2000	Abitur (3,1)
	Liebigschule Dahlem
Sept. 2000	Krankenhausküche
Okt. 2002	Studienanfang FU
	(Informatik/Anglistik)

Französischkenntnisse: Abitur
Ferienjobs: Studentenbar/Pizzeria
Auto: ja
Arbeitszeit: nach 17 Uhr

Extra!

11 Und was würden Sie gern machen?

 a You are listening to a radio programme from Germany. The presenter asks two young women who have just finished university about their education, situation now, and future plans. Draw up a grid and make a note of the relevant information – it doesn't matter if you do not understand everything.

	Ausbildung	Situation jetzt	Zukunftspläne
Alice			
Barbara			

 b Using your notes, write a profile of the two women in German.

 c **Was würden Sie gern machen?** Write a short paragraph about your own plans for the future.

12 Kein typischer Student?/Not a typical student?

> Herr Heydorn ist kein typischer Student. Er ist Rentner. Wann hat er sich entschieden, zur Universität zu gehen? „Das war vor vier Jahren", antwortet der Fünfundsechzigjährige. „Als meine jüngste Tochter ihr Studium begonnen hat, habe ich gedacht: Ich möchte so was machen! Ich habe mich informiert, bin zur Abendschule gegangen, habe das Abitur gemacht und … jetzt bin ich Student im ersten Semester." Warum wollte er studieren? „In meinem Alter studiert man, weil es Spaß macht", sagt er.

Fragen:
a In welchem Jahr hat Herr Heydorn sich entschieden, zur Universität zu gehen?
b Wie alt ist er jetzt? Wann ist er geboren?
c Was ist ein typischer Student?
d Warum wollte Herr Heydorn studieren?
e Und Sie? Warum studieren Sie? …

Grammatik

- **Perfect tense (continued)**

 - *Verbs with an infinitive ending in -ieren* are weak but their past participle omits the prefix **ge-**:
 Andreas hat nicht <u>studiert</u>. (← studieren)

 - *Verbs with an inseparable prefix* such as **be-**, **ver-**, **ent-**, **er-**, whether weak or strong, also omit the prefix **ge-** in their past participle:
 Wir haben unseren Großvater <u>besucht</u> (← besuchen weak);
 Meine Eltern haben es nicht <u>verstanden</u> (← verstehen strong).

 - *Mixed verbs* combine features of both weak verbs (a past participle ending in **-t**) and strong verbs (vowel change):
 Mandela hat viele Jahre im Gefängnis <u>verbracht</u>. (← verbringen)

- **Reflexive verbs**

 There are some *reflexive verbs* in the unit: these are formed with a reflexive pronoun:
 Ich interessiere mich für Bilder/Er interessiert sich für Literatur (← sich interessieren).
 See p. 154.

- **Expressing plans, wishes, hopes**

 ich würde gern + *infinitive* / **ich möchte gern** + *infinitive*

ich/er, sie, es	würde/möchte	wir/Sie/sie	würden/möchten
du	würdest/möchtest	ihr	würdet/möchtet

 Ich <u>würde gern</u> in einer Computerfirma <u>arbeiten</u>.
 Remember the infinitive comes at the end!

- **Subordinating conjunctions**

 - You have met the subordinating conjunctions **wenn**, **weil** and **dass**. In this unit two more were introduced: **als** (which means 'when' referring to the <u>past</u>: note that **wenn** is used in statements in the present tense, **wann** in questions) and **obwohl** ('although').

 - Remember subordinating conjunctions send the verb to the end:
 Wir waren glücklich, obwohl wir kein Geld <u>hatten</u>.
 Er ist oft sehr müde, weil er abends <u>ausgeht</u>. (note position of separable prefix **aus**)

 - When the subordinate clause (the part of the sentence introduced by the subordinating conjunction) comes first, the main verb follows immediately, preceded by a comma which separates the two clauses:
 Obwohl wir kein Geld hatten, <u>waren</u> wir glücklich.
 ⟵ subordinate clause ⟶, ⟵ main clause ⟶

Grammatikübungen

1 Complete the verb table. All these verbs can be found in this unit.

Infinitive	Past participle	Auxiliary	Meaning
sterben	————	————	————
————	geendet	————	————
————	————	————	to fall
————	gewonnen	————	————
komponieren	————	————	————
————	————	haben	to spend (time)
————	verstanden	————	————
————	————	————	to interest
finden	————	————	————
————	verdient	————	————
————	————	————	to move house
aufwachsen	————	sein	————
heiraten	————	————	————

2 Using an appropriate form of the **würde gern** construction, express the following in German:

Example: … work in a translation bureau. (I) .

Ich würde gern in einem Übersetzungsbüro arbeiten.

a … work in a team. (they)
b … attend the **Gymnasium** (grammar school). (she)
c … use your knowledge of languages? (you singular, informal)
d … find a job. (we)
e … move house. (he)

3 Subordinating conjunctions

a In the following two sentences, the two clauses are joined by **aber** ('but') – a *co-ordinating conjunction*. Join them with **obwohl** instead, remembering the word order rules.
 i Er hat viel Freizeit, aber er geht selten aus.
 ii Sie spricht fließend Italienisch, aber sie war noch nie in Italien.

b Insert the appropriate word for 'when':
 i (When) bist du geboren?
 ii (When) ich letzte Woche in Berlin war, habe ich deinen Bruder gesehen.
 iii (When) ich im Ausland arbeite, nutze ich meine Sprachkenntnisse.

Vokabeln

See Appendix on p. 191 for more vocabulary from exercises 7, 9, 10 and 11

Aufgabe 1

die Königin	queen
gestorben	pp of sterben*
sterben*	to die
der Mond	moon
gelandet	pp of landen
landen	to land
die Berliner Mauer	Berlin Wall
gefallen	here = pp of fallen*
fallen*	to fall
Brasilien	Brazil
die Weltmeisterschaft	World Cup
Südkorea	South Korea

Aufgabe 2

geboren	born
Opern *pl*	operas
Symphonien *pl*	symphonies
Violinkonzerte *pl*	violin concertos
Klavierkonzerte *pl*	piano concertos
komponiert	pp of komponieren
komponieren	to compose
Südafrika	South Africa
das Gefängnis	prison
verbracht	pp of verbringen
der Präsident	president
geworden	pp of werden*
werden*	to become
der Filmschauspieler	film actor
erhalten*	to receive (also pp)
die Rolle	role
„Der Pate"	'The Godfather'
„Wie ein wilder Stier"	'Raging Bull'
der Sänger	singer
der Songschreiber	songwriter
das Lied	song
geschrieben	pp of schreiben

Aufgabe 3

gar nicht	not at all
verstanden	pp of verstehen
verstehen	to understand
studiert	pp of studieren
einfach	simply
interessieren	to interest

leben	to live
die Stelle	job, position
mit 19	at 19
verlassen*	to leave (also pp)
weiter	further
die Bankangestellte	bank employee (f)
bald danach	soon afterwards
umgezogen	pp of umziehen
umziehen *sep*	to move (house)
aufgewachsen	pp of aufwachsen*
aufwachsen* *sep*	to grow up
aufgegeben	pp of aufgeben*
mehr	more
der Sportverein	sports club
kennen gelernt	pp of kennen lernen
geheiratet	pp of heiraten
heiraten	to marry
obwohl	although
reagiert	pp of reagieren
reagieren	to react

Aufgabe 5

der Lebenslauf	CV
das Gymnasium	grammar school
das Abitur	A Levels (equivalent)
die Durchschnittsnote	average grade
Anglistik	English (academic subject)
Computerlinguistik	computer linguistics
Studienabschluss	degree, diploma
der/die Assistent(in)	assistant (m/f)
die Berufserfahrung	professional experience
die Firma	firm
das Übersetzungsbüro	translation agency
Ferienjobs *pl*	holiday jobs
das Barpersonal	bar staff
Sprachkenntnisse *pl*	knowledge of languages
fließend	fluent

Aufgabe 6

Studienfächer *pl*	subjects studied
nutzen	to use
Semesterferien *pl*	vacation(s)
Erfahrung sammeln	to gain experience
die Arbeitswelt	world of work
das Studentenleben	student life
sich interessieren für	to be interested in
Fremdsprachen *pl*	foreign languages
Menschen *pl*	people
das Team	team

*Verb strong in present tense

Partnerarbeit

1 Elkes Lebenslauf

Ask your partner questions about Elke Schwarzer's CV and fill in the gaps with the relevant information.

Geburtsdatum:	*21.12.79*
Geburtsort:	*Schwerin*
August 86 – Juni 90:	
September 90 – Mai 99:	*Bert-Brecht-Schule, Jena, Abitur mit Durchschnittsnote 1,8*
Juni 99 – September 99:	
Dezember 99 – Januar 00:	*Verkaufsassistentin bei Karstadt, Abteilung Damenmode.*
Februar 00 – Februar 01:	
Mai 01 – September 01:	*Kellnerin Café Rosenthal, Berlin Mitte.*
September 01 –	

2 Sommer in der Schweiz/Summer in Switzerland

You are looking for a holiday job this summer and your partner helps by giving you a mock initial interview with the agency you are using.

Partnerarbeit

1 Elkes Lebenslauf

Ask your partner questions about Elke Schwarzer's CV and fill in the gaps in the grid with the relevant information.

Geburtsdatum:
Geburtsort:

August 86 – Juni 90: *Karl-Marx-Schule, Schwerin*

September 90 – Mai 99:

Juni 99 –September 99: *Büroangestellte im Arbeitsamt Jena*
 Computerkenntnisse: Word/Excel

Dezember 99 – Januar 00:

Februar 00 – Februar 01: *Buchgeschäft Humboldt, Berlin*
 Verkäuferin

Mai 01 – September 01:

September 01 – *Studienbeginn Humboldt-Universität*
 Studienfächer: Informatik und Graphik

2 Sommer in der Schweiz/Summer in Switzerland

Your partner is looking for a holiday job in Switzerland this summer. She/He is about to have an introductory interview with the agency and you have agreed to ask the questions in a mock interview. You have obtained the following outline from the agency's website, use it to formulate your questions.

```
FERIENJOBS IN DER SCHWEIZ

Vorstellungsgespräch - wir möchten Sie kennen lernen!

Name, wann und wo geboren, Familienstand (verheiratet/ledig),
Schule, Studium (Studienfächer), Qualifikationen, Sprachkenntnisse
(Deutsch, Französich, Italienisch), Berufserfahrung, Ferienjobs.
Was würden Sie gern tun? Warum?

Sind Sie: organisiert, zuverlässig, pünktlich?
Arbeiten Sie lieber im Team oder selbständig?
```

10 Zukunftspläne

In this unit you will learn how to express wishes and hopes for the future, compare situations in the past and in the present and talk about your holiday plans.

1 Im Ausland arbeiten/Working abroad

Markus Kühn hat Betriebswirtschaft und Politik studiert. Er arbeitet seit einem Jahr in einer akademischen Buchhandlung.

Read the following extract from an email Markus sent to his friend Gudrun, then translate it into English.

Ich weiß nicht, ob ich lange in diesem Job bleibe. Die Arbeit ist ziemlich monoton und langweilig, und ich würde gern eine interessantere Stelle finden – ich brauche Abwechslung im Leben! Ich würde gern im Ausland arbeiten, vielleicht in Großbritannien oder Italien. Mein Englisch ist besser als mein Italienisch, aber ich möchte wirklich gern in einem warmen Land leben und arbeiten, denn das regnerische Wetter hier im Norden macht mich ganz melancholisch. Warst du schon mal in Italien? Ich habe letztes Jahr fast einen Monat in Verona verbracht. Das Klima, die Leute, das Essen – alles war fantastisch. Ich würde gern mehr Zeit dort verbringen, um das Leben dort besser kennen zu lernen.

Grammatik

Comparative form of the adjective:

Die Stelle ist interessant
The job is interesting

Die Stelle ist interessanter
The job is more interesting

Irregular comparative: **gut – besser**.

eine interessante Stelle
an interesting job

eine interessantere Stelle
a more interesting job

2 Meine Zukunftspläne/My future plans

Markus explains his plans for the future to his parents. Listen carefully to the recording and then complete the sentences below using the cues. Remember **weil** sends the verb to the end!

a Markus würde gern eine andere Stelle finden, weil ... (langweilig)
b Die Atmosphäre ist oft schlecht, weil ... (nett)
c Er möchte einen Intensivkurs in Italienisch machen, weil ... (sprechen/arbeiten)
d Das Leben in Italien ist angenehm, weil ... (freundlicher)
e Markus würde gern in einem anderen Land arbeiten, weil ... (Erfahrung)

3 Und Sie? Würden Sie gern im Ausland arbeiten?

Explain to a partner why you would (or would not), where you would like to go and why.

4 Die ideale Partnerin

Markus ist ledig, aber er sucht eine Freundin. Er beschreibt seine ideale Partnerin.

a Listen to the recording and note down the key features of Markus' ideal partner (in German).

b Write a short description of this possible partner, and make sure you include the following key words and aspects:

Sinn für Humor – Sport – Kino – Politik – Musik – Freizeit – Ausland – Freunde

5 Er muss gern reisen/He must like travelling

Read this description of an ideal partner and check your understanding of it with a classmate. Would the woman who wrote this be interested in Markus? What evidence is there for your opinion? Explain in German.

> Mein idealer Partner...
> kann zwischen 1,58m und 1,78m groß sein
> muss sportlich sein
> muss flexibel und tolerant sein
> muss gern reisen
> darf mit seinen Freunden ausgehen
> darf nicht rauchen

Grammatik

Modal verb in addition to **müssen**, **können** and **wollen**:
dürfen: 'be allowed to', 'may'.

6 Ihre ideale Partnerin/Ihr idealer Partner

a Tell the others in the class about your ideal partner.

b Write a description of your perfect partner in German.

Für wen kauft er die Blumen?

7 Hoffnungen und Realität/Hopes and reality

Diese Woche besucht die Zeitschrift „Unser Leben" Marianne Hildebrandt in Jena. Marianne ist 1960 geboren, hat zwei Kinder – Jutta (17) und Klaus (15) – und ist seit 22 Jahren verheiratet. Sie hat ihr ganzes Leben in Jena gewohnt und möchte auch nicht umziehen. Nach der Wiedervereinigung ist sie natürlich mal nach Westdeutschland gefahren, um Verwandte zu besuchen. Ihr Bruder, die Schwester ihrer Mutter und der Bruder ihres Vaters wohnen alle im Westen. Aber sie ist auch gern wieder nach Jena zurückgekommen.

Natürlich hat die Wiedervereinigung viele Vorteile gebracht: mehr Freiheit zu reisen, mehr Auswahl beim Einkaufen, eine offenere Politik. Aber die Nachteile? Vor der Wiedervereinigung hatte Marianne einen relativ gut bezahlten Job als Bibliothekarin, heute ist sie arbeitslos. Vorher hat es in Jena wenig Kriminalität gegeben, heute haben viele Jugendliche keine Arbeit und zu viel Zeit – oft stehlen sie Autos und nehmen Drogen. Vorher war die Miete für die Wohnung billig, jetzt ist sie sehr viel teurer. Wir haben mit Marianne über ihre Hoffnungen und Zukunftspläne gesprochen.

UL *Frau Hildebrandt, vor der Wiedervereinigung war Ihr Leben ganz anders als jetzt. Welche Hoffnungen hatten Sie damals für die Zukunft?*

MH Ja, wissen Sie, ich war eigentlich ganz zufrieden. Meine Arbeit in der Bibliothek hat mir gut gefallen. Ich war unabhängig, weil ich auch Geld verdient habe. Das heißt, ich habe das Geld meines Mannes nicht gebraucht, wenn ich ein neues Kleid kaufen wollte. Ich habe gedacht, dass ich erst mit 65 aufhöre zu arbeiten. Als ich 1991 meine Stelle verloren habe, war das für mich ein Schock.

UL *Wie haben Ihre Kinder reagiert? Jutta und Klaus waren ja noch ziemlich klein?*

MH Damals war das okay, denn die Kinder haben sich gefreut, dass ich jeden Tag zu Hause war. Klaus ist nie gern in den Kindergarten gegangen, er war lieber hier, mit mir.

UL *Wie sehen Sie die Zukunft Ihrer Kinder jetzt?*

MH Sie haben viel schlechtere Chancen, einen Job zu finden. Sie wohnen natürlich im Moment beide zu Hause – Klaus geht ja noch in die Schule – und sie müssen keine Miete zahlen. Für mich war es damals leicht, eine Stelle zu bekommen. Nach der Hochzeit haben wir auch nicht lange gebraucht, eine schöne Wohnung zu finden. Das ist alles heute viel schwieriger.

 Fragen:

a Ist Marianne Hildebrandt ledig?

b Warum ist sie nach der Wiedervereinigung nach Westdeutschland gefahren?

c Welche Vorteile hat die Wiedervereinigung gebracht?

d Arbeitet Marianne?

e Wie ist die Situation jetzt in Jena?

f Warum hat Marianne gern gearbeitet?

g Wie sieht sie die Situation ihrer Kinder?

h Was ist ein anderes Wort für „die Schwester ihres Vaters"? (Suchen Sie im Wörterbuch.)

Grammatik

Genitive: possessive/indefinite article pattern

Die Schwester **ihres Vaters** (her father's sister) = '… of her father'

Der Bruder **ihrer Mutter** (her mother's brother) = '… of her mother'

Find the German equivalents of the following on page 113:

'My husband's money' (… 'of my husband') …

'Your children's future' ('of your children') …

 8 Damals und jetzt/Then and now

a You already know quite a lot about Marianne's situation before and after German reunification. Listen to the extract from an interview where Marianne talks in more detail about her hopes 20 years ago and her current situation. Then complete the grid:

Damals	Jetzt
Wenig Kriminalität	Teure Mieten
Alle hatten eine Stelle.	

 b With reference to the grid only, prepare a short talk in German on the contrast between life then and now. Give the talk to a group/the whole class.

c Write an account in German of Marianne's situation before and after reunification.

 9 Und welche Zukunftspläne und Hoffnungen haben Sie/hast du?

Get together with a partner and talk about plans and hopes for the future. Then present these to the class.

Example: *Michael möchte später in einer Großstadt wohnen. Er will …*

10 Zwei Wochen in der Sonne/Two weeks in the sun

Read the message. In a similar way, describe briefly (to a partner/the class) what you will be doing in the next few weeks.

> Liebe Eva und Max
>
> Hallo! Wie geht's? Es ist die letzte Woche des Semesters. Morgen um 11 Uhr habe ich meine letzte Vorlesung. Dann gibt es die Prüfungen! Und danach muss ich einige Wochen arbeiten, aber am 16. August gehe ich in Urlaub - zwei Wochen in der Sonne!
>
> Was macht ihr in den Sommerferien? Möchtet ihr nach Spanien fahren? Vielleicht sehe ich euch am Tag der letzten Prüfung. Wir können zusammen ein Bier trinken! Schreibt bald!
>
> Tschüss
> Mehmet

Grammatik

Genitive: definite article pattern
Masculine and neuter nouns: **das Ende des Semesters** 'the end of the semester'
Feminine and plural nouns: **der Tag der Prüfung(en)** 'the day of the exam(s)'

11 Wir müssen uns entscheiden/We must decide

Eva and Max are discussing their summer plans. Listen to the recording and fill in the gaps.

– Max, hast du die E-Mail von Mehmet gesehen?
– Nein, noch nicht.
– Er fährt im August **a** _____ Spanien und möchte wissen, was wir machen.
– Eine gute Frage: **b** _____ fahren wir eigentlich?
– Ich bin nicht sicher …
– Wir müssen uns entscheiden. Also … Deutschland oder **c** _____?
– Südeuropa ist zu warm …
– Also Deutschland. Fahren wir an die **d** _____ oder **e** _____ Land?
– An die **f** _____ – da kann man mehr machen.
– Nordsee oder Ostsee?
– Die Nordseeküste ist näher.
– Ok – An die Arbeit! Wir finden bestimmt was im Internet.

Grammatik

Wohin?/Wo? With the prepositions **auf**, **an** and **in** the accusative is used when the sense is 'to', the dative is used when the sense is 'at'.

ins Ausland/im Ausland	abroad (to/at)
an die See/an der See	to the seaside/at the seaside
aufs Land/auf dem Lande	to the country(side)/in the country(side)

Die ostfriesische Küste

Freizeit: Bootvermietung
Fahrradvermietung
Wanderungen
Ausflüge

Unterkunft: Hotels
Pensionen
Apartments
Ferienwohnungen
Campingplätze

 12 **Was kann man an der Nordseeküste machen?**

Eva and Max have decided to spend their summer holiday in Ostfriesland, on the North Sea coast. They are interviewed for a radio travel programme.

Given the location, decide which of these activities they are likely to be looking forward to, then check on the recording to see if you were right!

tanzen

Ski fahren

lesen

einkaufen

fernsehen

schwimmen

wandern

Kunstgalerien besuchen

Rad fahren

bergsteigen

in der Sonne liegen

 13 **Und du/Sie?**

Find out what your partner is doing this summer, when he/she is going away and what he/she is planning to do.

Was machst du/machen Sie…? *Wohin …?*
Wann gehst du/gehen Sie …? *Was kann man dort machen?*

14 **Meine Sommerpläne**

Draft an email to a German friend describing what you are doing this summer.

Extra!

15 Hoffnungen und Realität

a You will hear four people talk on a radio programme about their hopes when they were younger, and how their lives developed in reality. Draw up a grid with the headings given below, then listen carefully and note down in English their hopes and current situations in key words.

	Hopes	**Reality**
Helga Stein		
Benjamin Blume		
Renate Otto		
Dietmar Lang		

 b Using the information collected in your grid, write a short account in German of each person's life at present and their hopes.

16 Die deutsche Wiedervereinigung/German reunification

Zwischen 1949 und 1990 hat es zwei deutsche Staaten gegeben, die Bundesrepublik Deutschland im Westen und die Deutsche Demokratische Republik im Osten. Die kommunistische Regierung der DDR hat 1961 eine Mauer zwischen den Staaten gebaut, weil Tausende von Menschen die DDR verlassen haben, um ein neues Leben im Westen zu suchen.

DDR-Bürger durften nicht in den Westen fahren, wie sie wollten. Man konnte Verwandte nur selten sehen. Im Jahre 1989 haben Hunderttausende demonstriert, besonders in Leipzig. Sie wollten mehr Freiheit, vor allem die Freiheit zu reisen. Am Ende hat die Regierung verstanden, dass sie das kommunistische System reformieren musste. Am 9. November 1989 hat sie die Reisefreiheit eingeführt. Am selben Abend sind die Ost-Berliner zur Mauer gegangen – sie wollten den Westen sofort sehen! Das war das Ende der Mauer.

Es war auch das Ende des Staates DDR. Die Bürger haben in den freien Wahlen vom März 1990 für Parteien gewählt, die eine schnelle Wiedervereinigung wollten. Die ökonomische Situation der DDR war katastrophal. Im Oktober sind aus dem Territorium der DDR und Berlins fünf neue Bundesländer der Bundesrepublik Deutschland geworden.

Try out your reading skills. Remember, you are not being asked to translate but to show that you have understood information. Resist the temptation to focus on what you don't know! Read the whole text, then compare your understanding with a partner's.

Grammatik

- **The genitive**

masculine	**Er ist ein alter Freund mein<u>es</u> Vater<u>s</u>.**	(note **-s** on the noun!)
	He is an old friend of my father.	
feminine	**Das ist das neue Auto sein<u>er</u> Mutter.**	
	That is his mother's new car.	
neuter	**Hast du ein Foto dein<u>es</u> Baby<u>s</u>?**	(note **-s** on the noun!)
	Have you a photo of your baby?	
plural	**Von hier kann man das Haus unser<u>er</u> Eltern sehen.**	
	From here you can see our parents' house.	

The pattern is the same for the definite article:

die Jacke d<u>es</u> Lehrer<u>s</u> (m); **der Parkplatz d<u>er</u> Bibliothek** (f);
das Ende d<u>es</u> Semester<u>s</u> (n); **die Ankunft d<u>er</u> Züge** (pl).

- **Adjectives: the comparative**

(See the section on adjectives in the Grammar Overview beginning on page 147)

- German adjectives on their own after the verb 'to be' have no ending:
 Sein Computer ist neu; die Schule ist modern; das Bier ist kalt; die Kinder sind müde.
- They do take an ending after an article or possessive. For example, here is the indefinite article/possessive pattern in the nominative:
 ein neu<u>er</u> Computer (m); **eine modern<u>e</u> Schule** (f); **ein kalt<u>es</u> Bier** (n).
- In the accusative only the masculine is different: **einen neu<u>en</u> Computer**.
- Similarly, the comparative form of an adjective ('older', 'more intelligent') has no further ending than its distinctive **-er** in statements such as:
 Der Wein ist billiger in Italien. The wine is cheaper in Italy.
 Alles ist viel schwieriger. Everything is much more difficult.
- After an article or possessive it adds the adjectival ending to the existing **-er**:
 ein bess<u>er</u> Film (m) a better film/*accusative*: **einen bess<u>eren</u> Film**
 eine interessant<u>ere</u> Stelle (f) a more interesting job
 ein größ<u>eres</u> Haus (n) a bigger house
- Some adjectives add an umlaut in the comparative (**groß → größer**).
 Note: **schlecht<u>ere</u> Chancen** worse chances.

- *dürfen* **(to be allowed to, may)**
 Dürfen has an irregular present tense along the same lines as the other modals, **müssen**, **können** and **wollen**.
 Darf ich rauchen? May I smoke?
 ich darf, du darfst, er/sie/es darf, wir/Sie/sie dürfen, ihr dürft.
 Simple past: **ich durfte.**

Grammatikübungen

1 In the following exercise **von** and the dative is used to express the same idea as the genitive. Change into the genitive.

Example: Ein alter Freund von meinem Vater → *Ein alter Freund meines Vaters.*

a Ein alter Freund von meiner Schwester. _____

b Eine Freundin von seinem Bruder. _____

c Der Anfang von dem Semester. _____

d Die Handtasche von unserer Lehrerin. _____

e Die Bücher von den Studenten. _____

f Das Schlafzimmer von meinem Sohn. _____

g Der Parkplatz von dem Sportzentrum. _____

h Ein Foto von dem Baby. _____

2 Complete the following sentences with an appropriate comparative form from the list at the end of each paragraph. Make sure the adjectival ending, if any is needed, is correct.

Ich würde gern einen **a** _____ Job finden. In der Buchhandlung ist alles jetzt viel **b** _____ . Der neue Boss ist **c** _____ und ich habe endlich einen **d** _____ Computer. Aber ich brauche mehr Geld: ich möchte ein **e** _____ Haus kaufen, weil wir ein neues Baby haben.

a interessanteren/interessanter **b** besser/besseren/besseres
c netter/netterer/netteren **d** schneller/schnelleren **e** größeren/größeres/größer

Unsere Kinder haben **f** _____ Chancen, eine Stelle zu finden. Vor der Wiedervereinigung waren die Mieten **g** _____ und die Leute **h** _____ . Ich hatte ein **i** _____ Leben als jetzt.

f schlechter/schlechtere **g** billigere/billiger **h** glücklichere/glücklicher
i angenehmeren/angenehmer/angenehmeres

3 Your friend Sean has been advised by his doctor to adopt a healthier lifestyle. Explain in an email to your German friend Klaus that Sean:

may not eat chips, but has to eat fruit and vegetables and drink mineral water, isn't allowed to drink beer or wine, has to go for walks and must not smoke.

Vokabeln

See Appendix on p. 191 for vocabulary from exercises 11–12 and caption p. 112.

Aufgabe 1

die Betriebswirtschaft	business management
die Politik	politics
die Abwechslung	variety
das Leben	life
Großbritannien	Great Britain
besser als	better than
das Land	country
regnerisch	rainy
das Wetter	weather
im Norden	in the North
melancholisch	melancholy
Warst du schon in …?	have you ever been to …?
letztes Jahr	last year
das Klima	climate
die Leute *pl*	people

Aufgabe 2

die Atmosphäre	atmosphere
der Boss	boss
jeder	each (one)
billiger	cheaper
angenehm	pleasant
freundlicher	more friendly
kommunikativer	more communicative
das Straßencafé	pavement café
Städte *pl*	towns
die Kultur	culture
größer	bigger
mieten	to rent

Aufgabe 4

der Sinn für Humor	sense of humour
groß	(here =) tall
sportlich	sporty
der Federball	badminton
außerdem	besides
das Interesse an	interest in
Gespräche *pl*	conversations
modisch	fashionable
jeden Tag	every day
reisen	to travel
weggehen *sep*	to go away
öfters	often

unabhängig	independent

Aufgabe 7

die Zeitschrift	magazine
die Wiedervereinigung	reunification (of Germany, 1990)
Verwandte *pl*	relatives
alle	all, everybody
Vorteile *pl*	advantages
gebracht	pp of bringen
die Freiheit	freedom
die Auswahl	selection, choice
offener	more open
Nachteile *pl*	disadvantages
relativ	relatively
gut bezahlt	well paid
arbeitslos	unemployed
vorher	previously
wenig	little, not much
die Kriminalität	criminality
Jugendliche *pl*	young people
Drogen *pl*	drugs
die Miete	rent
teurer	dearer
über	about
ganz anders	totally different
damals	at that time
die Zukunft	future
eigentlich	really, actually
zufrieden	content
gedacht	pp of denken
denken	to think
aufhören *sep*	to finish
verloren	pp of verlieren
verlieren	to lose
der Schock	shock
sich freuen	to be glad
schlechter	worse
leicht	easy
die Hochzeit	wedding
schwieriger	more difficult

Aufgabe 10

die Sonne	sun
danach	after that
der Urlaub	holiday
in Urlaub fahren	to go on holiday

Aufgabe 11

wissen	to know (facts)
sicher	sure, certain
Südeuropa	Southern Europe

Partnerarbeit

1 Auf dem Auslandsamt/At the International Office

In this role-play, you are applying to spend a year of your studies working abroad and you go for an interview with the representative of a German firm which receives students on placement. The aim is to sustain a conversation about your reasons for wanting to work abroad and your plans for the future.

Take time to prepare for the interview. Do not refer to any notes during the role-play. The list below will give you some ideas.

Partner B starts the conversation off.

NB: Remember to use the correct verb forms!

- sich für die Kultur des Landes interessieren
- Sprachkenntnisse verbessern
- Erfahrungen in der Arbeitswelt sammeln
- ein anderes Land kennen lernen
- mit anderen Menschen zusammenarbeiten
- unabhängiger werden
- Abwechslung haben
- eine andere Lebensart/Küche kennen lernen
- bessere Chancen auf dem Arbeitsmarkt haben
- den Lebenslauf verbessern
- Flexibilität zeigen
- Geld verdienen
- ich möchte in … arbeiten, weil …

Mathildenhöhe Darmstadt

2 Im Ausland arbeiten – ja oder nein?

Discuss with your partner the advantages and disadvantages of living and working abroad. Take 10 minutes to prepare, summarising your points **for** working abroad in key words. Then discuss the question with your partner (who will argue against it), trying to respond to the arguments brought forward by him/her. You start the discussion.

Argumente für/ja

Ich glaube, dass …/Ich denke, dass …	I think that … (Beware word order!)
Meiner Meinung nach (*verb*) …	In my opinion …
Das ist nicht richtig, weil …	That is wrong because …
Du hast Recht, (aber …)	You are right (but…)
Das stimmt, aber …	

Partnerarbeit

1 Auf dem Auslandsamt/At the International Office

In this role-play, you are interviewing someone who has applied to work abroad for a year during their time at university. You ask questions in order to find out why he/she wants to do this and what his/her plans for the future are. Take time to prepare for the conversation but do not use any notes during it: refer to the checklist below. Begin with these items, and ask two further appropriate questions of your own. The aim is to sustain conversation successfully.

You start the conversation. Remember to use **Sie**, not **du**.

- Warum möchten Sie im Ausland arbeiten (mehrere Gründe!)
- persönliche Motivation
- Welche Vorteile bringt das Jahr im Ausland?
- In welchem Land möchten Sie arbeiten? Warum?

Mathildenhöhe Darmstadt

2 Im Ausland arbeiten – ja oder nein?

Discuss with your partner the advantages and disadvantages of living and working abroad. Take 10 minutes, summarising arguments **against** the notion in key-words. Then discuss the question with your partner (who will argue for it), trying to respond to the arguments brought forward by him/her. Partner A starts the discussion.

Argumente dagegen/nein

Ich glaube, dass …/Ich denke, dass …	I think that … (Beware word order!)
Meiner Meinung nach (*verb*) …	In my opinion …
Das ist nicht richtig, weil …	That is wrong because …
Du hast Recht, (aber …)	You are right (but…)
Das stimmt, aber …	

Weitere Übungen
FURTHER PRACTICE

1 Studenten

1 Länder/Countries

Give the missing countries or inhabitants.

a Deutschland <u>Deutscher/Deutsche</u>

b England _____

c Frankreich _____

d _____ Spanier(in)

e Italien _____

f _____ Österreicher(in)

g Schottland _____

h Irland _____

i _____ Belgier(in)

2 Sommerkurs/Summer course

Below is a completed registration form for a German language summer school. How much of the information can you give in complete German sentences? Use the pronoun **sie** (she), e.g. *Sie heißt* …

SOMMERKURS „DEUTSCH LERNEN IN BONN AM RHEIN"	
Familienname *Jenkinson*	Vorname *Anne*
Wohnort *Oxford*	Land *England*
Beruf *Sekretärin*	

3 Wer ist das?/Who is it?

Expand the following information into full sentences for each person. Do so first in sentences beginning **ich** 'I', as if you were the person concerned, then in sentences about each person, beginning **er** 'he' or **sie** 'she'. The sentences are on the recording for you to check your responses.

Name	aus …	Nationalität	Wohnort	Beruf
Lisa	Carlisle	Eng…	Sheffield	Studentin
Paul	Aberdeen	Schott…	Dortmund	Lehrer
Corinne	Lille	Franz…	München	Sekretärin
Wolfgang	Lüneburg	Deuts…	Hamburg	Busfahrer

 4 Anja und David

Summarise in English the information the two people give about themselves during their conversation.

 5 Brief von Alex/Letter from Alex

You receive the following message from a student. Give the contents in English.

```
Lieber (plus your name if m) or Liebe (plus your name if f)

Hallo! Mein Name ist Alex und ich komme aus Russland. Ich
studiere Geschichte und Politik. Ich bin auch Barmann im Red
Lion. Ich wohne in Redman Street. Ich lerne Deutsch. Die
Lehrerin ist Deutsche und heißt Frau Wolters. Kommst du aus
Deutschland oder lernst du Deutsch?

Alex
```

 6 Brief an Alex/Letter to Alex

Reply to Alex. If you ask any questions, use the informal **du**.

 7 Jutta und Peter

Fill in the gaps.

Das ist Peter Müller. Er **a** _____ aus Essen, er wohnt
b _____ Frankfurt am Main. Er **c** _____ als
Englischlehrer.

Jutta Schneider ist Peters **d** _____. Sie wohnt mit Peter in der
Taunusstraße und **e** _____ Psychologie an der Johann-Wolfgang-
Goethe-Universität in Frankfurt. Sie arbeitet **f** _____ Kellnerin in der
Studenten-Bar „Szene".

2 Bibliothek oder Diskothek?

 1 Zahlen/Numbers

Say the numbers out loud, then check them on the recording

32 44 76 59 81 23 67 55

 2 Wie viel Uhr ist es?/What time is it?

Write down (in figures) the times you hear.

a ____ b ____ c ____ d ____ e ____ f ____

 3 Am Morgen/In the morning

Listen to the account of a student's morning and give the information in English.

 4 Wann bist du frei?/When are you free?

You are trying to arrange a meeting with a German friend. You receive the following email. What is he doing today? When does he seem to be free?

> Heute habe ich am Morgen eine Vorlesung und ein Seminar. Ich gehe um 14 Uhr in das Sportzentrum und spiele Fußball. Trinkst du um 16 Uhr Kaffee? – Ich gehe in die Mensa. Die Englischstunde ist um 17 Uhr. Wann gehst du heute Abend nach Hause?
>
> Ralf

 5 Hallo, Ralf!

You ring Ralf. Speak after the prompts on the recording.

 6 Ralfs Abend/Ralf's evening

Using the outline, describe Ralf's evening.

18.00	fernsehen
20.00	ausgehen/Stadt
20.30	Kneipe/Bier trinken
22.15	Diskothek/tanzen
1.00	nach Hause
1.45	ins Bett gehen

✏ 7 **Schreiben**/Writing

Make complete sentences. Remember to check word order. Use the correct form of the verb given here in the infinitive.

a ich immer zu Hause bleiben.

b du oft Musik hören?

c sie manchmal ein Buch lesen

d er selten fernsehen

e Sie nie ausgehen?

8 **Wortsuche**/Wordsearch

Go through Unit 2 again and find as many nouns as you can which designate food and drink. Remember to give the definite article, too!

✏ 9 **Jutta und Peter**

Fill in the gaps.

Peter Müller steht immer **a** _____ 6.30 Uhr auf. Zum
b _____ isst er Toast mit Butter und er **c** _____
eine Tasse Kaffee. Er hört Radio und um 7.30 **d** _____ er zur Arbeit.
Mittags isst er normalerweise ein **e** _____ und er trinkt eine Cola.
Um 15 Uhr geht Peter nach **f** _____ . Er **g** _____
E-Mails und manchmal geht er in das Sportzentrum – er ist sehr fit! Peter
h _____ oft Basketball und Fußball. Abends **i** _____
er oft zu Hause und **j** _____ fern, zum Beispiel amerikanische Filme.

Jutta Schneider steht um 7.30 Uhr auf. Sie trinkt morgens Tee und isst ein Joghurt. Um 10
Uhr geht Jutta an die **k** _____ – die Vorlesung ist interessant. Um 12
Uhr geht sie immer in die **l** _____ und isst Pizza oder Omelett.
Nachmittags **m** _____ Jutta Spanisch. Die Spanischstunde
n _____ um 14.00 Uhr. Manchmal geht Jutta in die Stadt und kauft
für das Abendessen ein: Wein, Nudeln, Tomaten und Salat. Zu Hause
o _____ sie Musik und **p** _____ ein Buch.
Abends arbeitet sie oft in der Studentenbar und sie **q** _____ selten
zu Hause. Sie geht in die **r** _____ und tanzt. Um 0.30 Uhr geht Jutta
ins Bett.

3 Familie

1 Fragen und Antworten/Questions and answers

Here are the answers: what were the questions?

a Nein, ich bin ledig.

b Meine Freundin heißt Tina.

c Ja. Ich habe einen Sohn und eine Tochter.

d Ich bin Bibliothekar.

e Meine Mutter ist Architektin.

f Mein Großvater ist 81.

2 Stimmt das?/Is that right?

Look at Stephanie's family album on page 25 and decide whether these statements are true (**richtig**) or false (**falsch**). Where necessary, correct the statement.

a Andreas hat keinen Sohn. richtig/falsch

b Christian ist Stephanies Großvater. richtig/falsch

c Jessica ist Carolines Schwester. richtig/falsch

d Stephanie hat zwei Schwestern. richtig/falsch

e Martina hat zwei Töchter. richtig/falsch

f Stephanie hat einen Bruder. richtig/falsch

g Caroline ist ledig. richtig/falsch

3 Eine Familie

Listen to Dieter describing his family and sketch out a family tree.
Here are the names you will need: Ana/Carsten/Barbara/Silvia/Clara.

4 Mein oder dein?

Fill in the gaps with the correct form of the possessive from the list on the right.
Each word must be used once.

a Sie besuchen _____ Großeltern in Spanien.

b _____ Moped ist neu.

c _____ Tochter ist noch klein.

d Wir brauchen _____ Computer.

e Wie alt ist _____ Bruder?

| seine |
| dein |
| ihre |
| mein |
| unseren |

5 Passt das?/Does that belong here?

a Which is the odd word out in each group?

b Give the gender of each noun. Check in the vocabulary at the end of the book where necessary.

i Fahrrad/Auto/Moped/Schwimmbad

ii Fernseher/E-Mail/Handy/Computer

iii Tochter/Bruder/Sohn/Vater

iv Radio/Film/CD-Spieler/Handy

6 Dialog im Schwimmbad/Conversation at the swimming pool

Complete this dialogue with the help of the English prompts, then listen to the conversation on the recording.

- Hallo, Claudia. Sag mal, wo ist denn deine Schwester?
- *My sister is at home. She is watching* TV.
- Und was macht dein Bruder?
- *My brother is working. He goes to the library in the mornings.* ...
 I have got his Beatles CD. *Have you got your* CD *player*?
- Ja, den habe ich ... Komm, wir hören die CD. Sie ist sehr gut.
- *What are you doing this afternoon?*
- Meine Eltern sind in Marburg und wir gehen ins Restaurant.
- *I never go to the restaurant. We always eat at home!*
- ... Oh je, wie spät ist es denn?
- *It is almost one o'clock ... why?*
- [in a panic] So spät! Aber wir gehen um 1.30 Uhr ins Restaurant ...
- *Have you got your car?*
- Nein, ich habe mein Fahrrad!

7 Jutta und Peter

Fill in the gaps.

Juttas Familie ist groß – sie hat zwei Schwestern und einen **a** _____.
Ihr Bruder **b** _____ Jürgen und er ist verheiratet. Er hat
c _____ Kinder, aber er hat drei Katzen. Juttas große Schwester
Martina ist neunundzwanzig Jahre alt. Sie hat zwei **d** _____, Julia
und Klaus. Sie sind noch **e** _____ und gehen in den Kindergarten.
Martinas Mann ist Informatiker von **f** _____. Jutta ist
dreiundzwanzig Jahre alt und sie ist **g** _____, aber sie hat einen
Freund, Peter. Juttas „kleine" Schwester Ingrid ist zwanzig Jahre alt und sie studiert
Theaterwissenschaft, das ist sehr interessant. Jutta geht oft abends ins Theater. Theater
und Musik sind ihre **h** _____.

Peters Familie ist klein und er hat keine **i** _____. Manchmal besucht
er seine **j** _____. Sie wohnen in Offenbach und sie sind Rentner.
Peter hat ein Auto, aber Jutta hat ein **k** _____ – das ist sehr gesund!
Peter schreibt oft E-Mails und er braucht **l** _____ Computer. Seine
Hobbys sind Sport, Filme und Computerspiele. Normalerweise **m** _____
er abends zu Hause und manchmal sieht er mit Michael einen Film. Michael ist sein
Freund und er **n** _____ auch in Frankfurt. Michael und Peter
o _____ oft Pizza und trinken ein Bier. Abends
p _____ Jutta und Peter manchmal in ein Restaurant – „Bella Italia".
Das Restaurant ist sehr gut und Spaghetti Napoli fantastisch!

4 Am Wochenende

1 Was machst du gern am Wochenende?

Decide which verb form goes in which space, then check your decision by listening to the recording.

Silvia Ich **a** _____ spät _____! Ich **b** _____ gern zu Hause
und **c** _____ oder **d** _____ Musik …

Anna Und du **e** _____ .

Silvia Ja, ich **f** _____ gern.

Anna Ich **g** _____ nicht gern zu Hause. Samstags **h** _____ ich in die
Stadt – ich **i** _____ gern _____ . Manchmal **j** _____ ich
mit Markus _____ . Er **k** _____ gern Auto.

| gehe | lese | fährt | kochst | kaufe … ein | bleibe × 2 |
| höre | gehe … aus | koche | stehe … auf | | |

2 Das mache ich gern

Write to Katrin outlining your likes and preferences: you like going to the cinema, reading and shopping. You like walking but prefer cycling. What you like doing most of all at the weekend is cooking. You like smoking – but you do not like drinking wine or beer.
Ask her if she likes cooking.

3 Wann denn?

Fill in the gaps with the words below.

Wann **a** _____ Heinz mit Anja **b** _____? Am Montag und am
Dienstag **c** _____ er für sein Examen **d** _____ .
e _____ spielt sie Badminton. Am Donnerstag hat er **f** _____
Zeit: Seine Spanischstunde ist um 6 Uhr und dann **g** _____ er mit Martin
und Paul in die Kneipe **h** _____ . Am Freitag **i** _____ Anja
mit Sandra **j** _____ Theater und am Wochenende besucht sie ihre
k _____ in München.

| geht | Mittwochs | kann | ins | arbeiten | will |
| Eltern | ausgehen | keine | muss | gehen | |

4 Willst du mitkommen?

Listen to the short conversation between Anna and Christian and summarise what happens in English. Then check the answer at the end of the book.

5 Im Restaurant

Reconstruct the dialogue by putting what the diner and waiter say into the correct order. Then check by listening to the recording.

a Und was möchten Sie trinken?

b Ja, ich nehme den Tomatensalat, bitte.

c Guten Abend.

d Danke, das ist alles.

e Was bekommen Sie?

f Guten Abend, haben Sie einen Tisch für eine Person?

g Ja, hier am Fenster.

h Ich möchte das Steak, bitte

i Möchten Sie auch einen Salat?

j Danke.

k Sonst noch etwas?

l Ein Bier, bitte.

6 Jutta und Peter

Fill in the gaps.

Heute **a** _____ gehen Jutta und Peter ins Restaurant „Bella Italia". Jutta geht besonders **b** _____ italienisch essen, und auch Peter isst gern Pizza und Spaghetti. Um **c** _____ nach acht treffen sie Michael – Peters Freund – und um halb neun sind sie im Restaurant. Sie nehmen den **d** _____ am Fenster und der Kellner bringt die **e** _____. Jutta **f** _____ immer Spaghetti Napoli, aber Peter isst **g** _____ Pizza. Michael möchte Huhn mit Sahnesauce und einen Salat. Die drei Freunde wollen auch etwas **h** _____, und der Kellner bringt die Weinkarte. „Wir nehmen **i** _____ Rotwein Nummer 14", sagt Peter.

Das Essen ist **j** _____ und der Wein ist auch sehr gut. Um zwanzig vor zehn gehen Jutta, Peter und Michael. „Wir haben noch **k** _____ – was wollen wir machen?", sagt Jutta. Michael möchte gern in die Studentenbar „Szene" gehen, aber Jutta **l** _____ lieber tanzen! Der Kompromiss: Sie gehen in die Diskothek und um 11 Uhr in die Bar. Dort können sie noch ein Glas **m** _____ trinken und Freunde treffen. Um halb eins gehen sie nach **n** _____, denn morgen ist Donnerstag und Peter muss um halb sieben **o** _____ – das ist sehr früh! Michael muss auch früh arbeiten. Er ist Techniker von Beruf und arbeitet bei Siemens. Jutta **p** _____ bis neun Uhr schlafen. Ihre Vorlesung **q** _____ um 10 Uhr.

5 Zu Hause

1 **Wer wohnt da?**/Who lives there?

Read carefully the descriptions of three different sets of people. Decide which set of people lives in the room illustrated. Write a short description of the room.

Klaus und Marianne Schubert sind verheiratet und haben ein Kind. Ihre Tochter Annelie ist drei Jahre alt und geht in den Kindergarten. Klaus ist Ingenieur und muss jeden Tag eine halbe Stunde zur Arbeit fahren. Die Familie hat zwei Autos, denn Marianne muss Annelie jeden Tag in den Kindergarten bringen und dann zu ihrer Arbeit fahren. Sie arbeitet von 9 Uhr bis 12 Uhr in einem Eiscafé.

Herr und Frau Werner sind Rentner. Sie haben zwei Töchter und drei Enkelkinder, aber jetzt wohnen sie natürlich allein – fast allein, denn sie haben einen Hund. Der Hund heißt Fido und geht gern spazieren. Herr und Frau Werner fahren manchmal Rad, und sie lesen gern und telefonieren oft. Sie haben kein Auto, denn sie wohnen im Stadtzentrum.

Ulrike, Thomas und Jürgen sind Studenten in Leipzig. Ulrike studiert Architektur, und Thomas und Jürgen studieren Computerwissenschaften. Alle drei schlafen morgens gern lange und gehen abends oft aus. Sie kochen viel, denn Restaurants sind teuer. Sie waschen aber nicht gern ab und putzen auch nicht oft. Sie wohnen zentral und fahren normalerweise mit dem Fahrrad zur Universität. Sie brauchen kein Auto, aber Thomas hat ein altes Moped.

2 **Ute Schneiders Wohnung**

Listen to Ute talking about her flat in Bremen. Describe in German (**a**) the living room and (**b**) the kitchen. You will probably need to listen to the recording more than once.

3 Einladung

Listen to the telephone conversation between Christine and Axel and answer the questions.

a Wann will Christine grillen, und warum?
b Wo grillt sie?
c Was bringt Axel mit?
d Was braucht Christine noch?

e Wo muss Axel am Freitag einkaufen?
f Was macht Christine zum Essen?
g Wer kommt zum Barbecue?
h Warum muss Axel gehen?

4 Wo?

Read the sentences below carefully: the locations are mixed up – put each in the correct sentence so they all make better sense.

a Wir wohnen *im Restaurant*.
b Ich arbeite *in der Bismarckstraße*.
c Man kocht *auf einem Stuhl*.
d Sie essen *am Schreibtisch*.
e Er sitzt *in der Garage*.
f Das Auto ist *in der Diskothek*.
g Petra steht *in der Küche*.
h Ich tanze gern *unter der Dusche*.

> **PRINZ-CHRISTIANS-WEG**
> **13 – 25**

5 Jutta und Peter

Fill in the gaps.

Jutta arbeitet nachmittags oft in der Universitätsbibliothek. Heute geht sie auch in die Bibliothek, aber um vier Uhr will sie in die **a** _____ gehen. Sie muss eine gute Flasche **b** _____ kaufen, denn heute Abend gehen Jutta und Peter zu Michael. Michael hat eine neue **c** _____, im Prinz-Christians-Weg 25. Michael kocht ein gutes **d** _____, und seine Freunde bringen Wein und Bier mit. Um acht Uhr **e** _____ die Party – Musik gibt es auch. Michael hat ein sehr **f** _____ Wohnzimmer und man kann tanzen. Aber jetzt gibt es Essen! Michael kocht gern französisch, und heute **g** _____ es Quiche und Salat, mit Rotwein von Jutta. Das Esszimmer ist **h** _____ und gemütlich – es gibt sechs alte Stühle von Michaels **i** _____, einen Tisch und eine altmodische **j** _____.

Die Freunde sind jetzt **k** _____ Wohnzimmer und tanzen. Jutta tanzt sehr **l** _____, aber Peter will nach Hause gehen. Er muss früh **m** _____ und arbeiten. „Was machen **n** _____?", fragt Jutta. „Ich will jetzt ins Bett!", sagt Peter. „Stop – ihr müsst hier bleiben … ", sagt Michael. In Michaels Wohnung stehen Bierflaschen **o** _____ dem Fernseher, es gibt Gläser **p** _____ dem Stuhl und Tassen **q** _____ dem Computer. „Ich **r** _____ nicht allein aufräumen!", sagt Michael.

6 In der Stadt

1 Wo ist das Krankenhaus?

Summarise in English the directions given.

2 Gibt es eine Bank in der Nähe?

Listen to the prompts and speak in the gaps.

3 Das Geburtstagsgeschenk/The birthday present

a Answer the questions, without looking at the script:

 i Where are Marco and Fatma meeting?

 ii Where is the bookshop?

 iii What will Marco find there?

 iv Where is the flower shop?

b Now read the script to confirm your answers to **a**, and find the German equivalent of 'bouquet'.

Marco:	Es ist Fatmas Geburtstag heute, ich treffe sie in einer Stunde und ich habe kein Geschenk für sie!
Heike:	Wo triffst du sie?
Marco:	Vor dem Bahnhof.
Heike:	Einfach! … Am Bahnhof gibt's eine Buchhandlung. Fatma liest gern Krimis – du findest ganz bestimmt etwas für sie. … Und neben der Buchhandlung ist ein Blumengeschäft. Kauf einen schönen Blumenstrauß!
Marco:	Genial!

4 Die Jacke kann ich nicht kaufen

Without referring to the script, listen to the recording and answer the true/false questions. Then check your answers by reading the script. Alter them where necessary!

Julia und Hans sind im Kaufhaus.

Richtig/falsch:

a Hans nimmt die Jacke.

b Die Jacke gefällt Julia nicht.

c Die Jacke ist zu groß.

d Die Jacke ist nicht zu teuer.

e Karin kauft die Jacke.

H:	Nimm diese blaue Jacke!
J:	Ich weiß nicht …
H:	Gefällt sie dir nicht?
J:	Nein … sie gefällt mir sehr.
H:	Ist das nicht deine Größe?
J:	Nein … die Größe ist richtig.
H:	Ist sie zu teuer?
J:	Nein … sie kostet nur 81,50 Euro.
H:	Also … warum kaufst du sie nicht?
J:	Die Jacke kann ich nicht kaufen – Karin hat so eine!

5 Einkaufsbummel/Shopping trip

Ulrike and Klaus are going shopping. Listen to the dialogue and answer the following questions in English.

a What does Ulrike need?
b Why does Klaus object? (4 reasons)
c What would he rather buy with the money?
d What size is the garment?
e Where will Ulrike and Klaus meet?

6 Jutta und Peter

Fill in the gaps.

Heute ist Samstag, und wie jeden Samstag wollen Jutta und Peter in die
a _____ gehen und einkaufen. Jetzt ist es schon 11
b _____, und sie sind mit dem Frühstück fertig. „Fahren wir mit dem
c _____ oder laufen wir in die Stadt?", fragt Peter. „Wir laufen, denn
samstags ist das Parkhaus immer voll. Wir können aber auch mit dem
d _____ fahren." „Das ist zu teuer – das kostet 4,50 Euro. … Wir
laufen." Jutta und Peter wohnen in der **e** _____ von der Innenstadt,
und nach 20 Minuten sind sie im Zentrum. „Was brauchen wir?", fragt Jutta. „Wir müssen
Essen fürs Wochenende kaufen, und ich will heute **f** _____ einen
guten Video sehen … also erst ins Videogeschäft, und dann zum **g** _____."
Jutta will auch in ein Blumengeschäft **h** _____ – morgen ist
Muttertag, und sie braucht ein Geschenk für ihre Mutter. Aber sie hat kein Geld – also
müssen die beiden zur Bank gehen. Die Bank ist um die **i** _____,
und neben **j** _____ Bank ist das Videogeschäft. Jutta kauft den
Strauß für ihre Mutter, und dann **k** _____ sie Peter vor dem Café.
„Und was ist mit deiner Mutter?" fragt Jutta. „Meine Mutter … ich weiß nicht, ich habe
keine Idee." „Männer!"

7 Fahren

1 Paola

a On the train to Bonn Vijay gets to know Paola. What do you think he asks her to get the following answers?

 i Ich komme aus Rom.

 ii Ich lerne seit einem Jahr Deutsch.

 iii Weil ich im Ausland arbeiten will.

b Without looking at the text below, listen to the recording as the conversation continues. Answer the questions, then check your understanding against the text.

 i Wann kommt der Zug in Bonn an?

 ii Was macht Paola in Bonn?

 iii Warum?

 iv Was macht Vijay?

P: ... Ja, ich auch. Ich kann schon Französisch und jetzt …

„Meine Damen und Herren, in wenigen Minuten erreichen wir Bonn Hauptbahnhof."

P: Oh! Ich steige hier aus!

V: Ich auch! Was machst du in Bonn?

P: Ich mache einen Sprachkurs. Ich will mein Deutsch verbessern.

V: Ich auch! Ich helfe dir mit den Koffern, wenn du willst.

P: Oh ja, danke.

2 Der nächste Zug

Listen to the recording and take part in the dialogue, using the prompts given.

3 In den Sommerferien

Fill in the gaps in the letter.

a _____ 10. August fahre ich **b** _____ Bremen, um einen Sommerkurs zu **c** _____ . Ich lerne **d** _____ zwei Jahren Deutsch und will es **e** _____ . Der Kurs **f** _____ drei Wochen und man **g** _____ junge Leute aus der ganzen Welt kennen. Ich **h** _____ um 10.40 in Bremen an. Vom Flughafen fahre ich **i** _____ der Straßenbahn in die Stadtmitte. Ich **j** _____ dann mit dem Bus zur **k** _____ .

machen	mit	Universität	am	dauert	seit
fahre	nach	verbessern	lernt	komme	

 4 Ich darf nicht zu spät kommen!/I mustn't be late!

a Listen to the dialogue between Axel and Michael, and then answer the questions.

 i Warum kann Axel nicht mit ins Sportzentrum kommen?
 ii Was will Klaus am Samstag machen?
 iii Wie müssen sie nach Köln fahren?
 iv Warum will Axel nicht nach Köln fahren?
 v Was will er am Freitag machen?
 vi Was will Klaus in der Stadt kaufen?

b And you? Write down what you must/can/want to do on particular days of the week.

 5 Ich kann nicht so viel trinken …/I can't drink that much …

Listen to Gabi and Karl-Heinz and decide if the statements are true (**richtig**) or false (**falsch**).

a Gabi will mit ins Schwimmbad kommen. r/f
b Sie geht mit Karl-Heinz essen. r/f
c Karl-Heinz will mit Gabi in die Kneipe gehen. r/f
d Gabi trinkt gern Wein. r/f
e Sie hat morgen Abend keine Zeit. r/f

 6 Jutta und Peter

Fill in the gaps.

Heute ist der Freitag vor Ostern, und Jutta und Peter müssen zwei Wochen nicht **a** _____ , sie haben frei. Sie wollen für 10 Tage **b** _____ Cuxhaven fahren, denn sie haben eine Freundin dort und **c** _____ bei Sabine wohnen. Die Stadt ist sehr **d** _____ – direkt am Wasser! Jutta und Peter schwimmen gern, aber **e** _____ April ist das Wasser noch sehr kalt. Man **f** _____ in den Restaurants gut und billig Fisch essen, und man kann lange am Wasser **g** _____ . Die Koffer sind fertig und sehr schwer – Jutta und Peter wollen nicht mit dem **h** _____ fahren, sie nehmen ein Taxi zum Bahnhof. Dort **i** _____ sie eine Fahrkarte kaufen. Jutta geht zum **j** _____ und sagt: „Zwei **k** _____ nach Cuxhaven, bitte." Aber das ist sehr kompliziert. Mit Bahncard ist der Fahrschein billiger, aber Jutta und Peter haben keine Bahncard. Sie **l** _____ kein TwenTicket kaufen, **m** _____ Peter 26 Jahre alt ist – man muss jünger als 25 sein. „Und ein Guten Abend-Ticket?" – „Nein", antwortet Jutta, „wir wollen vor 19 Uhr fahren." „Wollen Sie den Super-Sparpreis?" Aber dann kann **n** _____ nicht freitags oder sonntags fahren! „Und das Wochenendticket?" Dann können wir nur am **o** _____ fahren. „Vielleicht bleiben wir zu **p** _____!", sagt Peter.

8 Gestern

1 Ich habe gelacht/I laughed

Read the following.

Ich bin gestern Abend spät ins Bett gegangen und habe gut geschlafen. Zu gut, denn ich bin heute Morgen spät aufgestanden. Ich habe nichts gegessen, nur ganz schnell ein Glas Wasser getrunken. Ich bin pünktlich um 7.30 an der Bushaltestelle angekommen, um ins Büro zu fahren. Erst dann habe ich gesehen, dass ich ganz allein war. „Oh Gott … es ist Samstag. Ich arbeite heute nicht!", habe ich laut gesagt. Dann habe ich gelacht.

Cover the text and write an account of what happened in the **er**-form of the perfect tense, using the following prompts:

spät ins Bett gehen – gut schlafen – aufstehen – essen – trinken
7.30 Haltestelle ankommen – sehen – allein – „Samstag!" – sagen – lachen

2 Mein Wochenende

„Wie war dein Wochenende?"

„Katastrophal! Man hat meine Kreditkarte gestohlen. Unsere Fußballmannschaft hat schlecht gespielt. Ich habe die Bücher für meinen Aufsatz nicht gefunden. … Und es hat stundenlang geregnet. Nächstes Wochenende bleibe ich im Bett!"

Give (in English) the negative features of this person's weekend. What conclusion does he draw?

3 Warum (nicht)?

You haven't been able to join your friend(s)/fulfil obligations because of other pressing engagements. Match up the two halves of each sentence to give a credible excuse.

1 Ich habe am Freitag nicht Tennis gespielt,

2 Ich bin gestern nicht in die Vorlesung gegangen,

3 Ich habe Peter nicht angerufen,

4 Ich bin gestern nicht nach Hause gekommen,

5 Ich bin am Samstag nicht zu deinen Eltern gefahren,

a ... weil meine Schwester mein Handy hat.

b ... weil ich samstags arbeite.

c ... weil der Professor so langweilig ist!

d ... weil ich die ganze Nacht in der Bibliothek war.

e ... weil ich nicht fit genug bin.

4 Gestern

The following sentences are in the present tense. Put them into the perfect. Make sure you know which verbs are strong and which weak, and which verbs take the auxiliary **sein**. Listen to the recording to check your version.

a Ich kaufe bei Aldi ein und koche für meine Freunde. Nach dem Essen hören wir Musik und später spielen wir Karten.

b Sie isst Brot mit Marmelade und trinkt eine Tasse Tee. Sie schreibt E-Mails an ihre Freunde. Dann liest sie die Zeitung.

c Ich stehe um sieben Uhr auf und fahre mit dem Bus zur Uni. Ich bleibe den ganzen Nachmittag in der Bibliothek. Ich suche ein Buch für meine Dissertation, aber finde es nicht.

5 Jutta und Peter

a Fill in the gaps.

Gestern war ein wichtiger Tag für Jutta und Peter: sie **a** _____ zu einem Rolling Stones Konzert nach Köln gefahren. Sie sind spät

b _____, so gegen halb elf, und haben dann gemütlich

c _____. Um drei Uhr mussten sie am

d _____ sein, weil samstags der schnelle ICE schon um 15.17 Uhr von Frankfurt nach Köln fährt. Peter war sehr aufgeregt, weil er ein großer Fan ist und die Stones noch nie live **e** _____ hat. Der Zug war pünktlich, die Fahrt angenehm, und um 17.32 Uhr sind Jutta und Peter in Köln

f _____. Sie **g** _____ noch viel Zeit – zwei Stunden! „Was wollen wir **h** _____?", hat Jutta gefragt. Peter hatte eine Idee: „Wir **i** _____ vielleicht in der Stadt in eine Kneipe gehen ..." Jutta war nicht enthusiastisch – sie wollte lieber den Dom sehen und am Rhein spazieren gehen. „Ich möchte nicht trinken oder rauchen. ... Ich will die Stadt

j _____." Jetzt war Peter enttäuscht: „Ein Kompromiss – ich gehe in die Kneipe, du **k** _____ zum Dom, und wir **l** _____ uns um zwanzig **m** _____ acht an der Konzerthalle." „Okay", hat Jutta gesagt. Zwei Stunden später war Jutta am Eingang. Um acht Uhr war Peter immer noch nicht da! Um Viertel nach acht

n _____ Peter endlich gekommen – viel zu spät! Das Konzert hat schon **o** _____, und Peter war sehr frustriert. „Meine Uhr ist kaputt – was machen wir denn jetzt?"

b Think of an ending to Jutta and Peter's story – what did they do when they realised that they could not see the concert? Write a short paragraph in German to conclude the story.

9 Lebensläufe

1 Wann?

Write out the following years in words, then check them on the recording.

a 1947 **b** 1921 **c** 2003 **d** 1912 **e** 1815 **f** 1993 **g** 1874 **h** 2005

2 Verben

The following sentences are in the present tense; put them into the perfect tense.

a Meine Eltern verstehen mich nicht.
b Seine Brüder studieren in Frankfurt.
c Er wird nach dem Studium Lehrer.
d Erhalten Sie gute Noten?
e Wir verlassen mit 16 die Schule.

3 Die Stelle gefällt mir nicht

a Ask the questions in this conversation, following the prompts on the recording.

b Listen to the conversation again and summarise in English what the interviewee tells you in reply.

4 Jobs!

Read the three job ads and decide for which of them the two people described are best suited.

a

> ### Studenten!
> Wir suchen selbständige Interviewer in der Marktforschung.
> Gute Bezahlung. Flexible Arbeitszeiten.
> Sie sind: Pünktlich, zuverlässig und mobil.

b

> **Fitness-Center** sucht Teamleiter/in für organisatorische und administrative Aufgaben.

c

> ### SERVICE/BAR
> Golfanlage „Schloss Jesinghausen"
> Wir suchen ab sofort Teil- oder Vollzeitkräfte.
> Nette, freundliche Persönlichkeit und soziale Kompetenz erforderlich.

Simon arbeitet am liebsten in einem Team. Er ist tolerant, populär und hat viel Humor. Er studiert Englisch und Sport.

Anja ist organisiert, fleißig und kommunikativ. Sie hat ein Auto. Sie studiert Soziologie.

5 Auf dem Arbeitsamt

a Listen to the conversation at the job centre and answer the following questions in English.

i When did Herr Helwig do his **Abitur**, and what was his grade?

ii For how long did he work as an ambulance driver?

iii Why did he do nothing for a while?

iv Where did he apply eventually?

v What was his job?

vi What are his qualities/abilities for the job market?

vii What did he do on Lanzarote?

b Listen to the recording again. Can you finish it by formulating a suitable reply for Herr Helwig? What do you think he might want to do now?

6 Sie möchte gern …

Finish the sentences by choosing a suitable reason from the list below.

Example: Ulrike möchte in der Bibliothek arbeiten, weil sie gern liest.

a Markus möchte im Krankenhaus arbeiten, weil …

b Carima möchte im Museum arbeiten, weil …

c Mehmet möchte im Sportzentrum arbeiten, weil …

d Helga möchte in einer Kneipe arbeiten, weil …

e Andreas möchte im Theater arbeiten, weil …

NB: The verbs must be put into an appropriate form as they are given in the infinitive below. Make sure your word order is right. And beware … there is one surplus reason in the list!

> gern sehr spät ins Bett gehen sich für Literatur interessieren sportlich sein
> gern anderen Menschen helfen gut Englisch sprechen sich für Bilder interessieren

7 Jutta und Peter

Fill in the gaps.

Jutta muss einen Ferienjob finden, weil sie kein **a** _____ mehr hat. Jutta und Peter **b** _____ gern im September nach Italien fahren, und Hotels sind teuer. Heute ist Samstag und Jutta **c** _____ beim Frühstück die Zeitung: „Peter, hier ist eine **d** _____ im Schwimmbad …" „Aber du **e** _____ doch überhaupt nicht gut schwimmen – das ist keine gute Idee." Jutta sieht eine andere Anzeige. „Im Krankenhaus suchen sie eine Küchenhilfe …" „Aber du kochst nicht gern, und du **f** _____ nicht gern ab." Jutta antwortet nicht. „Im Konferenzzentrum **g** _____ man Personal für die Cafeteria. ‚Muss abends arbeiten **h** _____ '. „Nein!", sagt Peter „Nicht in den Ferien! Ich will **i** _____ abends sehen." Jetzt ist Jutta wirklich böse auf Peter. „OK, dann **j** _____ wir den ganzen Sommer zu Hause – ohne Geld keine Toskana!"

10 Zukunftspläne

1 **Markus und die Zukunft**/Markus and the future

a Choose the right words to fill the gaps. Note that there are three more words than you need in the list at the end!

Markus findet seine Arbeit in **a** _____ Buchhandlung
b _____ . Er **c** _____ gern im
d _____ arbeiten. Das **e** _____ in einem
südeuropäischen **f** _____ ist **g** _____ und
die Kultur ist **h** _____ . Markus **i** _____
einen **j** _____ machen, um **k** _____ zu
lernen. Er geht **l** _____ Ausland, um neue **m** _____
zu sammeln. Wenn er **n** _____ , **o** _____ er
hoffentlich mehr Geld!

Land	zurückkommt	nach	langweilig	ins	der	würde	Italienisch
will	Erfahrungen	Ausland	Leben	interessanter	verdient	Jobs	
angenehmer	Sprachkurs	Italien					

b Then translate the passage into English.

2 **Die Badehose**/The swimming trunks

Complete the text below with an appropriate form of a modal verb. Then check your answers by listening to the recording.

Oskar **a** _____ heute Nachmittag ins Kino gehen, aber das ist leider nicht möglich. Er **b** _____ seine Eltern besuchen, denn sein Vater hat heute Geburtstag. Leider hat Oskar noch kein Geschenk für ihn ... Panik! Er hat ihm schon oft Bücher gegeben, denn er arbeitet in einer Buchhandlung. Sein Vater **c** _____ keinen Alkohol trinken, also **d** _____ er ihm keine Flasche Wein kaufen. Da sein Vater keine Hobbys hat, ist es wirklich schwierig, ein schönes Geschenk für ihn zu finden. Aber Oskar hat eine Idee – sein Vater **e** _____ einmal in der Woche schwimmen gehen, denn er ist nicht fit genug. Also eine Badehose!

3 Urlaub in Norddeutschland/Holidays in Northern Germany

Zwischen Nordsee und Ostsee – eine magische Landschaft

Fahrradtouren durch Holstein …

Malerische alte Dörfer, traditionelle Bauernhöfe, schöne Wälder und Seen, ruhige Strände, kleine Häfen … das ist Holstein.

Informieren Sie sich auch über unsere Touren … zu Fuß
auf dem Wasser
zu Pferde

Zwischen Nordsee und Ostsee – eine magische Landschaft

a Dictionary work: try to find the singular of the seven plural nouns in the advertisement. What is noteworthy about the noun **See** (plural **Seen**)?

b How many different ways of forming the plural are represented here?

c Which of the adjectives do you think means 'picturesque'?

d On the basis of this information, describe what you can do and see in Holstein:
In Holstein kann man … (Remember the word order rule: infinitive to end!)
es gibt …

4 Jutta und Peter

Fill in the gaps.

Zum Glück hat Jutta am Anfang der Semesterferien einen guten **a** _____ gefunden, und so **b** _____ Jutta und Peter doch in die Toskana in Italien fahren. Sie sind sehr glücklich . „Wir müssen das Hotel bald buchen, um ein **c** _____ Zimmer zu bekommen", sagt Peter. „Du hast Recht … Wir gehen morgen in die Stadt. Aber es gibt eine andere wichtige Frage: fahren wir **d** _____ dem Auto, oder mit **e** _____ Zug?", fragt Jutta. „Wir können fliegen! Fliegen ist viel schneller, aber vielleicht **f** _____ als mit dem Auto. Wir können nach Florenz fliegen und dann ein Auto mieten – ich glaube, das ist der beste Plan." Jutta ist nicht zufrieden … „Aber mit dem **g** _____ können wir **h** _____, wohin und wann wir wollen. Das finde ich viel besser. Außerdem muss man einen Flug früh buchen, und wir wissen noch nicht, an welchem Tag wir reisen wollen. Und wie kommen wir **i** _____ Flughafen? Mein Vater kann uns nicht fahren, **j** _____ meine Eltern sind auch in Urlaub. Und …" Jutta redet und redet.

Peter versteht das nicht. „Jutta, was ist denn **k** _____ Problem?" Nach einer langen Pause **l** _____ Jutta: „Ich habe Angst vor dem Fliegen." Peter lacht. „Jetzt kenne ich dich schon so lange, und ich habe nicht gewusst, dass du nicht **m** _____ fliegst! OK, dann fahren wir mit dem Auto …"

GUIDE TO GRAMMATICAL TERMS

Language learners often feel unsure about grammatical terms. The following list gives some simple definitions. Examples are underlined, terms used which are defined elsewhere in the list are given in bold. Examples are drawn from English: reference is made to German only when something distinctive about that language needs to be noted. This Guide is concerned only with the meanings of grammatical terms: there is a German Grammar Summary beginning on page 147.

Accusative In German, **case** used for the **direct object** and after certain **prepositions**.

Adjective A word used to describe a **noun** ('an <u>interesting</u> woman', 'the curry is <u>hot</u>'). See also **demonstrative adjective, possessive**.

Adverb A word which describes the action of a **verb** ('she sings <u>beautifully</u>', 'he cooks <u>well</u>') or modifies (= gives further information about) an **adjective** ('it's a <u>really</u> expensive car') or another adverb ('she sings <u>really</u> well').

Article <u>The</u> (called the definite article), <u>a</u> or <u>an</u> (the indefinite article).

Auxiliary verb A **verb** combining with another verb to form a compound tense. ('She has gone' = perfect tense formed by combining the auxiliary verb 'to have' with the past participle of 'to go'.)

Case In German, a category defined by function within the sentence. See **accusative, dative, genitive, nominative**.

Clause Subdivision of a sentence. Every clause has a verb. See also **main clause, subordinate clause**.

Coordinating conjunction A **conjunction** which joins two **clauses** of equal importance. ('The man is tall <u>and</u> his name is John.')

Comparative Form of an **adjective** ('that room is <u>bigger</u> than this one'; 'they've bought a <u>more expensive</u> car') or **adverb** ('it happens <u>more often</u> than you think') expressing a greater or lesser degree.

Conjunction A word which joins parts of a sentence ('he was tired <u>and</u> he wanted to go home'; 'they arrived early <u>because</u> they wanted a good seat'). See **coordinating conjunction, subordinating conjunction**.

Dative In German, **case** used for the **indirect object** and after certain **prepositions**.

Demonstrative adjective 'Points out' **nouns** (<u>this</u> chair/<u>these</u> chairs; <u>that</u> house/<u>those</u> houses).

Direct object The word which directly undergoes the action of the verb. In the sentence 'she sent her mother <u>a present</u>', what she sent was a present, so that is the direct object. She didn't send her mother! See also **indirect object**.

Gender In German, all **nouns** have a grammatical gender, masculine, feminine or neuter.

Genitive In German, **case** expressing ownership, belonging.

Imperative **Verb** form used in giving commands and instructions ('<u>Turn</u> left now!').

Indirect object A secondary object. In the sentence 'she sent <u>her mother</u> a present', the **direct object**, the thing which is sent, is the present. It was sent <u>to</u> her mother, the indirect object.

Infinitive The basic form of a **verb** ('<u>to sing</u>', '<u>to write</u>').

Irregular verb **Verb** that does not follow a standard pattern.

Main clause The principal statement in a sentence. To make sense, a **subordinate clause** depends upon the information in the main clause. '<u>Peter stayed at home</u> (because the weather was so bad.')

Mixed verb In German, a **verb** that combines features of both **strong** and **weak** verbs.

Modal verb E.g. '<u>can</u>', '<u>must</u>'. Often combines with another **verb**: 'he <u>can go</u> tomorrow'.

Nominative In German, **case** used for the **subject**.

Noun Word denoting a person ('<u>student</u>'), thing ('<u>book</u>') or abstract idea ('<u>happiness</u>').

Object see **direct object**, **indirect object**

Past participle Part of the **verb** which combines with an **auxiliary verb** to form the perfect tense ('they have <u>arrived</u>', 'I have <u>seen</u>').

Plural More than one: the plural of 'man' is '<u>men</u>'.

Possessive (also called 'possessive adjective' or 'possessive pronoun') e.g. '<u>my</u> house', '<u>your</u> friend', '<u>his</u> car' etc.

Preposition e.g. '<u>on</u> the table', '<u>under</u> the chair', '<u>to</u> the station', '<u>for</u> the teacher' etc.

Pronoun Word taking the place of a **noun**. 'Paul saw the waitress' becomes '<u>he</u> saw <u>her</u>'. See also **possessive**.

Reflexive verb In German, **verb** formed with an extra **pronoun** (called a 'reflexive pronoun'): e.g. <u>sich setzen</u> (to sit down), 'ich <u>setze mich</u>'.

Regular verb **Verb** that follows a standard pattern.

Separable verb In German, **verb** that has a detachable prefix: e.g. <u>aufstehen</u> → 'Ich stehe um 7 Uhr <u>auf</u>'.

Singular One rather than many: the singular of 'bananas' is '<u>banana</u>'.

Strong verb **Verb** which has an internal vowel change, e.g. in the English past tense (swim → swam).

Subject Who or what carries out the action of the **verb**. '<u>A student</u> sent me this email.'; '<u>We</u> are travelling next week.', '<u>The letter</u> arrived yesterday.'

Subordinate clause Part of a sentence introduced by a **subordinating conjunction**. To make sense it depends on the information in the **main clause**. '(Peter stayed at home) <u>because the weather was so bad</u>.'

Subordinating conjunction **Conjunction** that introduces a **subordinate clause**: e.g. <u>because</u>, <u>when</u>, <u>that</u>.

Tense Form taken by a **verb** to show when the action takes place, e.g. present tense: 'they <u>live</u> in New York'; past: 'they <u>lived</u> in New York'; future: 'they <u>will live</u> in New York' etc.

Weak verb In German, a regular verb without any internal vowel change. See also **verb**, **strong verb**.

Verb Word indicating an action ('they <u>ate</u> their dinner') or state ('the book <u>lay</u> on the table'). Different **tenses** are used to show when something happened. See also **irregular verb**, **mixed verb**, **modal verb**, **reflexive verb**, **regular verb**, **separable verb**, **strong verb**, **tense**, **weak verb**.

THE SOUNDS OF GERMAN

 ## Das Alphabet

a b c d e f g h i j k l m n o p q r s t u v w x y z

ä ö ü ß

Ich buchstabiere meinen Namen … / I'll spell my name …

 ## German spelling …

… is highly regular and predictable. Once you have learnt how the sounds are represented, you will be able to write down a word you hear but have not seen in print. Use these examples for some pronunciation practice, too!

ä	**Universität**	ö	**Köln**
ach	**Bach**	s	**Apfelsaft**
au	**Audi**	sch	**Schweiz**
äu	**Löwenbräu**	sp (initial)	**Sport**
d (final)	**Abend**	st (initial)	**Stuttgart**
e (final)	**Porsche**	u (long)	**Hut**
ee	**Kaffee**	ü	**München**
ei	**Wein**	v	**Volkswagen**
eu	**Deutschland**	w	**Wasser**
ich	**Zürich**	z	**Mozart**
ie	**Bier**	ss	**dass**
j	**ja**	ß	**Spaß**

 ## Using numbers

Geld:	€15,90	€0,75		
Gewicht:	74 kg	3,5 kg	500g	1 Pfund
	Ich wiege … ('I weigh …')			
Länge:	55 km	700 m	1,80m	30 cm
	Ich bin … groß ('I am … tall')			
Telefon:	00 49	2 28	67 43 10	
	Deutschland	*Vorwahlnummer*		
Temperatur:	23 °C			

GRAMMAR SUMMARY

This is a short summary of basic German grammar. If you are not familiar with grammatical terms, you will probably find the 'Guide to grammatical terms' on pages 144–5 very useful as an introduction to this section.

1 Nouns – gender

To use a German noun properly, you must know its gender: masculine, feminine or neuter. Words denoting males (**Mann**, **Vater**, **Lehrer**) are masculine and those denoting females are feminine (**Frau**, **Mutter**, **Lehrerin**; the exception: **Mädchen** 'girl' is neuter), but objects (**der Tisch** 'table' is masculine), and ideas (**die Hoffnung** 'hope' is feminine) have a grammatical gender too and can be any of the three genders. Learn a noun with its *definite article* and you will automatically learn its gender.

Feminine forms of nouns denoting a job often add **-in** to the masculine form: **Lehrer/Lehrerin**.

Compound nouns have the gender of the last element: **die Abendzeitung** 'evening paper' is feminine because **Zeitung** is.

2 Nouns – plurals

In English, the overwhelming majority of nouns form their plural by adding '-s' but there are other ways which survive from an earlier stage of the language: change of vowel (man → men); no change (sheep → sheep); addition of '-en' (ox → oxen).

German has these four ways of forming the plural of nouns but also has several others:

Add **-s**	**das Auto → Autos**
Vowel change (add Umlaut)	**der Bruder → Brüder**
No change	**der Amerikaner → Amerikaner**
Add **-en**	**das Bett → Betten**
Add **-n**	**die Schwester → Schwestern**
Add **-e**	**der Tag → Tage**
Vowel change (Umlaut) plus **-e**	**die Nacht → Nächte**
Add **-er**	**das Kind → Kinder**
Vowel change (Umlaut) plus **-er**	**das Land → Länder**

As you get to know the language better, you will see there are some patterns to this (e.g. feminine nouns ending in **-e** add an **-n** in the plural). The best advice is to learn the plural of each noun. The overall glossary beginning on page 160 gives the plurals of nouns in brackets.

3 Nouns – capitals

German nouns always begin with a capital letter.

4 The case system: articles, possessives and *dieser, welcher, jeder*

Nouns usually have accompanying words which give information on their function in the sentence. Here, we shall be looking at the *definite* and *indefinite* articles (**der** and **ein** etc.) and the *possessives* (**mein**, **dein**, **sein** etc.) as well as **dieser**, **welcher** and **jeder**, which follow the definite article pattern. Later sections deal with *adjectives* and *prepositions*.

As you have worked your way through the units of this book, you have seen a system of categories unfold. These categories, nominative, accusative, dative and genitive, are characterised by specific patterns, and using German grammar correctly is largely a matter of becoming familiar with the patterns. The categories are referred to as *cases*.

Nominative

This is the form used when the noun is the *subject*. It is also used after the verb **sein** 'to be':

	masc	fem	neut	pl
Definite article	**der**	**die**	**das**	**die**
dieser 'this', **welcher?** 'which?' **jeder** 'each'	**dieser**	**diese**	**dieses**	**diese** etc.
Indefinite article and **kein**	**(k)ein**	**(k)eine**	**(k)ein**	**keine**
Possessives	**mein**	**meine**	**mein**	**meine** etc.
(all possessives follow this pattern: see section 9 below)				

Dieser Rock ist zu teuer. **Wo ist mein Buch?**
Eine Limonade kostet €2,00. **Das Haus liegt in der Goethestraße.**

Accusative

• This is the form used when the noun is the *direct object*.
• It is also used after certain *prepositions* (see section 11 below) and the construction **es gibt**.

Only the masculine changes: the feminine, neuter and plural forms are all the same as the basic, nominative form:

Definite article	**den**
dieser/welcher/jeder	**diesen** etc.
Indefinite article and **kein**	**(k)einen**
Possessives	**meinen** etc.

Wann hast du diesen Computer gekauft? **Ich suche einen Job.**
Er arbeitet für seinen Bruder. **Es gibt einen Park in der Nähe.**

Dative

• This form is used when the noun is the *indirect object*.
• It has to be used after the verbs **helfen** and **gefallen**.
• It is also used after certain *prepositions* (see section 11).

	masc. + neut.	fem.	pl.
Definite article	**dem**	**der**	**den**
dieser/welcher/jeder	**diesem**	**dieser**	**diesen** etc.
Indefinite article and **kein**	**(k)einem**	**(k)einer**	**keinen**
Possessives	**meinem**	**meiner**	**meinen** etc.

* In the dative plural, nouns not already ending in an **-n** add one (except those with a plural ending in **-s**.)

Zu ihrem Geburtstag gebe ich <u>meiner</u> Schwester Blumen.
Klaus hilft <u>seinem</u> Großvater in <u>dem</u> Garten.
Wir bekommen oft Briefe von <u>unseren</u> Freunde<u>n</u> in Mexiko.

<u>Genitive</u>

This form is used to express belonging and ownership.

	masc. + neut.	fem. + pl.
Definite article	de<u>s</u>	de<u>r</u>
dieser/welcher/jeder	dies<u>es</u>	dies<u>er</u> etc.
Indefinite article and **kein**	(k)ein<u>es</u>	(k)ein<u>er</u>
Possessives	mein<u>es</u>	mein<u>er</u> etc.

* Masculine and neuter nouns add **-(e)s**.

Er ist ein Freund <u>meines</u> Vater<u>s</u>. **Das ist das Auto <u>der</u> Lehrerin.**
Am Ende <u>der</u> Ferien fahre ich nach Hause.

5 The case system: adjectives before the noun

When used before a noun and following a definite or indefinite article, **dieser**, **welcher**, **jeder** or a possessive, an adjective has an ending. The system is quite simple:

<u>The adjective has the ending **-en** in:</u>

– the masculine accusative singular (after **den/einen** etc.)
– the dative singular (any gender) (after **dem/einem** and **der/einer** etc.)
– the genitive singular (any gender) (after **des/eines** and **der/einer** etc.)
– the plural (all cases) (after **die/der/den** and **keine/keiner/keinen** etc.)

Ich trage gern diesen blau<u>en</u> Rock. (masculine accusative)
Es ist das Haus eines alt<u>en</u> Freundes. (masculine genitive)
Die neu<u>en</u> Stühle sind im Wohnzimmer. (plural nominative)

<u>Otherwise, the adjective has the following endings:</u>

(a) **-e** after the *definite* article and **dieser, welcher, jeder**:
 – masc. nominative (after **der/dieser**)
 – fem. nominative + accusative (after **die/diese**)
 – neut. nominative + accusative: (after **das/dieses**)

(b) **-er**, **-e**, or **-es** as follows after the *indefinite* article and **kein/mein** etc:
 – masc. nominative (**ein/kein/mein** etc.) **-er**
 – fem. nominative + accusative (after **eine/keine/meine** etc.) **-e**
 – neut. nominative + accusative (after **ein/kein/mein** etc.) **-es**

a **b**
Der italienisch<u>e</u> Anzug ist zu teuer. **Ein neu<u>er</u> Computer kostet mehr!**
Diese weiß<u>e</u> Bluse gefällt mir nicht. **Deine blau<u>e</u> Bluse ist schön.**
Heinz hat das alt<u>e</u> Fahrrad da, aber … **Lucy hat ein klein<u>es</u> Auto gekauft.**

Grammar summary

At-a-glance summary of articles/adjectival endings

	masc.	fem.	neut.	pl.
nom.	der -E	die -E	das -E	die -EN
	ein -ER	eine -E	ein -ES	keine -EN
acc.	den -EN	die -E	das -E	die -EN
	einen -EN	eine -E	ein -ES	keine -EN
dat.	dem -EN	der -EN	dem -EN	den -EN
	einem -EN	einer -EN	einem -EN	keinen -EN
gen.	des -EN	der -EN	des -EN	der -EN
	eines -EN	einer -EN	eines -EN	keiner -EN

6 Adjective after the noun: no ending

Das Haus ist sehr modern. **Die Arbeit ist langweilig.**

7 Adjective + plural noun

When there is no article, the nominative and accusative plural adjectival ending is **-e**.
Ihr habt tolle Sessel.

8 Comparison of adjectives

Add **-er** to the adjective: **interessant → interessanter**.
Some adjectives change their internal vowel (Umlaut): **groß → größer**, **lang → länger**.
Irregular comparative: **gut → besser**

The resulting forms then follow the normal pattern for adjectives:
Das war ein besserer Film. **Ich habe einen schnelleren Computer gekauft.**
masculine nominative masculine accusative

Ist dein Job jetzt interessanter?
no ending

9 Possessives

These are sometimes referred to as possessive adjectives, sometimes as possessive
pronouns. They follow the pattern of the indefinite article **ein** (see section 4 above).

my	**mein**	our	**unser**
your (informal)	**dein/euer** (sing./pl.)	your (formal)	**Ihr**
his/its (m/n)	**sein**	their	**ihr**
her/its (f)	**ihr**		

10 Amount, number

viel/viele	much/many	**viel Geld/viele Studenten**
wenig/wenige	little (not much)/ few (not many)	**wenig Geld/wenige Studenten**
weniger	less	**Andrew bekommt weniger Geld als Kevin.**
mehr	more	**Kevin bekommt mehr Geld als Andrew.**
einige	some	**Gundula hat einige Freunde eingeladen.**
mehrere	several	**Mehrere Studenten warten im Korridor.**

11 Prepositions

<u>Always followed by the accusative:</u>

für ('for'), **um** ('around', 'at' – time), **durch** ('through'), **gegen** ('towards', 'against', 'about' – time), **bis** ('until'), **ohne** ('without').

Er arbeitet für seinen Bruder. **Sie gehen durch den Park.** **Wir fahren ohne ihn.**

<u>Always followed by the dative:</u>

aus ('out of'), **bei** ('at someone's house', 'for a firm (working)'), **gegenüber** ('opposite'), **mit** ('with'), **nach** ('after'), **seit** '(since'), **von** ('from', 'of'), **zu** ('to').

Er kommt um drei Uhr aus dem Bahnhof. **Er wohnt gegenüber einer Bäckerei.**

<u>Followed by accusative or dative:</u>

an ('at'), **auf** ('on'), **in** ('in'), **über** ('over', 'about'), **unter** ('under') are the prepositions most commonly found in both cases.

The following are followed by the accusative when the rule below requires it, but are much more likely to be found in contexts which require a dative:

hinter ('behind'), **neben** ('next to'), **vor** ('in front of', 'before'), **zwischen** ('between').

<u>Rule:</u> These prepositions are followed by a dative when they are just giving a location but by an accusative form when they express a change of place:

Example: **Sie tanzt in <u>der</u> Diskothek** is in the *dative* because this sentence is telling us <u>where</u> she is dancing (location): i.e. in the disco. If we used the *accusative* **Sie tanzt in die Diskothek** it would be talking about a change of place and it would be telling us that she dances <u>into</u> the disco!

In fact, 'into' in English expresses the same idea as **in** + accusative in German. In the example, she is doing the same thing in each sentence (dancing) but in one she is going from outside into the disco.

Sein Buch liegt auf <u>dem</u> Tisch. Here **liegen auf** + *dative* tells us where the book is – on the table.

Er legt das Buch auf <u>den</u> Tisch. Legen auf + *accusative* describes a change of place – he puts the book on(to) the table.

The verbs **liegen** 'to lie' and **legen** 'to lay, put down' underline the difference in context between using one of these prepositions with the dative and using it with accusative.

Er steht unter <u>der</u> Dusche. 'He is standing under the shower.'– **Unter** + *dative* gives location.

Er geht unter <u>die</u> Dusche. 'He is going under the shower.' – **Unter** + *accusative* describes a change of place.

<u>Meaning of prepositions</u>

English and German often use prepositions differently, so beware when translating them!

For example, English has a different equivalent of the German preposition **auf** in each of the following:

Die Katze sitzt auf meinem Schreibtisch. The cat is sitting <u>on</u> my desk.

Wir wohnen auf dem Lande. We live <u>in</u> the country.

Sie fahren auf das Land. They are going <u>to</u> the country.

Ich warte auf den Bus. I am waiting <u>for</u> the bus.

Sie ist böse auf mich. She is angry <u>with</u> me.

12 Pronouns

nominative		accusative		dative	
ich	I	**mich**	me	**mir**	(to) me
du	you – familiar sing.	**dich**	you	**dir**	(to) you
er	he, it	**ihn**	him/it	**ihm**	(to) him/it
sie	she, it	**sie**	her/it	**ihr**	(to) her/it
es	it	**es**	it	**ihm**	(to) it
wir	we	**uns**	us	**uns**	(to) us
Sie	you – formal sing & pl.	**Sie**	you	**Ihnen**	(to) you
sie	they	**sie**	they	**ihnen**	(to) them
ihr	you – familiar pl.	**euch**	you	**euch**	(to) you

Ich liebe dich. **Er hat ihr ein Geschenk gegeben.** **Arbeitest du mit ihnen?**
nom *acc* *nom* *dat* *nom* *dat*
I love you. He gave her a present. ('to her') Do you work with them?

Gefällt dir dieser Rock? – Nein, er ist zu kurz.
Do you like this skirt? – No, it is too short.

Er = 'it' here because it refers to **Rock**, a masculine noun.

13 Verbs – the infinitive

This is the basic form of the verb and the one given in dictionaries and word-lists.

The infinitive of all verbs ends in **-n**. With very few exceptions the ending is **-en**: e.g. **wohnen** 'to live', **ausgehen** 'to go out', **sich waschen** 'to get washed'.

14 Verbs – present tense

German has no continuous present ('She is eating a pizza'). The present tense outlined here covers both that and the English simple present ('She eats pizza every day').

As in English, the German present tense can also refer to the future:
Wir fahren nächste Woche nach Spanien. We are travelling to Spain next week.

Regular verb pattern (also called weak pattern)

ich wohn**e**	wir wohnen
du wohn**st**	Sie wohnen
er/sie/es wohn**t**	sie wohnen
ihr wohn**t**	

The three forms on the right are identical with the *infinitive*. The other four forms add the endings **-e**, **-st** and **-t** to the *stem* of the infinitive: **wohn-**. Most verbs follow this pattern.
If the stem ends in **-t** or **-d**, or in a consonant combination such as **-gn**, an **-e** is put in before the normal endings of the **du-** and **er/sie/es**-forms to make pronunciation possible: e.g. **er arbeitet**.

Note also that verbs with a stem ending in **-s**, **-ß** or **-z** don't add an extra **-s** in the **du**-form: **du heißt, du sitzt**.

Strong verb pattern

ich schlafe	wir schlafen
du schl**ä**fst	Sie schlafen
er/sie/es schl**ä**ft	sie schlafen
ihr schlaft	

The endings are the same as in the regular pattern but there is an internal vowel change (here it is from **a** to **ä**) in two forms: the **du**-form and the **er/sie/es**-form. Other common strong verbs in the present tense include: **fahren, essen, nehmen, lesen**. There is a list on page 158.

Separable verbs

In verbs such as **aufstehen**, the prefix separates off and comes at the end of the clause: **Anna steht um 7 Uhr auf.** Other examples include: **ausgehen, umsteigen, einkaufen, anrufen**. Some separable verbs are weak, some are strong. They follow the appropriate pattern as outlined earlier.

Modal verbs

ich kann	wir können
du kannst	Sie können
er/sie/es kann	sie können
ihr könnt	

Modals all have a distinctive form without an ending for the **ich**-form and **er/sie/es**-form, which also provides the basis of the **du**-form. The other forms are regular. Modals are typically used with the infinitive of another verb, which comes at the end of the clause.

Ich kann nächsten Montag um 4 Uhr kommen. I can come next Monday at 4 o'clock.

Other modals: **müssen** 'must, to have to' – **ich muss**; **wollen** 'to want to' – **ich will**; **dürfen** 'may, to be allowed to' – **ich darf**.

Reflexive verbs

e.g. **sich setzen** 'to sit down'

ich setze <u>mich</u>	**wir setzen <u>uns</u>**	Imperative:
du setzt <u>dich</u>	**Sie setzen <u>sich</u>**	**Setz dich!/Setzt euch!/Setzen Sie sich!**
er/sie/es setzt <u>sich</u>	**sie setzen <u>sich</u>**	
ihr setzt <u>euch</u>		

These have a *reflexive pronoun* in each form. Some are weak and some strong.

Er setzt sich an seinen Schreibtisch. He sits down at his desk.
(Do not confuse this verb with **sitzen** 'to be sitting': **Er sitzt an seinem Schreibtisch.**)

Other reflexives include: **sich freuen (auf)** 'to look forward (to)'; **sich waschen** 'to get washed'.

Two irregular verbs: **sein** and **haben**

sein 'to be'		**haben** 'to have'	
ich bin	**wir sind**	**ich habe**	**wir haben**
du bist	**Sie sind**	**du hast**	**Sie haben**
er/sie/es ist	**sie sind**	**er/sie/es hat**	**sie haben**
ihr seid		**ihr habt**	

15 The imperative

This is the form used to give instructions. It is based on the three 'you'-forms of the present tense.

– Familiar singular: **du**-form of the verb minus its **-st** ending.
 Geh geradeaus. Go straight on. **Ruf morgen an.** Phone tomorrow.

– Familiar plural: **ihr**-form of the verb without the pronoun.
 Geht geradeaus.

– Formal singular and plural: **Sie**-form of the verb, with the pronoun second.
 Gehen Sie geradeaus.

Irregular: **sein** **sei/seid/seien Sie**

16 The perfect tense

Like the perfect tense in English ('Have you ever been to America?'), the German perfect tense is a *compound* tense: it is made up of two elements, an *auxiliary* verb (**haben** or **sein**) combined with the *past participle* of the verb you are using.

Unlike its English equivalent, it is the tense most often used for talking about the past: **Ich habe um ein Uhr gegessen** is used where English would have 'I ate at one o'clock'. It is also used when English requires a perfect tense: **Wir haben schon gegessen.** 'We have already eaten.'

<u>Weak verbs</u>

auxiliary	present tense of **haben**	past participle (at end of clause)
	ich habe ... etc.	**ge____t** e.g. **gekocht** ← **kochen**
		separable verb: **eingekauft** ← **einkaufen**

Er hat eine wunderbare Paella gekocht. **Ich habe den ganzen Abend getanzt.**
Am Nachmittag haben wir eingekauft.

A few weak verbs have **sein** as their auxiliary: **Sie sind gelandet. (← landen)**

<u>Strong verbs</u>

auxiliary:	present tense of **haben**	past participle (at end of clause)
	ich habe ... etc.	**ge____en** e.g. **gegessen** ← **essen**
or	present tense of **sein**	e.g. **gefahren** ← **fahren**
	ich bin ... etc.	
		separable verb: **ferngesehen** ← **fernsehen**

Wir haben Paella gegessen. **Hast du das Buch schon gelesen?**
Er ist nach Rom gefahren. **Sie hat bis 11 Uhr ferngesehen.**

* With the perfect tense, the simplest approach is to learn the strong verbs as a category: those that have a past participle ending in **-en**. Some verbs (e.g. **gehen** → **gegangen**) are strong in the perfect tense but do not have a vowel change in the present tense **du-** and **er/sie-**forms. Equally, not all strong verbs have a vowel change in the perfect (e.g. **sehen** → **gesehen**). See the list on p. 158.

<u>Special past participle patterns</u>

Verbs ending with an infinitive ending in **-ieren** have a weak past participle without the prefix **ge-**.
Er hat in Amerika studiert. (← studieren).

Verbs with an inseparable prefix (e.g. **be-**, **er-**, **ent-**, **ver-**) also have a past participle without the **ge-**: **ich habe meine Eltern besucht (← besuchen).**

As in the present tense, verbs with a stem ending in **-t**, **-d**, or consonant combinations such as **-gn** add **-et** rather than **-t**: **es hat geregnet.**

17 Simple past tense

haben to have

		Modals follow the same pattern:	
ich hatte I had etc.	**wir hatten**	**wollen** → **ich wollte**	I wanted to
du hattest	**Sie hatten**	**müssen** → **ich musste**	I had to
er/sie/es hatte	**sie hatten**	**können** → **ich konnte**	I was able to
ihr hattet		**dürfen** → **ich durfte**	I was allowed to

sein 'to be' is irregular:

ich war I was etc.	**wir waren**
du warst	**Sie waren**
er/sie/es war	**sie waren**
ihr wart	

When talking about the past using **sein**, **haben** or a modal verb, the simple past tense, or imperfect, is preferred to the perfect.

Wir wollten heute ins Restaurant gehen, aber wir konnten nicht, weil Petra babysitten musste.

18 'Would like to'

There are two verb forms we can use: **möchte (gern)**/**würde gern** + infinitive

ich möchte; du möchtest; er/sie/es möchte; wir/Sie/sie möchten; ihr möchtet
ich würde, du würdest, er/sie/es würde, wir/Sie/sie würden, ihr würdet

Ich würde gern im Ausland arbeiten.

19 Verbs and word order

The verb is the second item in a sentence but not necessarily the second word.

Peter studiert in Manchester.
1 2

Die drei deutschen Studenten sind jetzt in Manchester.

The subject is one word in the first sentence and four words in the second, but it is still a single item, so the verb comes next. The verb is still the second item if the sentence does not begin with the subject:

Jetzt sind die drei deutschen Studenten in Manchester.

Note that here the subject follows the verb. This is unlike English where, if something other than the verb begins the sentence, the subject still comes in its normal place, before the verb:

Now the three German students are in Manchester.

Questions are formed by inverting the subject and the verb:

Geht er oft ins Kino? Hast du Michael gesehen? Wann können Sie uns besuchen?

Note that in the first examples the inversion of subject and verb means that the verb is in first place in the sentence. When the question begins with one of the question-forms in **w-** (**warum** 'why', **was** 'what', **wann** 'when', **wie** 'how', **wer** 'who', **wo** 'where') the verb comes second.

An infinitive comes at the end of the clause.

The two constructions you have met where this comes into play are: (i) **um ... zu** 'in order to' followed by an infinitive and (ii) modal verbs with an infinitive, where the modal verb takes second position in the clause.

(i) **Sie macht einen Intensivkurs, um ihr Deutsch zu verbessern.**
(ii) **Ich will im Ausland arbeiten.**

Like infinitives, past participles come at the end of the clause.

The auxiliary verb comes in second place:
Ich habe am Nachmittag Basketball gespielt.

In a subordinate clause, the verb comes at the end:

Wir bleiben zu Hause, weil wir im Moment viel Arbeit haben.
◄— Main clause —► ◄——— Subordinate clause ———►

When the subordinate clause begins the sentence, the verb in the main clause follows immediately because the subordinate clause is then the first item and the main verb must be the second item:

Weil wir viel Arbeit haben, bleiben wir zu Hause.
◄— Subordinate clause —► 2

TMP: Time, Manner, Place

Time expressions precede place expressions:

Der Zug kommt um drei Uhr in Heidelberg an.

English usually has them the other way round: 'The train arrives in Heidelberg at three o'clock.' Expressions of manner ('how') come between time and place expressions:

Ich fahre im Sommer mit meinem Bruder nach Spanien.

◄— T —►◄——— M ———►◄— P —►

20 Adverbs

In German, the adverb has the same form as the adjective without an ending:

Er schreibt gut. He writes well.

Adverbs come immediately after the verb, unlike in English:

Er schreibt <u>oft</u> an seine Mutter. He often writes to his mother.

Gern, lieber, am liebsten

The useful adverb **gern** means that the subject of the preceding verb likes doing whatever that verb denotes:

Er <u>spielt gern</u> Karten. He <u>likes playing</u> cards.
<u>Gehst</u> du <u>gern</u> ins Kino? Do you <u>like going</u> to the cinema?
Ja, aber ich <u>gehe lieber</u> in die Diskothek. Yes, but I <u>like going</u> to the disco <u>more</u>.
Ich <u>bleibe am liebsten</u> zu Hause. I <u>like staying</u> at home <u>most of all</u>.

21 Negation

Nouns: think of **kein** as the negative form of **ein** (it also follows the same pattern, see section 4 above): **Ich habe einen Computer**, negative: **Ich habe <u>keinen</u> Computer** 'I don't have a computer'. Unlike **ein**, it can be used in the plural: **Er hat <u>keine</u> Freunde** 'He hasn't any friends'.

Verbs are negated by **nicht**: **Er geht <u>nicht</u> in die Bibliothek.**

157

22 Some common strong verbs

Separable verbs are not listed: for **fernsehen** see **sehen** etc.

infinitive	meaning	er/sie-form present	past participle
beginnen	to begin	X	**begonnen**
bleiben	to stay, remain	X	**geblieben***
essen	to eat	**isst**	**gegessen**
fahren	to go (in vehicle)	**fährt**	**gefahren***
fallen	to fall	**fällt**	**gefallen***
fliegen	to fly	X	**geflogen***
geben	to give	**gibt**	**gegeben**
gehen	to go	X	**gegangen***
gewinnen	to win	X	**gewonnen**
kommen	to come	X	**gekommen***
laufen	to run, walk	**läuft**	**gelaufen***
nehmen	to take	**nimmt**	**genommen**
rufen	to call	X	**gerufen**
sehen	to see	**sieht**	**gesehen**
sitzen	to sit	X	**gesessen**
sprechen	to speak	**spricht**	**gesprochen**
sterben	to die	**stirbt**	**gestorben***
steigen	to climb	X	**gestiegen***
tragen	to wear, carry	**trägt**	**getragen**
treffen	to meet	**trifft**	**getroffen**
trinken	to drink	X	**getrunken**
tun	to do	X	**getan**
vergessen	to forget	**vergisst**	**vergessen**
verlieren	to lose	X	**verloren**
wachsen	to grow	**wächst**	**gewachsen***
waschen	to wash	**wäscht**	**gewaschen**
werden	to become	**wird**	**geworden***

X Not strong in present tense
* Forms perfect tense with **sein** as auxiliary

23 Mixed and irregular verbs

infinitive	meaning	er/sie-form present	past participle
bringen	to bring	X	**gebracht**
denken	to think	X	**gedacht**
haben	to have	**hat**	**gehabt**
sein	to be	**ist**	**gewesen***

* Forms perfect tense with **sein** as auxiliary.

In this book, **sein**, **haben** and the modals are encountered in the simple past, not the perfect.

VOCABULARY

Plurals of nouns (see Grammar summary, section 2) are given in brackets after the noun.

pl after a noun means it is already in the plural.

/in at the end of a noun means that the feminine form has **-in** added to it:
(**Amerikaner/Amerikanerin**).

* after a verb means the verb is strong in the present tense; *sep* means the verb is separable; *refl* means it is reflexive

pp = past participle

ab	from (time)
der Abend (e)	evening
am Abend	in the evening
das Abendessen (-)	dinner, evening meal
zum Abendessen	for dinner
abends	in the evening(regularly)
die Abendschule (n)	evening classes
aber	but
abfahren* *sep*	to depart (train, bus)
abgeschlossen	pp of **abschließen**
abholen *sep*	to collect (someone)
das Abitur	A-Levels (equivalent)
die Abreise (n)	departure (person from hotel)
abschließen *sep*	to complete
abwaschen* *sep*	to wash up
die Abwechslung (en)	variety
die Adresse (n)	address
(das) Aerobic	aerobics
der Alkohol (e)	alcohol
alle	everybody, all
allein	alone
alles	everything
als	as; when (past)
also	so, therefore
alt	old
das Alter	age
altmodisch	old-fashioned
am = an dem	at the, by the
der/die Amerikaner/in (-/nen)	American (m/f)
die Ampel (n)	(set of) traffic lights
an	at, by, to, on
anders	different(ly)
anfangen* *sep*	to begin, start
angenehm	pleasant
angerufen	pp of **anrufen**
angeschaltet	pp of **anschalten**
die Anglistik	English (academic subject)
die Angst (vor)	fear (of)
Angst haben	to be afraid
ängstlich	anxious, afraid

ankommen *sep*	to arrive
die Ankunft (Ankünfte)	arrival (train)
anprobieren *sep*	to try on
die Anreise (n)	arrival (person in hotel)
anrufen *sep*	to phone
anschalten *sep*	to switch on
antworten	to answer
die Anzeige (n)	advert
der Anzug (Anzüge)	suit
die Apotheke (n)	pharmacy
die Arbeit	work
zur Arbeit	to work
arbeiten	to work
das Arbeitsfeld (er)	area of work
arbeitslos	unemployed
die Arbeitswelt (en)	world of work
der/die Architekt/in (e/nen)	architect (m/f)
die Architektur (en)	architecture
der/die Assistent/in (en/nen)	assistant
die Atmosphäre (n)	atmosphere
auch	also, as well
auf	on
die Aufgabe (n)	exercise
aufgeben* *sep*	to give up
aufgegeben	pp of **aufgeben**
aufgemacht	pp of **aufmachen**
aufgeregt	excited
aufgestanden	pp of **aufstehen**
aufgewachsen	pp of **aufwachsen**
aufhören *sep*	to finish
aufmachen *sep*	to open
aufräumen *sep*	to tidy up
der Aufsatz (Aufsätze)	essay
aufstehen *sep*	to get up
aufwachsen* *sep*	to grow up
aus	out of; from (place)
der Ausflug (Ausflüge)	trip
ausgehen *sep*	to go out
ausgezeichnet	excellent
das Ausland	foreign countries
im Ausland	abroad
außerdem	besides
die Aussicht (en)	view
aussteigen *sep*	to get off (transport)
Australien	Australia
die Auswahl	selection, choice
das Auto (s)	car
Auto fahren*	to drive a car
die Autobahn (en)	motorway
der Automat (en)	vending machine
der/die Automechaniker/in (-/nen)	motor mechanic (m/f)

babysitten	to babysit
backen	to bake
der Bäcker (-)	baker
die Bäckerei (en)	baker's/bakery
die Badehose (n)	swimming trunks
die Badewanne (n)	bath(tub)
das Badezimmer (-)	bathroom
die Bahncard	railcard
der Bahnhof (Bahnhöfe)	railway station
bald (danach)	soon (afterwards)
der Balkon (s)	balcony
die Bank (en)	bank
der/die Bankangestellte	bank employee (m/f)
der Barmann	barman
das Barpersonal	bar staff
der Basketball	basketball
bauen	to build
der Bauernhof (Bauernhöfe)	farm
beginnen	to begin
bei	at (someone's house or shop); for (a company)
beide	both
beige	beige
bekommen	to get
Belgien	Belgium
der/die Belgier/in (-/nen)	Belgian (m/f)
bequem	comfortable
der Berg (e)	mountain
bergsteigen	to go mountain-climbing
die Berliner Mauer	Berlin Wall
der Beruf (e)	profession
die Berufserfahrung	professional experience
besitzen	to possess
besonders	especially
besser (als)	better (than)
bestätigen	to confirm
die Bestätigung (en)	confirmation
bestimmt	definitely
besuchen	to visit
die Betriebswirtschaft	business management
das Bett (en)	bed
im Bett	in bed
ins Bett gehen	to go to bed
sich bewerben um* *refl*	to apply for
der/die Bewerber/in (-/nen)	applicant (m/f)
die Bewerbung (en)	application
bewirbt	**er/sie**-form of **bewerben**
die Bibliothek (en)	library
der/die Bibliothekar/in (e/nen)	librarian (m/f)
das Bier (e)	beer
die Bierflasche (n)	beer bottle
der Biergarten (Biergärten)	beer garden
bieten	to offer
billig(er)	cheap(er)
bin	**ich**-form of **sein**
die Biologie	biology
bis	until
bis wann?	until when?
bis zu	as far as
bisschen	bit
bist du?	are you?
bitte	please
Bitte?	How can I help you?
blau	blue
bleiben	to stay, remain
die Blume (n)	flower
das Blumengeschäft (e)	flower shop
der Blumenstrauß (-sträuße)	bouquet
die Bluse (n)	blouse
böse	angry
der Boss (e)	boss
das Brandenburger Tor	Brandenburg Gate, Berlin
Brasilien	Brazil
brauchen	to need
braun	brown
die BRD	Federal Repubic of Germany
der Brief (e)	letter
die Brieftasche (n)	wallet
bringen	to bring; to take
das Brötchen (-)	bread roll
der Bruder (Brüder)	brother
das Buch (Bücher)	book
buchen	to book
das Bücherregal (e)	bookshelves
der Buchladen (-läden)	bookshop
Bundesländer *pl*	federal states
die Bundesrepublik	Federal Republic
bunt	colourful
der Bürger (-)	citizen
das Büro(s)	office
der Bus (se)	bus
der/die Busfahrer/in (-/nen)	bus driver (m/f)
die Butter	butter
ca. = circa = zirka	about
der Campingplatz (-plätze)	campsite
der CD-Spieler (-)	CD-player
die/das Cola (s)	cola
der Computer (-)	computer
die Computerlinguistik	computer linguistics
das Computerspiel (e)	computer game
die Computerwissenschaften *pl*	computer science
damals	at that time
danach	after that
der/die Däne/Dänin (n/nen)	Dane (m/f)
Dänemark	Denmark
dann	then

Vocabulary

das geht	that's OK
das ist alles	that's all
das stimmt	that's right
das war schade	that was a pity
dass	that (conjunction)
dauern	to last
die DDR	GDR, Communist East Germany 1949–1990
dein	your *informal sing*
demonstrieren	to demonstrate
denken	to think
denn	because
deshalb	therefore
Deutsch	German (language)
(die/der) Deutsche(r)	German (f/m)
Deutschland	Germany
die Deutschstunde (n)	German class
Dienstag	Tuesday
direkt	directly
die Diskothek (en)	discotheque, club
der Dom (e)	cathedral
Donnerstag	Thursday
das Doppelzimmer (-)	double room
das Dorf (Dörfer)	village
dort	there
dort drüben	over there
draußen	outside
dritt... (der dritte etc.)	third
die Droge (n)	drug
die Drogerie (n)	chemist's, drug store
drücken	to press
du	you *informal sing*
dunkel	dark
durch	through
die Durchschnittsnote (n)	average grade
die Dusche (n)	shower
die Ecke (n)	corner
an der Ecke	on the corner
um die Ecke	round the corner
das Ei (er)	egg
eigentlich	really
einfach	simple/simply; single (ticket)
einführen *sep*	to introduce
eingekauft	pp of **einkaufen**
einige	some
einkaufen *sep*	to go shopping
einladen* *sep*	to invite
die Einladung (en)	invitation
einmal	once (when ordering a meal = 'one')
einschließlich	including
einsteigen *sep*	to get on, board
der Eintritt	entrance, admission
das Einzelzimmer (-)	single room
das Eiscafé (s)	ice-cream parlour
der Elektroherd (e)	electric cooker

Eltern *pl*	parents
die E-Mail (s)	email
das Ende (n)	end
endlich	finally
der/die Engländer/in (-/nen)	Englishman/woman
Englisch	English (language)
Enkelkinder *pl*	grandchildren
enthusiastisch	enthusiastic
sich entscheiden *refl*	to decide
entschuldigen Sie ...	excuse me (formal)
entsprechend	appropriate
enttäuscht	disappointed
die Enttäuschung (en)	disappointment
er	he; it (*masc*)
die Erfahrung (en)	experience
Erfahrung sammeln	to gain experience
erhält	**er/sie**-form of **erhalten**
erhalten*	to receive (also pp)
erkältet	suffering from a cold
erreichen	to get to
erst... (der erste etc.)	first
erst	only, not until
der/die Erwachsene	adult
erzählen	to tell
erzählt	pp of **erzählen** (also **er/sie**-form)
es	it
essen*	to eat
das Essen (-)	food, meal, eating
das Esszimmer (-)	dining room
etwa	about, roughly
etwas	something
euer/eure etc.	your (*pl*, informal)
Europa	Europe
der/die Europäer/in (-/nen)	European (m/f)
europaweit	throughout Europe
das Examen (-)	exam
exklusiv	exclusive
die Fähigkeit (en)	ability, capability
fahren*	to go, drive
die Fahrkarte (n)	ticket
der Fahrpreis (e)	fare
das Fahrrad (Fahrräder)	bicycle
die Fahrradvermietung	bicycle hire
der Fahrschein (e)	ticket
der Fahrstuhl (-stühle)	lift
fährt	**er/sie**-form of **fahren**
das Fahrtziel (e)	destination
fallen*	to fall
fällt	**er/sie**-form of **fallen**
der Fan (s)	fan
fängt ... an	**er/sie**-form of **anfangen**
fantastisch	fantastic
die Farbe (n)	colour
fast	almost
der Federball	badminton

feiern	to celebrate; party
das Fenster (-)	window
der Ferienjob (s)	holiday job
ferngesehen	pp of **fernsehen**
fernsehen* *sep*	to watch TV
der Fernseher (-)	TV set
fertig	finished
der Film (e)	film
der Filmschauspieler (-)	film actor
finden	to find
die Firma (Firmen)	firm
der Fisch (e)	fish
Fitnessgeräte *pl*	fitness equipment
das Fitness-Studio	keep-fit centre
das Fitnesstraining	fitness training
das Fleisch	meat
fleißig	hard-working
flexibel	flexible
fliegen	to fly
fließend	fluent(ly)
Florenz	Florence
der Flughafen (-häfen)	airport
Flugreisen *pl*	air travel
folgend	following
Frankreich	France
der/die Franzose/	
Französin (n/nen)	Frenchman/woman
französisch	French
Frau	Mrs, Ms
die Frau (en)	woman; wife
frei	free
die Freiheit	freedom
Freitag	Friday
Freizeitmöglichkeiten *pl*	leisure opportunities
die Fremdsprache (n)	foreign language
sich freuen *refl*	to be glad
sich freuen auf *refl*	
(+ accusative)	to look forward to
freut mich, Sie kennen	
zu lernen	pleased to meet you
der Freund (e)	(boy)friend
die Freundin (nen)	(girl)friend
freundlich	friendly
froh	glad, pleased
das Frühstück (e)	breakfast
zum Frühstück	for breakfast
frühstücken	to have/eat breakfast
frustriert	frustrated
der/die Fünfundsechzigjährige	
	65-year-old (m/f)
für	for
furchtbar	terrible
der Fußball	football
der Fußboden (-böden)	floor
ganz	complete(ly)
gar nicht	not at all
die Garage (n)	garage

der Garten (Gärten)	garden
der Gasherd (e)	gas cooker
gastronomisch	gastronomic
gebaut	pp of **bauen**
geben*	to give
geblieben	pp of **bleiben**
geboren	born
gebracht	pp of **bringen**
der Geburtstag (e)	birthday
gedacht	pp of **denken**
gefahren	pp of **fahren***
gefallen	pp of **fallen***
gefallen*	lit. 'to please' (but see
	unit 6 grammar page 70)
gefällt	**er/sie**-form of **gefallen**
das Gefängnis (se)	prison
gefunden	pp of **finden**
gegangen	pp of **gehen**
gegen	about (time); against
gegenüber	opposite
gegessen	pp of **essen***
das Gehalt (Gehälter)	salary
geheiratet	pp of **heiraten**
gehen	to go
geholt	pp of **holen**
gehört	pp of **hören**
der Geist (er)	spirit
gekocht	pp of **kochen**
gekommen	pp of **kommen**
gelandet	pp of **landen**
gelangweilt	bored
gelb	yellow
das Geld	money
der Geldschein (e)	banknote
gelernt	pp of **lernen**
gemacht	past participle of **machen**
die Gemeinschaftsküche	
(n)	communal kitchen
das Gemüse (-)	vegetable(s)
die Gemüsesuppe (n)	vegetable soup
gemütlich	cosy
genau	exactly
gerade	just now
geradeaus	straight on
geredet	pp of **reden**
geregnet	pp of **regnen**
gern	(see grammar summary
	page 157)
die Geschichte (n)	history; story
geschmeckt	pp of **schmecken**
geschrieben	pp of **schreiben**
Geschwister *pl*	brothers and sisters,
	siblings
gesessen	pp of **sitzen**
gespielt	pp of **spielen**
das Gespräch (e)	conversation
gesprochen	pp of **sprechen***
gestohlen	pp of **stehlen***

Vocabulary

gestorben	pp of **sterben***
gestresst	stressed
gesucht	pp of **suchen**
gesund	healthy
getanzt	pp of **tanzen**
getrunken	pp of **trinken**
gewinnen	to win
gewonnen	pp of **gewinnen**
geworden	pp of **werden***
gewünscht	desired
gibt	**er/sie**-form of **geben**
die Gitarre (n)	guitar
die Gitarrenstunde (n)	guitar lesson
das Glas (Gläser)	glass
glauben	to think, believe
gleich	immediately
Gleis x	Platform x
das Glück	luck, happiness
zum Glück	fortunately
glücklich	happy, lucky
der/die Grieche/Griechin (n/nen)	Greek (m/f)
Griechenland	Greece
grillen	to barbecue
groß	big; tall
Großbritannien	Great Britain
die Größe (n)	size
Großeltern *pl*	grandparents
größer	bigger
der Großvater (-väter)	grandfather
grün	green
gut	good, well
gut bezahlt	well paid
gut, danke	fine, thanks
guten Abend	good evening
guten Morgen	good morning
guten Tag	hello
das Gymnasium (Gymnasien)	grammar school
haben	to have
der Hafen (Häfen)	harbour, port
halb	half (<u>to</u> the next hour)
halb…	half
halblinks	fork left
das Hallenbad (-bäder)	indoor swimming pool
hallo	hello (*informal*)
die Haltestelle (n)	stop (bus, tram)
die Handtasche (n)	handbag
das Handy (s)	mobile phone, cellphone
Hannover	Hanover
hat	**er/sie**-form of **haben**
hatte	had
die Hauptstadt (-städte)	capital city
das Haus (Häuser)	house
nach Hause	(to) home
zu Hause	at home
heiraten	to marry
heiß	hot

heißen	to be called
helfen*	to help
hell	bright
das Hemd (en)	shirt
die Herrenabteilung (en)	men's department
Herzlich willkommen!	Welcome!
heute	today
heute Nachmittag	this afternoon
hier	here
hiermit	herewith
die Hilfe	help
hilft	**er/sie**-form of **helfen**
hin und zurück	return
hinter	behind
Hobby (s)	hobby
die Hochzeit (en)	wedding
hoffentlich	hopefully
holen	to fetch; go and get
Holstein	region of N. Germany to the north of Hamburg
die Hose (n)	(pair of) trousers
hübsch	pretty
das Huhn (Hühner)	chicken
der Hund (e)	dog
hungrig	hungry
ich	I
ich bin's	it's me
die Idee (n)	idea
ihm	him, it (*dative*)
ihr	her/their; you (*pl, familiar*); to her
Ihr	your (*formal*)
im = in dem	in the
immer	always
die Informatik	computer science
sich informieren *refl*	to inform oneself
der/die Ingenieur/in (e/nen)	engineer (m/f)
inklusive	including
die Innenstadt (-städte)	town/city centre
innerhalb von	within
ins = in das	into
intensiv	intensive
interessant	interesting
das Interesse (n) (an + dative)	interest (in)
interessieren	to interest
sich interessieren für *refl*	to be interested in
der/die Ire/Irin (n/nen)	Irishman/woman
Irland	Ireland
isst	**er/sie**-form of **essen**
ist	is
Italien	Italy
Italiener/in (-/nen)	Italian (m/f)
italienisch	Italian
die italienische Küche	Italian cuisine
Italienisch	Italian language
ja	yes

die Jacke (n)	jacket
das Jackett (s)	(elegant) jacket
das Jahr (e)	year
jeden Tag	every day
jeder	each (one)
jetzt	now
der or das Joghurt	yoghurt
der/die Journalist/in (en/nen)	journalist (m/f)
Jugendliche *pl*	young people
jung	young
jüngst	youngest
das Kabelfernsehen	cable TV
der Kaffee	coffee
die Kantine (n)	canteen
kann	can – **ich-**, **er/sie-**form of **können**
kaputt	broken
Karten *pl*	cards
das Käsebrot (e)	cheese sandwich
katastrophal	catastrophic
die Katze (n)	cat
kaufen	to buy
das Kaufhaus (-häuser)	department store
der/die Kellner/in (-/nen)	waiter/waitress
kennen	to know (be familiar with)
kennen lernen	to get to know
das Kind (er)	child
kinderfreundlich	welcoming to children
der Kindergarten (-gärten)	kindergarten
das Kino (s)	cinema
die Kirche (n)	church
das Kissen (-)	cushion
kitschig	kitschy
das Klavierkonzert (e)	piano concerto
das Kleid (er)	dress; *pl* (also) clothes
der Kleiderschrank (-schränke)	wardrobe
klein	small
das Kleingeld	small change
das Klima	climate
die Kneipe (n)	pub
kochen	to cook
der Koffer (-)	suitcase
der Kollege (n)	colleague
Köln	Cologne
kommen (aus)	to come (from)
kommunikativ	communicative
kommunistisch	communist
kompakt	compact
kompliziert	complicated
komponieren	to compose
komponiert	pp of **komponiert**
die Königin (nen)	queen
konnte	was able to, could – simple past of **können** (**ich**, **er/sie-**forms)

das Konzert (-e)	concert
kosten	to cost
köstlich	delicious
krank	ill
das Krankenhaus (-häuser)	hospital
die Krawatte (n)	tie
die Kreditkarte (n)	credit card
der Kreisverkehr	roundabout
die Kreuzung (en)	junction, crossroads
der Krimi (s)	detective story
die Kriminalität	criminality
die Küche (n)	kitchen; cuisine
der Kuchen (-)	cake
die Küchenhilfe (n)	kitchen assistant
der Kugelschreiber (-)	ballpoint pen
der Kühlschrank (-schränke)	refrigerator
die Kultur	culture
die Kundenberatung	advising customers
die Kunstgalerie (n)	art gallery
kurz	short
küssen	to kiss
die Küste (n)	coast
der Laden (Läden)	shop, branch
lädt … ein	**er/sie-**form of **einladen**
die Lage (n)	situation
die Lampe (n)	lamp
das Land (Länder)	country
landen	to land
lang	long
lange	a long time
langweilig	boring
laufen*	to go on foot
läuft	**er/sie-**form of **laufen**
laut	(a)loud
leben	to live
das Leben (-)	life
der Lebenslauf (-läufe)	CV
ledig	single, unmarried
legen	to lay, put down
der/die Lehrer/in (-/nen)	teacher (m/f)
leicht	easy
das Leid	sorrow
es tut mir Leid	I'm sorry
leider	unfortunately
lernen	to learn
lesen*	to read
letzt	last
letztes Jahr	last year
Leute *pl*	people
lieben	to love
das Lied (er)	song
liegen	to lie
liest	**er/sie-**form of **lesen**
die Linie (n)	bus/tram route
links	left
links von	to the left of

Vocabulary

die Literatur	literature
machen	to do; make
die Mahlzeit (en)	meal
manchmal	sometimes
der Mann (Männer)	man; husband
die Mannschaft (en)	team
der Mantel (Mäntel)	coat
die Markthalle (n)	market hall
die Marmelade (n)	jam
Mathematik	mathematics
mehr	more
mein	my
melancholisch	melancholy
die Mensa	student canteen
der Mensch (en)	person, human being; *plural* – people
das Menü (s)	set menu
das Metier (s)	profession
die Miete (n)	rent
mieten	to rent
die Mikrowelle (n)	microwave
die Milch	milk
das Mineralwasser	mineral water
mit	with
mit 19	at 19
mit dem Bus	by bus
mit dem InterCity	by Intercity
mitkommen *sep*	to come along/come too
das Mittagessen (-)	lunch
zum Mittagessen	for lunch
der Mittagstisch	lunchtime menu
Mittwoch	Wednesday
mobil	mobile
möchte(n) *irreg*	would like (to)
modern	modern
modisch	fashionable
der Moment (e)	moment
im Moment	at the moment
der Monat (e)	month
der Mond	moon
Montag	Monday
montags	on Mondays (regularly)
das Moped (s)	moped
morgen	tomorrow
der Morgen (-)	morning
am Morgen	in the morning
morgens	in the morning (regularly)
motiviert	motivated
müde	tired
München	Munich
die Münze (n)	coin
das Museum (Museen)	museum
die Musik	music
Musik hören	to listen to music
musste	had to – simple past of **müssen (ich, er/sie-**forms)

die Mutter (Mütter)	mother
nach	after; to (a place)
der Nachmittag (e)	afternoon
am Nachmittag	in the afternoon
nachmittags	in the afternoon (regularly)
nächst	next; nearest
nächste Woche	next week
nächstes Jahr	next year
die Nacht (Nächte)	night
der Nachteil (e)	disadvantage
der Nachttisch (e)	bedside table
nahe	near
in der Nähe	nearby
nähen	to sew
näher	nearer
der Name (n)	name
natürlich	of course
neben	next to
das Neckarufer	bank of the River Neckar
nehmen*	to take
nein	no
nett	nice
neu	new
nicht	not
nicht weit von	not far from
nichts	nothing
nie	never
nimmt	**er/sie**-form of **nehmen**
noch	still
Norddeutschland	N. Germany
der Norden	the North
die Nordsee	North Sea
normalerweise	normally
die Note (n)	grade
Nudeln *pl*	pasta, noodles
die Nummer (-n)	number
nutzen	to use
das Obst	fruit
obwohl	although
oder	or
oder?	isn't it?
offener	more open
Öffnungszeiten *pl*	opening hours
oft	often
öfters	often
ohne	without
ökonomisch	economic
das Omelett (e or s)	omelette
die Oper (n)	opera
optimistisch	optimistic
der Orangensaft	orange juice
die Ordnung	order
in Ordnung	ok, all right
organisiert	organised
der Osten	East

Ostern	Easter
zu Ostern	at Easter
Österreich	Austria
der/die Österreicher/in (-/nen)	Austrian (m/f)
Ostfriesland	island and coastal region on the North Sea coast
die Ostsee	Baltic Sea
das Papier (e)	paper
der Park (s)	park
das Parkhaus (-häuser)	multi-storey car park
der Parkplatz (-plätze)	car park
die Partei (en)	political party
die Party (s)	party
Partys feiern	have parties
die Pension (en)	boarding house
das Personal	personnel, staff
Personen pl	persons
das Pferd (e)	horse
zu Pferde	on horseback
der Pförtner (-)	porter
die Pizza (s) or (Pizzen)	pizza
der Plan (Pläne)	plan, map (town)
die Politik	politics
der/die Polizist/in (en/nen)	policeman/woman
Pommes frites pl	chips, French fries
die Post	post office
praktisch	practical
der Präsident (en)	president
prima!	great!
pro Tag/Nacht	per day/night
die Prüfung (en)	exam
die Psychologie	psychology
der Pullover (-)	pullover
pünktlich	punctual, on time
putzen	to clean
Rad fahren*	to cycle
das Radio (s)	radio
im Radio	on the radio
das Rathaus	town hall
rauchen	to smoke
reagieren	to react
reagiert	pp of **reagieren**
Recht haben	to be right
rechts	right
rechts von	to the right of
reden	to talk
reformieren	to reform
die Regierung (en)	government
regnen	to rain
regnerisch	rainy
der Reichstag	German parliament building, Berlin
... rein	into ...
die Reise (n)	journey

das Reisebüro (s)	travel agency
reisen	to travel
relativ	relatively
der/die Rentner/in (-/nen)	pensioner
reparieren	to repair
reservieren	to reserve, book
das Restgeld	change
der Rhein	River Rhine
richtig	right, correct
der Rock (Röcke)	skirt
die Rolle (n)	role
rot	red
der Rotwein (e)	red wine
die Rückfahrkarte	return ticket
ruhig	quiet
Russland	Russia
sagen	to say
die Sahne	cream
die Sahnesauce	cream sauce
der Salat (e)	salad
Samstag	Saturday
der Sänger (-)	singer
die Sauna	sauna
schade	(that's a) pity
Schau mal	Look!
schick	elegant, chic
das Schinkenbrot (e)	ham sandwich
schlafen*	to sleep
schläft	**er/sie**-form of **schlafen**
das Schlafzimmer (-)	bedroom
schlank	slim
schlecht	bad(ly)
schlechter	worse
der Schlüssel (-)	key
schmecken	to taste (good)
schnell	fast
die Schnellwahl	rapid choice
der Schock (s)	shock
die Schokolade	chocolate
das Schokoladeneis	chocolate ice cream
der Schokoladenkuchen (-)	chocolate cake
schon	already
schön	beautiful
der/die Schotte/Schottin (n/nen)	Scot (m/f)
Schottland	Scotland
der Schrank (Schränke)	cupboards
schrecklich	terrible/terribly
schreiben (an)	to write (to)
der Schreibtisch (e)	desk
der Schuh (e)	shoe
die Schule (n)	school
schwarz	black
Schwedisch	Swedish (language)
die Schweiz	Switzerland

Vocabulary

schwer	heavy	die Speisekarte (n)	menu
die Schwester (n)	sister	der Sperrmüll	bulky refuse (often picked up by bargain-hunters)
schwierig	difficult		
das Schwimmbad	swimming pool	sich spezialisieren auf	
schwimmen	to swim	(+ accusative) *refl*	to specialise in
das Schwimmen	swimming	spielen	to play
der See (n)	lake	der Sport	sport
die See (n)	sea	sportlich	sporty
segeln	to sail	der Sportverein (e)	sports club
sehen*	to see	das Sportzentrum	
die Sehenswürdigkeit		(-zentren)	sports centre
(en)	sight worth seeing	die Sprache (n)	language
sehr	very	Sprachkenntnisse *pl*	knowledge of languages
sein (*possessive*)	his; its	der Sprachkurs (e)	language course
sein (*verb*)	to be	sprechen*	to speak
seit	since	spricht	**er/sie**-form of **sprechen**
die Seite (n)	side	der Staat (en)	state
auf der rechten Seite	on the right-hand side	die Stadt (Städte)	town
die Seitenstraße (n)	side street	die Stadtmitte	town centre
die Sekretärin (nen)	secretary (f)	das Stadtzentrum (-tren)	town centre
selbständig	independent	der Stammbaum	
selten	seldom, rarely	(-bäume)	family tree
Semesterferien *pl*	university vacation	die Station (en)	station (on underground)
das Seminar (e)	seminar	stattfinden *sep*	to take place
der Seminarraum		das Steak (s)	steak
(-räume)	seminar room	stehen	to stand
der Sessel (-)	armchair	stehlen*	to steal
sich setzen *refl*	to sit down	die Stelle (n)	job
sicher	sure, certain	die Stellenanzeige (n)	job advert
sie	she, they	sterben*	to die
Sie	you (*formal*)	stirbt	**er/sie** form of **sterben**
sieht	**er/sie**-form of **sehen**	der Stock (-)	floor (of building)
der Sinn für Humor	sense of humour	im ersten Stock	on the first floor
sitzen	to sit	der Strand (Strände)	beach
Ski fahren	to ski	die Straße (n)	street
so	so	die Straßenbahn (en)	tram
so was	something like that	das Straßencafé (s)	pavement café
die Socke (n)	sock	der Strauß (Sträuße)	bouquet
das Sofa (s)	couch	das Studentenleben	student life
sofort	at once, immediately	das Studentenwohnheim	
der Sohn (Söhne)	son	(e)	hall of residence
das Solarium	solarium	der Studienabschluss	degree, diploma
der Sommer	summer	das Studienfach (-fächer)	subject
Sommerferien *pl*	summer holidays	studieren	to study
der Songschreiber (-)	songwriter	studiert	pp of **studieren** (also **er/sie**-form)
Sonnabend	Saturday (N. Germany)		
die Sonne	sun	das Studium (Studien)	study/studies
Sonntag	Sunday	der Stuhl (Stühle)	chair
sonst noch etwas?	anything else?	die Stunde (n)	hour; lesson
Spanien	Spain	stundenlang	for hours
der/die Spanier/in (-/nen)	Spaniard (m/f)	suchen	to look for
Spanisch	Spanish (language)	Südafrika	South Africa
spannend	exciting	Südeuropa	Southern Europe
der Sparpreis (e)	low price	Südkorea	South Korea
Spaß haben	to have fun	der Supermarkt	
Spaß machen	to be fun	(-märkte)	supermarket
später	later	die Symphonie (n)	symphony
spazieren gehen	to go for a walk	das System (e)	system

der Tag (e)	day
die Tageskarte (n)	day ticket
täglich	daily
die Tankstelle (n)	petrol station
tanzen	to dance
die Tanznacht (-nächte)	dance night
die Tasse (n)	cup
die Taste (n)	button, key
tausend	a thousand
das Taxi (s)	taxi
das Team (s)	team
der/die Teamleiter/in (-)/(nen)	team leader
teamorientiert	team-orientated
technisch	technical
der Tee	tea
das Telefon (e)	telephone
telefonieren	to phone
die Telefonnummer (-n)	phone number
das Teller (-)	plate
der Termin (e)	appointment, deadline
die Terrasse (n)	terrace
das Territorium (-orien)	territory
der Test (s)	test
einen Test schreiben	to do/take a test
teuer	dear, expensive
teurer	dearer
das Theater (-)	theatre
die Theaterwissenschaft	theatre studies
tippen	to type
der Tisch (e)	table
der Tischtennis	table tennis
der Toast	toast
die Tochter (Töchter)	daugher
die Toilette (n)	toilet
toll	great
die Tomate (n)	tomato
die Tomatensuppe	tomato soup
die Toskana	Tuscany
die Tour (en)	tour
tragen*	to wear; carry
trägt	**er/sie**-form of **tragen**
traurig	sad
treffen*	to meet
sich treffen*refl	to meet up
trifft	**er/sie**-form of **treffen**
trinken	to drink
das T-Shirt (s)	T-shirt
tun	to do
die Tür (en)	door
tut mir Leid	I'm sorry
das TwenTicket	young person's ticket
typisch	typical
die U-Bahn	underground
über	about, over, across
überrascht	surprised
der/die Übersetzer/in (-/nen)	translator

das Übersetzungsbüro (s)	translation agency
die Uhr (en)	clock, watch
zwei Uhr	two o'clock
um	at (time); around (place)
um wie viel Uhr?	what time?
um … zu	in order to
umgezogen	pp of **umziehen**
umsteigen *sep*	to change (trains/buses)
umziehen *sep*	to move (house)
unabhängig	independent
und	and
Und dir?	And how are you?
unglücklich	unhappy, unlucky
die Universität (en)	university
unser	our
unter	under
die Unterkunft	accommodation
der Unterricht	lesson(s), class(es)
im Unterricht	in class
unterwegs	on the way
der Urlaub (e)	holiday
in Urlaub fahren	to go on holiday
das Vanilleeis	vanilla ice-cream
der Vater (Väter)	father
verbessern	to improve
verbracht	pp of **verbringen**
verbringen	to spend (time)
verdienen	to earn
verheiratet	married
verlassen*	to leave (also pp)
verlässt	**er/sie**-form of **verlassen**
verliebt	in love
verlieren	to lose
verloren	pp of **verlieren**
die Vermietung	hire
die Verpflegung	catering
verstanden	pp of **verstehen**
verstehen	to understand
Verwandte *pl*	relatives
das Verzeichnis (se)	index
der Video	video
das Videogeschäft (e)	video shop
der Videorekorder (-)	VCR
viel	a lot
viel zu machen	a lot to do
viele	many
vielen Dank	many thanks
vielleicht	perhaps
das Viertel (-)	quarter
Viertel nach/vor	quarter past/to
das Violinkonzert (e)	violin concerto
voll	full
von	from; of
vor	before, in front of; (before time expression) ago
vorbeigehen *sep* am Krankenhaus vorbei	to go past past the hospital

vorher	previously	Wie heißt du?	What's your name?
die Vorlesung (en)	lecture	Wie kann ich Ihnen	
der Vorteil (e)	advantage	helfen?	How can I help you?
		wie komme ich zu …	how do I get to …
wächst auf	**er/sie**-form of	wie lange	how long (time)
	aufwachsen	wieder	again
Wahlen *pl*	elections	die Wiedervereinigung	reunification (of Germany,
wählen	to choose		1990)
die Wahrheit	truth	Wien	Vienna
der Wald (Wälder)	forest	wird	**er/sie**-form of **werden**
der/die Waliser/in (-/nen)	Welshman/woman	wirklich	really
wandern	to go on a hike, walk	wirst	**du**-form of **werden**
Wanderungen *pl*	hikes, walks	wissen*	to know
wann	when (in questions)	wo(her)	where (from)
war	was	die Woche (n)	week
warm	hot	das Wochenende (-)	weekend
Warst du schon in … ?	have you ever been to	wohin?	where to?
	…?	wohnen	to live
warum	why	der Wohnort	place of residence
was	what	die Wohnung (en)	flat
Was ist los?	What's the matter?	das Wohnzimmer (-)	living room
die Waschmaschine (n)	washing machine	wollte	wanted (to) – simple past
wäscht … ab	**er/sie**-form of		of **wollen** (**ich**, **er/sie**-
	abwaschen		forms)
das Wasser	water	das Wörterbuch	
wechseln	to change money	(-bücher)	dictionary
weggehen *sep*	to go away	wunderbar	wonderful
weil	because	die Wurst (Würste)	sausage
der Wein (e)	wine	das Würstchen (-)	(small) sausage
die Weinkarte (n)	wine-list		
weiß	white	zahlen	to pay
weiß	**ich-**, **er/sie-**form of	die Zahlung (en)	payment
	wissen	der Zahnarzt (Zahnärzte)	dentist
der Weißwein (e)	white wine	zeigen	to show
weiter	further	die Zeit (en)	time
welche(r/s)	which	die Zeitschrift (en)	magazine
der Wellness-Bereich (e)	health and fitness area	die Zeitung (en)	newspaper
weltberühmt	world-famous	das Zentrum (Zentren)	centre
die Weltmeisterschaft		ziemlich	quite
(en)	World Championship	das Zimmer (-)	room
wen	whom	die Zimmerreservierung	room booking
wenig	little, not much	zu	to; too (+ adjective)
wenn	if, when	zufrieden	content
wer	who	der Zug (Züge)	train
werden*	to become	die Zukunft	future
der Westen	West	zurückerhalten* *sep*	to get back
das Wetter	weather	zurückkommen *sep*	to come back
wichtig	important	zusammen	together
wie	how	zusammenleben mit *sep*	to live with
wie alt	how old	zuverlässig	reliable
Wie geht's?	How are you?	zwischen	between

ANSWERS

UNIT 1

5 **a** Deutschland **b** Österreich **c** England
d Griechenland **e** Frankreich **f** Schottland
g Belgien **h** Irland **i** Spanien **j** Dänemark
k Wales **l** Italien

6 **a** Spanien **b** Deutschland **c** Frankreich
d Österreich **e** Griechenland

8 **a** Wie heißt du? **b** Wie heißen Sie?
c Woher kommst du? **d** Woher kommen
Sie? **e** Wo wohnst du? **f** Wo wohnen Sie?
g Bist du Engländer(in)? **h** Sind Sie
Engländer(in)? **i** Bist du Student(in)?
j Sind Sie Student(in)?

9 **a** **i** Sind Sie Engländer? **ii** Wo wohnen Sie?
iii Kommen Sie aus Frankfurt?
b **i** Wo wohnen Sie? **ii** Sind Sie
Engländerin? **iii** Sind Sie Studentin?

11 **a** **i** Das ist Marianne Möller. **ii** Nein, sie ist
Lehrerin. **iii** Sie wohnt in Manchester.
iv Sie kommt aus Hamburg. **v** Nein, sie
ist Deutsche.
b **i** Er heißt Tom Paschke. **ii** Nein, er ist
Lehrer. **iii** Nein, er wohnt in London.
iv Nein, er kommt aus Berlin. **v** Ja, er ist
Deutscher.
c **i** Nein, er heißt Marc Berlande. **ii** Nein,
er ist Student. **iii** Er wohnt in Glasgow.
iv Er kommt aus Marseille. **v** Nein, er ist
Franzose.
d **i** Das ist Sue Edwards. **ii** Sie kommt aus
Birmingham. **iii** Sie wohnt in Leipzig.
iv Nein, sie lernt Deutsch. **v** Nein, sie ist
Engländerin.

12 **a** **i** bin, heiße, komme **ii** heiße, bin, lerne
iii heiße, komme, bin, lerne **iv** heiße,
komme, bin, wohne
b **i** Sie ist Deutsche. Sie heißt Silke und
kommt aus Stuttgart. Sie studiert Sport
und Englisch. **ii** Sie heißt Eva. Sie ist

Spanierin, aber sie studiert in England.
Sie studiert Literatur und lernt Englisch
– und Deutsch! **iii** Er heißt Michael. Er
kommt aus Cork in Irland. Er ist Student
in Birmingham. Er studiert Biologie. Er
lernt auch Deutsch. **iv** Er heißt Yannis
und er kommt aus Griechenland. Er ist
Student hier in England. Er wohnt in
Brighton und studiert Psychologie.

15 **a** **i** Er kommt aus Leipzig. **ii** Nein, er
studiert in Marburg. **iii** Cristina ist
Martins Freundin. **iv** Nein, sie ist
Italienerin. **v** Sie ist Sekretärin. **vi** Sie
arbeitet in Frankfurt.
b **i** Ja, sie arbeitet als Kellnerin. **ii** Nein, sie
ist Französin. **iii** Lyon ist in Frankreich.
iv Sie wohnt in London.
c **i** Er heißt Bernd Voigt. **ii** Bremen ist in
Deutschland. **iii** Nein, er ist Deutscher.
iv Er ist Journalist.

Extra!

18 **Annie** studiert Literatur. Sie kommt aus
Frankreich, aber sie wohnt in Düsseldorf.
Sie arbeitet als Kellnerin.
Jürgen kommt aus Österreich. Er wohnt in
London und er ist Journalist von Beruf.
(Seine Freundin ist Engländerin.)
Padma ist Engländerin und sie kommt aus
Birmingham. Sie studiert Psychologie in
Leeds.

19 **a** *Your summary should be similar to the
following:* Ursula Eggebrecht is from
America, but she is studying psychology
at Bremen University. She is studying in
Europe because her father is German
and her mother Dutch, and she feels
European as well as American. She has
also got a job as a car mechanic.

b i Sie wohnt in Bremen. **ii** Sie kommt aus New York. **iii** Sie studiert Psychologie. **iv** Nein, sie studiert in Deutschland. **v** Ja, sie ist Automechanikerin / sie repariert Autos.

Grammatikübungen

1 **a** Studentin/Deutsche **b** Student/ Deutscher **c** Spanierin/Lehrerin **d** Italiener/Journalist

2 **a** Er **b** Sie **c** ich **d** ich **e** er **f** du **g** ich

3 **a** heißt **b** wohnt (arbeitet) **c** kommt **d** kommen **e** komme **f** Ist **g** bin **h** sind

4 **a** Wie heißt sie? **b** Wo wohnst du? / Wo wohnen Sie? **c** Bist du Student? / Sind Sie Student? **d** Wo arbeitet er? **e** Woher kommst du? / Woher kommen Sie? **f** Bist du / Sind Sie Franzose/ Spanier/Italiener...? **g** Was ist er von Beruf? **h** Was lernt sie?

5 **a** Wer **b** Wo **c** Wie **d** Woher **e** Was **f** Was

UNIT 2

1 **b** 5, 9, 12, 14, 17
c 13, 8, 6, 11, 16, 2, 1, 15

3 **a** **73** dreiundsiebzig
54 vierundfünfzig
66 sechsundsechzig
47 siebenundvierzig
95 fünfundneunzig
81 einundachtzig
38 achtunddreißig
b **30** dreißig **40** vierzig **50** fünfzig
60 sechzig **70** siebzig **80** achtzig
90 neunzig
c **i** 34 **ii** 54 **iii** 56 **iv** 87 **v** 98

5 **a** **i** 7.45 **ii** 8.05 **iii** 8.30 **iv** 9.00 **v** 10.15 **vi** 11.00

b **i** Nein, er steht um 7.45 auf. **ii** Er frühstückt um 8.05. **iii** Er geht um 8.30 an die Universität. **iv** Die Vorlesung beginnt um 9.00. **v** Nein, er trinkt um 10.15 Kaffee. **vi** Er geht um 11.00 in die Bibliothek.

9 *Note possible variations in word order!* Er geht um 13.30 in die Bibliothek. **oder:** Um 13.30 geht er in die Bibliothek. Er geht um 14.30 in die Stadt. Um 16.00 hat er eine Deutschstunde. Er spielt um 17.10 Fußball./Er geht um 17.10 in das Sportzentrum. Um 18.45 geht er nach Hause.

10 1c 2e 3f 4a 5g 6h 7d 8b

11 **Bernd:** Ich gehe oft aus. Manchmal trinke ich ein Bier, manchmal spiele ich Fußball.
Petra goes out rarely, but she often watches TV or listens to music. She sometimes reads.
Ralf never stays at home. He goes to the pub or the disco.
Jasmin always stays at home. She writes emails, but rarely watches TV. She goes to bed at 11 pm.
Bernd goes out a lot. He sometimes goes for a beer, and sometimes he plays football.

14 **a** Sie trinkt (morgens) eine Tasse Kaffee. / Morgens trinkt sie eine Tasse Kaffee. **b** Sie geht immer in die Mensa. **c** Sie isst um 13.00 Uhr (zum Mittagessen) ein Käsebrot. **d** Nein, sie trinkt zum Mittagessen eine Cola. **e** Sie isst Nudeln mit Fisch oder Salat. **f** Sie trinkt ein Glas Orangensaft.

Extra!

16 **a** Nein, Vera trinkt mit Susanne Kaffee. **b** Nein, Veras Vorlesung beginnt um 16.00. **c** Am Abend geht sie ins Kino und in die Bar. **d** Sie geht um 20.30 ins

Kino. **e** Walter steht um 7.00 auf. **f** Er frühstückt, geht schwimmen und in die Vorlesung. **g** Um 12.00 geht er in die Bibliothek. **h** Nein, er bleibt zu Hause. / Nein, er liest ein Buch.

17 **Some important points:**
Annette is studying psychology. She goes out in the evenings to the theatre or pub. She has lectures during the day and fish or pasta for dinner.

Klaus is studying sports and literature. He usually stays in in the evenings. In the morning he goes to the library and he often eats pizza. (*This is an informal conversation.*)

Herr Wolf comes from Magdeburg and is a teacher. He now lives in Heidelberg and he is in town to do some shopping. He often goes for a coffee and he watches TV in the evenings. He is also learning French.

Frau Petri comes from Heidelberg. She is a stewardess and works in Frankfurt. She often stays at home in the evenings, but sometimes goes to the fitness centre. She plays the guitar and listens to music. (*Formal conversation*)

Grammatikübungen

1 der Orangensaft, die Kneipe, die Diskothek, der Lehrer, das Bier, der Kaffee, die Tasse, die E-Mail, der Abend, das Sportzentrum, der Fisch, das Glas, der Toast, die Studentin, das Käsebrot, die Deutschstunde

2 **a** beginnt **b** trinke **c** geht **d** liest **e** essen **f** gehe … aus, bleibe **g** Hast **h** steht … auf

3 **i** Eva geht nachmittags in die Bibliothek. / Nachmittags geht Eva in die Bibliothek. **ii** Ich esse manchmal Toast. / Manchmal esse ich Toast. **iii** Er sieht immer fern. / Immer sieht er fern. **iv** Ich gehe um 17.00 nach Hause. / Um

17.00 gehe ich nach Hause. **v** Sie spielt oft Tischtennis. / Oft spielt sie Tischtennis. **vi** Ich habe heute eine Deutschstunde. / Heute habe ich eine Deutschstunde.

UNIT 3

2 **a** **i** Stephanie ist 19 Jahre alt. **ii** Nein, sie ist ledig. **iii** Sie studiert Mathematik und Informatik. **iv** Ihre Mutter / Sie ist Architektin von Beruf. **v** Ihr Vater / Er arbeitet bei Siemens. **vi** Carolines Mann / Er heißt Heinz. **vii** Ja, Caroline hat zwei Kinder. **viii** Ja, er hat eine Freundin. Sie heißt Tina.

b *Your talk should be similar to the following*: Ich heiße Stephanie. Ich bin 19 Jahre alt. Meine Mutter heißt Martina und ist 51 Jahre alt. Mein Vater heißt Christian und er ist 53 Jahre alt. Meine Schwester Caroline ist 25 Jahre alt und sie ist verheiratet. Ihr Mann heißt Heinz und ist 29. Sie hat zwei Kinder, Jessica ist 3 und Michael ist 2. Mein Bruder Andreas ist 22 Jahre alt. Er ist ledig, aber er hat eine Freundin. Seine Freundin heißt Tina und ist 23. Mein Freund Alex ist 21 Jahre alt.

3 **a** ihr **b** Ihre **c** ihr **d** Ihr **e** Ihre **f** Ihr **g** Ihre **h** Seine **i** Seine **j** Sein **k** Sein **l** Seine

4 **a** **i** Mein **ii** 22 **iii** ledig **iv** Meine **v** 2 **vi** Ingenieur **vii** 51
b **i** Wie alt sind Sie? **ii** Sind Sie ledig? **iii** Wie heißt Ihr Mann? **iv** Haben Sie Kinder? **v** Wie alt ist Ihre Tochter? **vi** Haben Sie Geschwister? **vii** Was ist Ihre Mutter von Beruf?

7 Stephanies Großvater hat ein Fahrrad, ein Radio, ein Telefon und eine Katze. Er hat kein Auto, keinen Fernseher, keinen Computer und kein Handy.

8 a/b 1 Auto (n) **2** Fahrrad (n)
3 Kugelschreiber (m) **4** CD-Spieler (m)
5 Brieftasche (f) **6** Handy (n)
7 Fernseher (m) **8** Radio (n)
9 Computer (m) **10** Handtasche (f)
11 Wörterbuch (n) **12** Kreditkarte (f)
13 Katze (f)

10 a f Sie wohnen in Mannheim. **b** r **c** r
d f Sie essen viel Obst und Gemüse.
e f Sie haben kein Auto. **f** f Beide sind
80 Jahre alt. **g** f Sie haben ein Auto.
h r **i** r **j** f Sie gehen nie in das
Sportzentrum.

11 a They often watch TV. **b** They some-
times drink wine.

Extra!

13 *Your key words should include several of the
following*:
Annelie: ledig / zwei Brüder, Paul und
Richard / Paul (23) studiert, Richard (19)
arbeitet im Café / Annelies Freundin
Marion wohnt in Kiel / Annelie und
Marion gehen oft ins Sportzentrum /
Annelie liest viel und hört Musik
Markus: seine Mutter ist Managerin, sein
Vater Elektriker / seine Schwester Barbara
(25) ist verheiratet und hat ein Kind (2
Jahre alt), ihr Mann ist Student / hat
Freunde und geht ins Theater / fährt Rad
und geht in die Kneipe
Hanna: ledig / hat eine Tochter (10) /
Sekretärin, arbeitet vormittags / lernt
abends (Abendschule) / wohnt mit
Mutter / Freundin Vera / Kollegin / gehen
manchmal ins Restaurant oder
schwimmen / bleibt zu Hause und sieht
fern

14 *More variations possible!*
Junge Frauen haben oft einen
Computer / fast immer einen Fernseher
/ oft (manchmal) ein Auto / fast immer
ein Handy / fast nie (selten) einen Hund
/ oft eine Kreditkarte

Rentnerinnen haben selten einen
Computer / fast immer einen Fernseher
/ manchmal ein Auto / selten ein Handy
/ oft einen Hund / fast nie eine
Kreditkarte
Junge Männer haben oft einen
Computer / fast immer einen Fernseher
/ manchmal (oft) ein Auto / oft ein
Handy / fast nie einen Hund / fast
immer eine Kreditkarte
Rentner haben fast nie einen
Computer / fast immer einen Fernseher
/ oft ein Auto / selten ein Handy / oft
einen Hund / manchmal (selten) eine
Kreditkarte.

Grammatikübungen

1 a eine **b** ein, ein **c** einen, kein
d einen, eine **e** ein **f** eine, einen
g keine
2 a sind **b** wohnen (studieren) **c** haben
d bleiben (sind) **e** essen **f** trinken
3 a Sie ist Sekretärin von Beruf. **b** Sein
Bruder heißt Oliver. **c** Seine Freundin
wohnt in Leipzig. **d** Ihre Katze heißt
Minka. **e** Seine Mutter arbeitet (im
Moment) nicht. **f** Ihre Schwester ist 12
Jahre alt. **g** Ihre beste Freundin heißt
Hanna. **h** Sein Hund heißt Wolf. **i** Sein
Vater ist Mathematikprofessor von
Beruf. **j** Ihre Mutter ist 43 Jahre alt.
4 1 f mein **2 d** seinen **3 e** ihr **4 c** sein
5 a mein **6 b** ihre

UNIT 4

1 a Felix **b** geht **c** gern **d** raucht **e** Anna
f Auto
4 a t **b** t **c** t **d** f **e** f
5 Gudrun trinkt gern Tee / lieber Cola /
am liebsten Wein / nicht gern Bier.
Gudrun isst gern Käse / lieber Salat /
am liebsten Fisch / nicht gern Pizza.
Frank trinkt gern Wein / lieber Tee / am

liebsten Bier / nicht gern Cola.
Frank isst gern Salat / lieber Käse / am
liebsten Pizza / nicht gern Fisch.
Gabi trinkt gern Cola / lieber Wein / am
liebsten Tee / nicht gern Bier.
Gabi isst gern Pizza / lieber Fisch / am
liebsten Käse / nicht gern Salat.

7 **Astrid** likes going to the disco or for a
walk. She doesn't like going to the pub
because she neither smokes nor drinks
beer.
Christoph doesn't like dancing, he
prefers the pub. He too enjoys going
for a walk, but prefers to stay at home
and watch TV – especially football!

8 **b i** 5.45 **ii** 2.30 **iii** 9.15 **iv** 4.10 **v** 9.35

10 **a** They agree to meet for an Italian
meal at about 9 on Friday.
b i Schade **ii** Ist das in Ordnung?
iii tut mir Leid. **iv** Kommst du mit?
v das geht. **vi** vielleicht **vii** bis
Freitag. **viii** Wie geht's? **ix** Tschüss
x Wo treffen wir uns? **xi** fängt … an
xii leider
c muss … arbeiten, will … essen
gehen, kann … ausgehen, können …
gehen, kannst … ausgehen, müssen
… gehen, muss … gehen

11 **a** Er muss in die Bibliothek gehen.
b Sie will ins Sportzentrum gehen.
c Nein, er hat am Mittwoch keine Zeit.
Er will mit Klaus nach München fahren.
d Sie trifft ihre Freundinnen am
Donnerstag. **e** Sie können am Freitag
Tennis spielen. **f** Er will das Fußballspiel
sehen.

12 **a i** Öffnungszeiten **ii** Eintritt
iii italienische Küche **iv** ab 23 Uhr
v täglich **vi** Weinkarte
vii kinderfreundlich
b i Man kann ins Restaurant / in die
altdeutsche Bierstube / ins Kino
gehen. **ii** Man kann in Charly's

Diskothek gehen. **iii** Man kann ins
Restaurant / ins Kino gehen. **iv** Man
kann um 15.30 oder um 19.30 ins
Kino gehen. **v** Man kann von 17 Uhr
bis 23 Uhr ins Restaurant gehen.
vi Man kann am Samstagabend um
20 Uhr ins Theater gehen.

Extra!

14 **Montag:** 10.00 Vorlesung (Philosophie) /
12.00 Mittagessen Kantine mit Markus /
13.30 Einkaufen / 16.00 Gitarrenstunde /
19.15 Fernsehen, kochen, lesen / 22.30
Bett
Donnerstag: 8.15 Schwimmen / 11.00
Vorlesung / 13.00 Spanischstunde / 15.45
Café mit Mutter / 17.00 Sportzentrum /
20.15 Kino / 22.30 Kneipe
Samstag: 11.00 Aufstehen /
Mittagessen mit Schwester und Freund
/ 16.00 Stadt (Einkaufen) / Musik hören
(zu Hause) / 20.15 Kneipe mit Anja /
21.30 Chinesisches Restaurant / 23.00
bis 2.00 Disko

15 **Sabine und Rolf können zusammen**
ins Kino gehen / in die Diskothek gehen
/ Apfelwein trinken / italienisch essen /
schwimmen gehen
Sie können nicht zusammen in die
Kneipe gehen / Fußball spielen / ins
Restaurant gehen / ins Sportzentrum
gehen

Grammatikübungen

1 **a** Ich trinke gern Mineralwasser / lieber
Cola / am liebsten Orangensaft / nicht
gern Bier. **b** Er isst gern Pasta / lieber
Pizza / am liebsten Pommes frites /
nicht gern Salat. **c** Ich lese gern / höre
lieber Musik / spiele am liebsten Gitarre
/ gehe nicht gern spazieren. **d** Sie
gehen gern ins Kino / lieber in die Stadt
/ am liebsten ins Sportzentrum / nicht
gern in die Diskothek.

175

2 **a** Willst **b** gehen **c** kann **d** ausgehen **e** muss **f** bleiben **g** wollen **h** trinken **i** Können **j** sehen

3 *Your suggestions should include the following*: Man kann in Clubs und in die Diskothek gehen, und man kann in die Kneipe oder ins Kino gehen. Man kann ins Restaurant gehen / indisch essen gehen. Man kann ins Theater gehen oder einkaufen gehen. Man kann auch im Peak District spazieren gehen.

4 den Fernseher, das Radio, den Videorekorder, den CD-Spieler, das Handy, die Katze, den Hund, das Wörterbuch, die CDs (*pl.*), das Moped, den Computer

UNIT 5

1 **i** Nein, sie ist unter der Dusche. **ii** Astrid ist im Unterricht. **iii** Sie arbeitet am Computer. **iv** Sie sitzt am Computer. / Sie ist in ihrem Zimmer. **v** Markus ist mit Anna und Jens im Eiscafé. **vi** Er ruft später an.

2 **a** **i** Sportzentrum **ii** Mensa **iii** Sportzentrum **iv** Kneipe

3 **das Wohnzimmer** – living room, **die Küche** – kitchen, **das Schlafzimmer** – bedroom, **das Badezimmer** – bathroom, **die Garage** – garage, **der Balkon** – balcony, **das Esszimmer** – dining room

4 **a** first left: **Esszimmer**, second left: **Wohnzimmer**, middle: **Küche**, top right: **Schlafzimmer**, bottom right: **Badezimmer/Toilette (WC)**
b lamp – **die Lampe** / wardrobe – **der Kleiderschrank** / electric cooker – **der Elektroherd** / bookcase – **das Bücherregal** / washing machine – **die Waschmaschine** / bed – **das Bett** / bath – **die Badewanne** /

cupboards – **die Schränke** (pl.) / sofa – **das Sofa** / fridge – **der Kühlschrank** / bedside tables – **die Nachttische** (pl.) / armchairs – **die Sessel** (pl.) / microwave – **die Mikrowelle** / shower – **die Dusche**

5 Es gibt einen Tisch und vier Stühle / ein Sofa / einen Sessel / ein Bücherregal / einen Fernseher / ein Radio.

7 **a** **i** unter dem Bett **ii** Bücher und Papiere **iii** auf seinem Computer **iv** Tassen und Teller

8 **1** hell **2** gemütlich **3** modern **4** wunderbar **5** dunkel **6** kalt **7** bequem **8** klein **9** kompakt **10** groß **11** toll **12** warm **13** neu **14** kitschig **15** altmodisch **16** exklusiv **17** teuer **18** köstlich

9 **a** *Your list should include some of the following*: Sie haben tolle Sessel / einen praktischen Balkon / moderne Stühle / wunderbare Kissen / ein kaltes, dunkles Schlafzimmer / ein neues (bequemes) Bett / ein großes Schlafzimmer / eine kitschige (altmodische/exklusive/teure) Lampe / eine kleine (kompakte/ gemütliche) Küche.

Extra!

10 *Your notes should include some of the following*:
Volker: wohnt in Berlin (Zentrum) mit Freundin Simone; ein Zimmer für Volker und ein Zimmer für Simone, ein Wohnzimmer, Küche und Badezimmer; Volker hat: ein großes Bett, einen CD-Spieler, einen Tisch und Computer, einen kleinen Schrank, ein Bücherregal, einen alten Tisch (vom Sperrmüll)
Silvia: wohnt in Dresden ; nicht zentral (hat ein Auto); hat eine große Wohnung; Wohnung hat einen großen Balkon, ein Schlafzimmer, Wohnzimmer, Esszimmer,

Badezimmer (Dusche und Badewanne), Küche; Im Wohnzimmer hat Silvia ein Ledercouch und Sessel, einen Tisch, moderne Bilder, ein kleines Bücherregal, einen CD-Player und Fernseher, eine Art Nouveau Lampe

Oliver: wohnt bei Ulm (kleine Stadt) mit Eltern; das Haus hat 5 Zimmer (Wohnzimmer, Esszimmer, Schlafzimmer, Olivers Zimmer, Zimmer für seine Schwester), 2 Badezimmer, Küche, Garage und Garten; großes Esszimmer, Esstisch und 6 Stühle, Schrank, eine altmodische Lampe

11 **i** Uschi ist 8 Wochen in Exeter. **ii** Auf dem Campus gibt es einen Park und viele Studenten. **iii** Nein, sie wohnt mit zwei englischen Studentinnen zusammen. **iv** Es gibt 5 Zimmer. **v** Sie sieht fern oder geht in die Studentenbar. **vi** In der Küche gibt es einen Gasherd und einen Kühlschrank.

Grammatikübungen

1　ein Radio, einen Computer, eine Lampe, einen Fernseher, einen Schreibtisch, einen Kühlschrank, einen Elektroherd, einen Tisch, eine Waschmaschine, eine Mikrowelle

2　**a** der **b** ins **c** der **d** meinem **e** ins **f** im

3　**a** beim, in der **b** von einem **c** auf einem, im **d** mit seiner **e** zum

4　**a** schöne **b** neue, modern **c** kleines **d** elegant, bequem **e** kleinen **f** teure

5　**a** Wohnen Sie hier in Rostock? **b** Du backst köstliche Kuchen. **c** Haben Sie eine Wohnung mit Garage? **d** Habt ihr eine Dusche oder eine Badewanne?

UNIT 6

1　**a** **i** auf der linken Seite **ii** Geh über die Straße. **iii** Geh am Krankenhaus vorbei. **iv** wir sind um die Ecke. **v** an der Ecke **vi** die nächste Straße links **vii** direkt gegenüber der Schule **viii** nicht weit von dem Krankenhaus **ix** in der Nähe **x** im ersten Stock

2　Ich nehme den Bus. Es gibt eine Haltestelle in der Humboldtstraße. Ich gehe über die Straße und dann rechts und die nächste Straße links. Ich gehe am Krankenhaus vorbei und nehme die zweite Straße rechts. Die Nummer 72 ist auf der linken Seite.

3　**a** **a** weit **b** rechts **c** Parkhaus **d** Seite **e** erste Straße **f** rechts **g** geradeaus **h** über

4　**a** Entschuldigen Sie bitte, wie komme ich zum Museum für moderne Kunst? **b** Entschuldigen Sie, wie komme ich zum Parkhaus Bendergasse?

6　1 d 2 g 3 a 4 j 5 m 6 l 7 k 8 f 9 b 10 e 11 c 12 h 13 i

7　**a** **a** rechts **b** zweite **c** Kreuzung **d** gegenüber **b** **e** links **f** rechts **g** rechten

9　1 x 2 z 3 w

10　**b** **i** gegenüber einer, einem **ii** einem Blumengeschäft **iii** dem **iv** zwischen einer Kirche und einer Tankstelle **v** dem Parkhaus

c *Some possible answers:* **i** Die Bar ist gegenüber dem Hotel / gegenüber der Kirche / neben dem Schwimmbad. **ii** Das Kino ist neben dem Restaurant / gegenüber dem Krankenhaus. **iii** Die Schule ist gegenüber der Kneipe / neben der Mensa. **iv** Die Bibliothek ist zwischen der Universität und dem Museum / gegenüber der Mensa.

Answers

v Der Park ist gegenüber der Universität/der Kneipe / neben der Mensa.

12 a Das Kleid ist zu lang. **b** Sie kauft einen Rock. **c** Sie will ein Hemd für Michael kaufen.

13 a i Dieses T-Shirt gefällt mir nicht. **ii** Diese Jacke gefällt mir nicht. **iii** Dieses Hemd gefällt mir nicht. **iv** Dieser Pullover gefällt mir nicht. **v** Diese Socken gefallen mir nicht. **vi** Dieser Rock gefällt mir nicht. **vii** Dieses Kleid gefällt mir nicht. **viii** Dieses Jackett gefällt mir nicht. **ix** Diese Schuhe gefallen mir nicht.

Extra!

15 a Brandenburger Tor **b** Berliner Dom **c** Königliche Bibliothek

16 *You should mention three of the places below in your answer:*
Reichstag Germany's parliament; designed by British architect Sir Norman Foster; after WW2, the Reichstag was a ruin
Unter den Linden most famous street in Berlin
Staatsbibliothek 6 million books; lovely garden
Humboldt-Universität Berlin's first university; today it has 23,000 students, Karl Marx studied there
Deutsche Staatsoper destroyed twice in WW2; restored 1955; this week they are performing Mozart's "Marriage of Figaro", with Pavarotti
Deutsche Historische Museum oldest baroque building in Berlin; you can see 600 years of history
Museumsinsel cultural centre of Berlin; 5 buildings – museums and galleries

Grammatikübungen

1 i Trink **ii** Gehen Sie **iii** Kommt **iv** Bring **v** Geht **vi** Arbeite

2 i Gefällt dir dieses Kleid? – Ja, es gefällt mir sehr. **ii** Gefällt dir diese Jacke? – Nein, sie gefällt mir nicht. **iii** Gefällt dir dieser Rock? – Ja, er gefällt mir sehr. **iv** Gefällt dir diese Krawatte? – Nein, sie gefällt mir nicht. **v** Gefallen dir diese Schuhe? – Nein, sie gefallen mir nicht. **vi** Gefällt dir dieser Pullover? – Ja, er gefällt mir sehr.

3 1 f **2** e **3** d **4** h/c **5** g **6** a **7** b **8** c/h

UNIT 7

3 b i der vierundzwanzigste Januar **ii** der fünfzehnte April **iii** der neunte Juni **iv** der dritte Oktober **v** der zehnte Dezember
c i 5.11 **ii** 17.3 **iii** 22.8 **iv** 30.5 **v** 1.7

4 a Ich lerne seit sechs Monaten Deutsch. **b** Ich mache einen intensiven Sprachkurs. **c** Ich mache den Kurs, um mein Deutsch zu verbessern. **d** Er dauert zehn Tage. **e** Ich lerne Deutsch, weil ich im Ausland arbeiten möchte.

5 This letter confirms Vijay Basran's room booking for the students' hall of residence in Bonn. He has booked a single room with bath and shower, TV, video and telephone. There is a communal kitchen and a student refectory (open for lunch). The room is booked from 31 March till 9 April, price €16.50 a night without breakfast. The hall of residence is situated in the centre of Bonn, tram stop is 5 minutes away. Leisure activities include a sports centre, cinema and theatre, swimming pool and gym as well as bicycle hire.

6 **b** **a** Kiel **b** 15.04 **c** 14.23 **d** 3 **e** €48
 c **i** Muss ich umsteigen? **ii** Wann kommt
 der Zug an? **iii** Was kostet eine
 Rückfahrkarte? **iv** Einmal Bonn hin
 und zurück, bitte. **v** Zweimal einfach
 nach Kiel, bitte. **vi** der nächste Zug
 vii Wann fährt der Zug nach Kiel ab?
 viii von Gleis 3

7 **a** vom 4. bis zum 12. April / Zimmer
 Nummer 47, im vierten Stock /
 Johannes / Marion / die Vorlesungen
 b Vijay arrives at reception and is
 handed the key to his room. There is
 no lift, but a porter can carry the
 suitcase upstairs. Vijay declines, as
 his suitcase is not heavy. He is
 introduced to Ms Schubert, the team
 leader.

9 **a** The rapid choice option is for central
 destinations. You only need to press
 the appropriate button. **b** You find your
 destination in the alphabetical list,
 which gives you a destination number.
 c You press the rapid choice button
 and then choose the type of ticket you
 want. The machine will display the fare.
 Alternatively, you type in the
 destination number. **d** Adult / child /
 day ticket **e** You can pay with coins or
 notes. The machine gives change.

Extra!

10 *Your grid should contain some of the*
 information listed below:
 Paloma: *Personal:* comes from Madrid
 Course: is on a three-week course at
 university and has six hours of teaching
 a day / the course is interesting and the
 group is small / course very expensive;
 Homework/duties: a lot of homework
 (one to two hours per day) / likes
 talking, but finds writing difficult / exam
 at the end of the course: *Friends:* Italian

friend Paola / they go shopping
together (and to the disco and pubs) /
Paola hopes to visit her some time
Jean-Paul: *Personal:* comes from
France; *Course:* six week-course in
Munich / classes only in the morning /
teachers a bit boring / enjoys the role
plays; *Homework:* not much homework,
but projects on topics related to
Munich / listens to cassettes to
improve language; *Friends:* met nice
French girl, Nathalie (speak French –
bad for his German) / also made friends
with a German, Manfred

11 *Suggested summary:* The hotel is only
 1.5 km from the motorway. Rooms from
 €69, which includes breakfast, fitness
 centre and car park. All have a toilet
 and shower, cable TV, telephone and a
 mini-bar. It's on the river-bank, with a
 terrace (beautiful view) and beer-
 garden. There's also a restaurant and a
 cosy bar. It's located just a few minutes
 from the sights of Old Heidelberg.

Grammatikübungen

1 **a** Sie kann leider nicht kommen, weil sie
 am vierzehnten einen Test schreibt. **b** Ich
 weiß, dass er sehr gute Noten bekommt.
 c Wir haben keine Zeit, weil wir jeden
 Abend arbeiten. **d** Wenn das Wetter
 schlecht ist, komme ich schon am
 neunzehnten zurück. **e** Sie fahren nach
 Deutschland, um einen Deutschkurs zu
 machen. **f** Ich habe einen Job, um Geld
 für die Sommerferien zu verdienen.

2 **a** Seit drei Jahren wohnt Dieter mit
 seinen Freunden Uwe und Hans
 zusammen. **b** Seit November hilft er
 seinen Eltern im Büro.

3 **a** Klaus gibt ihm einen Brief. **b** Markus
 geht mit ihr ins Kino. **c** Ich kann Ihnen
 ein gutes Café zeigen. **d** Sagen Sie mir,

wenn Sie Probleme haben. **e** Wie geht es dir? **f** Ali zeigt ihnen sein neues Auto.

4 **a** **i** der erste März **ii** der sechsundzwanzigste Juni **iii** der dritte Oktober **iv** der fünfzehnte Mai **v** der dreißigste Januar **vi** der siebte August **vii** der elfte November **viii** der siebenundzwanzigste Februar

b **i** Am ersten März fahre ich nach London. **ii** Am sechsundzwanzigsten Juni hat sie Geburtstag. **iii** Am dritten Oktober geht er zum Zahnarzt. **iv** Am fünfzehnten Mai ziehen wir um. **v** Am dreißigsten Januar schreibe ich einen Test. **vi** Am siebten August fahren wir zum Sprachkurs. **vii** Am elften November fängt der Sprachkurs an. **viii** Am siebenundzwanzigsten Februar gehen wir essen.

UNIT 8

1 **a** Und du, was hast du gestern gemacht? – Ich habe Fußball gespielt.

b **i** Sabine hat bei Aldi eingekauft. **ii** Sie hat Nudeln, Tomaten, Salat, Rotwein und Parmesan gekauft. **iii** Nach dem Essen haben die Freunde Musik gehört und ein bisschen getanzt. **iv** Sie haben Karten gespielt.

2 **Um Viertel nach acht** hat Verena **heute Toast** mit Marmelade gegessen, und dazu hat sie **ein Glas Mineralwasser** getrunken. Nach dem Frühstück hat sie einige E-Mails an ihre Freunde **in Norddeutschland** geschrieben. Sie hat **ein Buch** gelesen und dann **um 12 Uhr** im Café Bauer **ihre Schwester** getroffen. Sie haben beide **eine Cola** getrunken. Am Abend

hat Verena **ihren Freund Andreas** angerufen, um **ihn** ins Kino einzuladen. **Der Film war langweilig**.

3 **a** bin aufgestanden – aufstehen / bin gefahren – fahren / bin geblieben – bleiben / ist gekommen – kommen / sind gegangen – gehen

b Harald got up too late and had no time for breakfast. It was raining, so he went to university by bus. There was no lecture because the professor was ill. Harald spent all afternoon in the library, looking for a book he needs for his dissertation – no luck. He went to the café with his friend Julius, then went home to watch TV all evening.

c *Your answer should read something like this*: Harald ist spät aufgestanden und mit dem Bus zur Uni gefahren, weil es geregnet hat. Der Professor war krank und Harald ist den ganzen Nachmittag in der Bibliothek geblieben. Er hat ein Buch gesucht, aber nicht gefunden. Sein Freund ist gekommen und sie sind ins Café gegangen. Am Abend hat Harald ferngesehen.

4 **a** Carima ist aufgestanden. **b** Sie hat gefrühstückt. **c** Sie ist mit dem Bus zur Uni gefahren. **d** Sie ist in die Bibliothek gegangen. **e** Sie hat mit einem Freund Kaffee getrunken. **f** Sie ist ins Kino gegangen. **g** Sie ist am Abend nach Hause gegangen. **h** Sie hat ferngesehen und hat eine Pizza gegessen.

5 **a** **i** Sie war krank und musste zu Hause bleiben. **ii** Sie hat eingekauft und ist ins Café am Marktplatz gegangen. **iii** Herr Schulz von ihrer Arbeit war auch im Café. **iv** Er ist sofort zurück zur Arbeit gegangen und hat allen Kollegen erzählt, dass er sie gesehen hat.

b i Horst hat eine Freundin in Bielefeld. **ii** Er hat sie in einer Vorlesung getroffen. **iii** Sie sind essen gegangen. **iv** Sie ist schon fünf Jahre mit ihrem Freund zusammen.

7 a i Er war in der Bibliothek. **ii** Er war müde. **iii** Er ist in die Campus-Bar gegangen. **iv** Er hat mit Antje gesprochen und hat sie geküsst.

8 a i noch schlimmer **ii** hat erzählt **iii** die Wahrheit **iv** böse **v** liebt

9 a 1 i 2 g 3 e 4 l 5 b 6 k 7 j 8 n 9 f 10 d 11 h 12 m 13 a 14 c
b i glücklich (froh) **ii** gestresst (müde) **iii** krank (erkältet) **iv** optimistisch **v** verliebt **vi** gestresst

Extra!

10 a Sie ist drei Wochen in München geblieben. **b** Der Unterricht hat um halb neun (8.30) angefangen. **c** Sie ist zweimal jede Woche schwimmen gegangen, wenn es warm war. Sie ist auch ins Kino gegangen und hat ferngesehen. **d** Paola ist Palomas Freundin (aus Italien). Sie haben oft am Wochenende etwas gemacht. **e** Der Sprachkurs hat Jean-Paul nicht so gut gefallen, (weil die Lehrer langweilig waren.) **f** Er hatte nur morgens Unterricht und die Lehrer waren langweilig. **g** Er ist viel Rad gefahren und nach Regensburg gefahren. Er ist ins Museum und in den Park gegangen, und oft mit der U-Bahn gefahren. **h** Nathalie ist Französin und sie ist sehr nett.

11 a Karin had a terrible weekend. She overslept and then went into town to buy herself a new dress. She tried on a lot of dresses, but couldn't find one that she liked. She was frustrated and it was raining, so she went home by bus. The ticket machine was broken, she had no change and the bus driver could not change her €10 note. Her boyfriend called and said he could not go to the cinema with her. She opened a bottle of wine and switched the TV on.

Kurt had a great weekend. His girlfriend got breakfast and they went on a trip to the mountains. They had lunch in a nice restaurant and the weather was brilliant. In the afternoon they had a glass of wine in the garden and then went to a party in the evening. They had a lovely time there, meeting old friends and dancing.

Grammatikübungen

1 a haben … gewohnt **b** haben … gekauft **c** hat … geküsst **d** Hast … geschlafen **e** Haben … geschrieben **f** habe … gefrühstückt **g** sind … gefahren **h** seid … gegangen **i** ist … gekommen; ist … geblieben **j** ist … aufgestanden

2 a i sie **ii** uns **iii** dich **iv** ihn **v** euch **vi** sie
b i ihn **ii** ihr **iii** ihm **iv** mich **v** dich **vi** sie **vii** mir **viii** sie

Answers

UNIT 9

1 **a** 1901 **b** 1945 **c** 1969 **d** 1989 **e** 2002
 i neunzehnhundertneunundachtzig

2 **a** 1 Wolfgang Amadeus Mozart
 2 Nelson Mandela **3** Robert De Niro
 4 John Lennon
 b 1 siebzehnhundertsechsundfünfzig
 2 neunzehnhundertachtzehn
 3 neunzehnhundertdreiundvierzig
 4 neunzehnhundertvierzig

3 **a** C, B, A, E, D
 b **i** Ich habe eine Stelle gefunden.
 ii Ich habe geheiratet. **iii** Ich bin in
 Hamburg aufgewachsen. **iv** Ich habe
 meine Stelle aufgegeben. **v** Ich habe
 die Schule verlassen. **vi** Ich habe
 meinen Mann kennen gelernt.
 vii Meine Eltern sind umgezogen.
 viii Ich bin geboren. **ix** Ich habe
 immer gute Noten bekommen.
 c **i** Nein, sie ist in Hamburg
 aufgewachsen. **ii** Ihre Eltern sind
 umgezogen. **iii** Das Studium hat sie
 nicht interessiert. **iv** Sie hat 1978
 geheiratet. **v** Sie hat die Stelle
 aufgegeben, weil sie mehr Zeit mit
 den Kindern verbringen wollte. **vi** Sie
 arbeitet jetzt nicht mehr.

4 *Your version should read something like
 this*: Maria ist in Berlin geboren, aber
 ihre Eltern sind umgezogen und sie ist in
 Hamburg aufgewachsen. Sie hat immer
 gute Noten bekommen, aber sie hat mit
 19 die Schule verlassen und eine Stelle
 gefunden. Sie hat ihren Mann im
 Sportverein kennen gelernt. Sie hat 1978
 geheiratet. Sie hat die Stelle aufgegeben,
 weil sie drei Kinder hat.

6 **a** Von **b** Abitur **c** nach **d** angefangen
 e April **f** spreche **g** bisschen
 h Computerfirma **i** abends **j** gearbeitet
 k Computer **l** weil

7 **Hanna:** Viktoriaschule / Studium:
 Psychologie in Düsseldorf, jetzt in
 Heilbronn / Ferienjob in einem
 Reisebüro / würde gern als Psychologin
 im Krankenhaus arbeiten
 Jens: Viktoriaschule, dann Bert-Brecht-
 Schule / studiert Sport / arbeitet im
 Supermarkt (Aldi) / möchte gern
 Sportlehrer werden

10 *Your letter should be similar to the one
 below.*
 Sehr geehrter …, / Sehr geehrte …,
 ich habe Ihre Stellenanzeige mit
 Interesse gelesen und möchte mich um
 die Stelle als Kellner bewerben. Ich
 studiere Anglistik und Informatik an der
 FU und spreche fließend Englisch.
 Meine Französischkenntnisse sind gut.
 Ich habe Erfahrung im
 Restaurantmetier: Im September 2002
 habe ich in einer Krankenhausküche
 gearbeitet, und in den Ferien hatte ich
 Jobs in einer Studentenbar und in einer
 Pizzeria. Dort habe ich im Team
 gearbeitet. Ich habe ein Auto und kann
 ab 17 Uhr arbeiten.
 Mit freundlichen Grüßen,
 Uwe Heimann

Extra!

11 **Alice:** studiert Politik und Literatur /
 wohnt mit zwei Frauen zusammen und
 will nach dem Studium ein Jahr in Afrika
 arbeiten / hat einen Freund, aber sie
 sind unabhängig und wohnen nicht
 zusammen / möchte weiter studieren /
 Thema: Frauen in der Dritten Welt
 Barbara: hat gleich nach dem Abitur
 studiert – Mathematik / wohnt bei den
 Eltern, das ist billig / hat einen Freund
 (seit 2 Jahren) / sie wollen heiraten / will
 als Lehrerin arbeiten / hat sich um zwei
 Stellen beworben / will Kinder haben und
 nicht arbeiten, wenn die Kinder klein sind

12 a Er hat sich im Jahr 20.. entschieden, zur Universität zu gehen. **b** Er ist jetzt fünfundsechzig Jahre alt. Er ist 19.. geboren. **c** Ein typischer Student ist jung – kein Rentner! **d** Seine jüngste Tochter hat ihr Studium begonnen, und er wollte auch studieren. (… so was auch machen.)

Grammatikübungen

1 sterben, **gestorben**, **sein**, **to die** / **enden**, geendet, **haben**, **to end** / **fallen**, **gefallen**, **sein**, to fall / **gewinnen**, gewonnen, **haben**, **to win** / komponieren, **komponiert**, **haben**, **to compose** / **verbringen**, verbracht, haben, to spend (time) / **verstehen**, verstanden, **haben**, **to understand** / **interessieren**, **interessiert**, **haben**, to interest / finden, **gefunden**, **haben**, **to find** / **verdienen**, verdient, **haben**, **to earn** / **umziehen**, **umgezogen**, **sein**, to move house / aufwachsen, **aufgewachsen**, sein, **to grow up** / heiraten, **geheiratet**, **haben**, **to marry**

2 a Sie würden gern in einem Team arbeiten. **b** Sie würde gern das Gymnasium besuchen. **c** Würdest du gern deine Sprachkenntnisse nutzen? **d** Wir würden gern eine Stelle finden. **e** Er würde gern umziehen.

3 a i Obwohl er viel Freizeit hat, geht er selten aus. **ii** Obwohl sie fließend Italienisch spricht, war sie noch nie in Italien. **oder** Obwohl sie noch nie in Italien war, spricht sie fließend Italienisch.
b i Wann bist du geboren? **ii** Als ich letzte Woche in Berlin war, habe ich deinen Bruder gesehen. **iii** Wenn ich im Ausland arbeite, nutze ich meine Sprachkenntnisse.

UNIT 10

1 I don't know if I'll stay in this job for long. The work is rather monotonous and boring and I'd like to find a more interesting job – I need variety in life! I'd like to work abroad: perhaps in Britain or Italy. My English is better than my Italian but I'd really like to live and work in a hot country because the rainy weather here in the north makes me all gloomy. Have you ever been to Italy? Last year I spent almost a month in Verona. The climate, the people, the food – everything was fantastic. I'd like to spend more time there to get to know the life there better.

2 a weil es in der Buchhandlung (manchmal) (sehr) langweilig ist. **b** weil sein/der Boss nicht sehr nett ist. **c** weil er die Sprache fließend sprechen möchte / weil er im Ausland / in Italien arbeiten möchte. **d** weil die Leute freundlicher und kommunikativer sind. **e** weil es/das eine wichtige Erfahrung ist.

4 a Sinn für Humor, klein
Sport – Schwimmen und Federball. Markus geht gern ins Kino: sie interessiert sich auch für Filme
Politik – interessante Gespräche – modisch
Musik – Pop und Jazz
Freizeit – mit Freunden in der Kneipe oder in einem Restaurant. Manchmal tanzen.
Reist gern – Italien, vielleicht im Ausland arbeiten.
Nicht böse wenn ich mit Freunden weggehe, geht auch mit Freundinnen aus.

7 a Nein, sie ist (seit 22 Jahren) verheiratet. **b** Sie ist nach Westdeutschland gefahren, um Verwandte zu besuchen. **c** Es gibt

mehr Freiheit zu reisen, mehr Auswahl beim Einkaufen und eine offenere Politik. **d** Nein, sie ist arbeitslos. **e** Es gibt mehr Kriminalität – Jugendliche stehlen Autos und nehmen Drogen. **f** Sie hat gern gearbeitet, weil sie unabhängig war. **g** Die Kinder haben schlechtere Chancen, einen Job zu finden. **h** Tante

8 **a** *Your grid should contain several of the following*:

Damals: wenig Kriminalität / große, alte Wohnung / Man musste viel reparieren. / Miete war billig, aber keine Toilette in der Wohnung/ Alle hatten eine Stelle. / Kinder hatten freie Kindergartenplätze. / Man konnte nur nach Ungarn fahren. / Kinder sind meistens in der gleichen Stadt geblieben. / Man konnte die Familie in Westdeutschland nicht sehen.

Jetzt: Kleine, aber moderne Wohnung / 20 Minuten mit dem Bus ins Stadtzentrum / teure Mieten / Viele Leute haben keine Arbeit, besonders Frauen. / Freiheit zu reisen / viel Kriminalität und Drogen / Viele junge Leute gehen nach Westdeutschland. / Man kann die Familie in Westdeutschland besuchen.

11 **a** nach **b** wohin **c** Ausland **d** See **e** aufs **f** See

12 wandern, schwimmen, Rad fahren, lesen

Extra!

15 **Helga S.:** wanted to study architecture and share a big flat in Berlin / didn't want to get married / wanted to travel and be independent / had a baby and stopped studying / lives with boyfriend and baby and goes to evening classes / hopes to continue her studies
Benjamin B.: wanted to be a policeman and get married and have children / met his wife in South Africa / worked there in a hospital for 5 years / returned to Germany 2 years ago / now has a daughter and works in a hospital in Regensburg
Renate O.: left school at 16 to work in a florist's / wanted to marry, have children / got married at 21 and had 2 children / now divorced, children both at school / needs money and is working part-time / hopes to find a better job in the future
Dietmar L.: wanted to become a teacher / studied languages and went on exchange visit to France / met French girl but went back to Germany / his girlfriend came to Germany / he had job as a teacher, but his girlfriend wasn't very happy in Germany / he now teaches in France

16 There were two German states between 1949 and 1990. Communists built a wall between in 1961, to stop thousands of people leaving. East Germans weren't free to travel. In 1989 there were large demonstrations for the freedom to travel. The government understood that they had to reform the system. On 9 November 1989 they gave freedom to travel and the East Berliners went straight to the wall to see the west. That was the end of the wall and of East Germany. In March 1990 parties were elected that wanted to re-unify. In October five new Länder joined the Federal Republic.

Grammatikübungen

1 **a** Ein alter Freund **meiner Schwester** **b** Eine Freundin **seines Bruders** **c** Der Anfang **des Semesters** **d** Die Handtasche **unserer Lehrerin** **e** Die Bücher **der Studenten** **f** Das Schlafzimmer **meines Sohnes** **g** Der

Parkplatz **des Sportzentrums** h Ein Foto **des Babys**

2 **a** interessanteren **b** besser **c** netter **d** schnelleren **e** größeres **f** schlechtere **g** billiger **h** glücklicher **i** angenehmeres

3 Sean darf keine Pommes frites essen – er muss Obst und Gemüse essen und Mineralwasser trinken. Er darf kein Bier und keinen Wein trinken und er muss spazieren gehen. Er darf nicht rauchen.

WEITERE ÜBUNGEN

Unit 1

1 **b** Engländer/Engländerin
c Franzose/Französin **d** Spanien
e Italiener/Italienerin **f** Österreich
g Schotte/Schottin **h** Ire/Irin **i** Belgien

2 Sie heißt Anne Jenkinson. Sie kommt aus England und sie wohnt in Oxford. Sie ist Sekretärin von Beruf.

4 **Anja** is German and she comes from Hamburg. She works as a teacher in Glasgow.
David is a student and he lives in Manchester, but he comes from Bristol.

5 **Alex** is a student from Russia. He is studying history and politics, but he also works behind the bar at *The Red Lion*. He lives in Redman Street and he is learning German. The teacher is German and is called Frau Wolters. Alex asks whether you are German or are learning German.

7 **a** kommt **b** in **c** arbeitet **d** Freundin **e** studiert **f** als

Unit 2

2 **a** 18.20 **b** 7.55 **c** 4.19 **d** 20.27 **e** 11.12 **f** 13.38

3 Anna gets up at 7.10 am and has breakfast at 7.30 am. At 7.50 am she goes to the university. At 8.35 am she goes to the library, and her lecture starts at 10 am. At 11.15 am she has coffee.

4 He has a lecture and a seminar in the morning, and in the afternoon he's going to the sports centre to play football. He has an English lesson at 5 pm. He seems to be free for coffee at 4 pm and after his English class.

6 *Note that different word order would also be acceptable.* Um 18.00 sieht Ralf fern. Um 20.00 geht er in die Stadt. Er geht um 20.30 in die Kneipe und trinkt ein Bier. Um 22.15 geht er in die Diskothek und tanzt. Er geht um 1.00 nach Hause und um 1.45 geht er ins Bett.

7 **a** Ich bleibe immer zu Hause. **b** Hörst du oft Musik? **c** Sie liest manchmal ein Buch. **d** Er sieht selten fern. **e** Gehen Sie nie aus?

8 der Kaffee, die Cola, das Bier, der Toast, der (das) Joghurt, das Käsebrot, das Schinkenbrot, die Nudeln (pl.), der Fisch, der Salat, der Orangensaft, die Pizza, der Wein, das Müsli

9 **a** um **b** Frühstück **c** trinkt **d** geht **e** Käsebrot (Schinkenbrot) **f** Hause **g** schreibt (liest) **h** spielt **i** bleibt **j** sieht **k** Universität **l** Mensa **m** lernt **n** beginnt **o** hört **p** liest **q** bleibt (ist) **r** Diskothek

Unit 3

1 **a** Sind Sie (Bist du) verheiratet? **b** Wie heißt Ihre (deine) Freundin? **c** Haben Sie (Hast du) Kinder? **d** Was sind Sie (bist du) von Beruf? **e** Was ist Ihre (deine) Mutter von Beruf? **f** Wie alt ist Ihr (dein) Großvater?

Answers

2 **a** richtig **b** falsch **c** falsch **d** falsch
e richtig **f** richtig **g** falsch

3 **Dieter** (58), verheiratet mit **Clara** (57);
Dieter (29) verheiratet mit **Ana** (25);
Carsten (34) (ledig), **Silvia** (36),
Barbara (9, Silvias Tochter)

4 **a** seine/ihre **b** mein **c** ihre/seine
d unseren **e** dein

5 **a** **i** Schwimmbad **ii** E-Mail **iii** Tochter
iv Film
b **i** das/das/das/das **ii** der/die/das/der
iii die/der/der/der **iv** das/der/der/das

7 **a** Bruder **b** heißt **c** keine **d** Kinder
e klein **f** Beruf **g** ledig **h** Hobbys
i Geschwister **j** Eltern **k** Fahrrad
l seinen (einen) **m** bleibt **n** wohnt
o essen **p** gehen

Unit 4

1 **a** stehe….auf **b** bleibe **c** lese **d** höre
e kochst **f** koche **g** bleibe **h** gehe
i kaufe … ein **j** gehe … aus **k** fährt

2 *Your letter should look similar to the
following*:
Liebe Karin,
ich gehe gern ins Kino, lese gern und
ich kaufe auch gern ein. Ich gehe gern
spazieren, aber ich fahre lieber Rad. Am
Wochenende koche ich am liebsten. Ich
rauche gern, aber ich trinke nicht gern
Wein oder Bier. Kochst du auch gern?

3 **a** kann **b** ausgehen **c** muss **d** arbeiten
e Mittwochs **f** keine **g** will **h** gehen
i geht **j** ins **k** Eltern

4 Christian asks Anna if she would like to
go with him to Munich on Saturday. She
isn't sure because she has to revise for
a test on Monday. Christian suggests
that she can do that on Sunday, and
Anna is easily persuaded to come
along.

5 c, f, g, j, e, h, i, b, a, l, k, d

6 **a** Abend **b** gern **c** Viertel (zehn, …)
d Tisch **e** Speisekarte **f** nimmt **g** lieber
h trinken **i** den **j** fantastisch (sehr gut,
…) **k** Zeit **l** will **m** Wein (Bier, …)
n Hause **o** aufstehen **p** kann **q** beginnt

Unit 5

1 Herr und Frau Werner

2 **a** Wohnzimmer: großes Fenster, hell,
Sofa, Tisch, Sessel, Balkon
b Küche: groß, großen Tisch, 4 Stühle,
Elektroherd, Kühlschrank,
Waschmaschine

3 **a** Sie will am Freitagabend grillen. **b** Sie
grillt im Garten. **c** Er bringt eine
Flasche Wein mit. **d** Sie braucht noch
zwei große Baguettes. **e** Er muss beim
Bäcker einkaufen. **f** Sie macht
Nudelsalat und Reissalat. **g** Hanna,
Ursula und vielleicht Martin kommen
zum Barbecue. **h** Er will einen Film
sehen. / Es gibt einen guten
amerikanischen Film.

4 **a** Wir wohnen in **der Bismarckstraße**
b Ich arbeite **am Schreibtisch c** Man
kocht **in der Küche d** Sie essen **im
Restaurant e** Er sitzt **auf einem Stuhl**
f Das Auto ist **in der Garage g** Petra
steht **unter der Dusche h** Ich tanze
gern **in der Diskothek**

5 **a** Stadt **b** Wein **c** Wohnung **d** Essen
e beginnt **f** großes (schönes) **g** gibt
h klein (schön/groß) **i** Mutter
(Großmutter/Schwester) **j** Lampe **k** im
l gern **m** aufstehen **n** wir **o** auf
p unter (auf) **q** auf (neben/unter) **r** will
(kann)

Unit 6

1 Get off at the bus stop in
Bismarckstraße. Go straight on, then
first right. Go past the park – you then
come to a big crossroads. Cross the

road and go right. The hospital is on the left-hand side.

3 **a i** in front of the station **ii** at the station **iii** something/a detective novel for Fatma **iv** next to the bookshop
b der Blumenstrauß

4 **a** f **b** f **c** f **d** r **e** f

5 **a** She needs a summer skirt. **b** Ulrike already has 6 or 7 skirts, the skirt is too long, too colourful and too expensive. **c** He would rather buy 7 CDs with the money. **d** The skirt is size 38. **e** They will meet in the CD department.

6 **a** Stadt **b** Uhr **c** Auto **d** Bus **e** Nähe **f** Abend **g** Supermarkt **h** gehen **i** Ecke **j** der **k** trifft

Unit 7

1 **a i** Woher kommst du? **ii** Wie lange lernst du (schon) Deutsch? **iii** Warum lernst du Deutsch?
b i Der Zug kommt in wenigen Minuten in Bonn an. **ii** Sie macht einen Sprachkurs. **iii** Sie will ihr Deutsch verbessern. **iv** Vijay hilft ihr mit den Koffern.

3 **a** Am **b** nach **c** machen **d** seit **e** verbessern **f** dauert **g** lernt **h** komme **i** mit **j** fahre **k** Universität

4 **a i** Er kann nicht mit ins Sportzentrum kommen, weil er eine Vorlesung hat. **ii** Er will am Samstag (zum Einkaufen) nach Köln fahren. **iii** Sie müssen mit dem Zug fahren. **iv** Er will nicht nach Köln fahren, weil er in Moment nicht so viel Geld hat. **v** Am Freitag will er die Wohnung aufräumen. **vi** Klaus will neue Schuhe und eine CD kaufen.

5 **a** f **b** f **c** r **d** f **e** r

6 **a** arbeiten **b** nach **c** können **d** schön **e** im **f** kann **g** spazieren gehen **h** Bus

i müssen (können) **j** Fahrkartenschalter **k** Rückfahrkarten **l** können **m** weil **n** man **o** Wochenende (Samstag/Sonntag) **p** Hause

Unit 8

1 Er ist spät ins Bett gegangen und hat gut geschlafen. Heute Morgen ist er spät aufgestanden. Er hat nichts gegessen und nur ein Glas Wasser getrunken. Um 7.30 ist er an der Bushaltestelle angekommen, um ins Büro zu fahren. Er hat gesehen, dass er ganz allein war. „Es ist Samstag! Ich arbeite heute nicht!" hat er laut gesagt. Und dann hat er gelacht …

2 credit card was stolen / football team did not perform well / couldn't find books for essay / it rained for hours … Conclusion: will stay in bed next weekend.

3 **1** e **2** c **3** a **4** d **5** b

4 **a** Ich habe bei Aldi eingekauft und (habe) für meine Freunde gekocht. Nach dem Essen haben wir Musik gehört und später haben wir Karten gespielt. **b** Sie hat Brot mit Marmelade gegessen und eine Tasse Tee getrunken. Sie hat E-Mails an ihre Freunde geschrieben. Dann hat sie die Zeitung gelesen. **c** Ich bin um sieben Uhr aufgestanden und (bin) mit dem Bus zur Uni gefahren. Ich bin den ganzen Nachmittag in der Bibliothek geblieben. Ich habe ein Buch für meine Dissertation gesucht, aber habe es nicht gefunden.

5 **a** sind **b** aufgestanden **c** gefrühstückt **d** Bahnhof **e** gesehen **f** angekommen **g** hatten **h** machen **i** können **j** sehen **k** gehst **l** treffen **m** vor **n** ist **o** angefangen

Answers

Unit 9

1. **a** neunzehnhundertsiebenundvierzig
 b neunzehnhunderteinundzwanzig
 c zweitausend(und)drei
 d neunzehnhundertzwölf
 e achtzehnhundertfünfzehn
 f neunzehnhundertdreiundneunzig
 g achtzehnhundertvierundsiebzig
 h zweitausend(und)fünf

2. **a** Meine Eltern haben mich nicht verstanden. **b** Seine Brüder haben in Frankfurt studiert. **c** Er ist nach dem Studium Lehrer geworden. **d** Haben Sie gute Noten erhalten? **e** Wir haben mit 16 die Schule verlassen.

3. **b** The interviewee was born in Stuttgart in 1973, but grew up in Hanover. He passed his *Abitur* with a good grade. He really wanted to find a job and get married. He didn't get married till 1999 and he now has a small daughter. They still live with his parents. He studied psychology and sociology and has found a job at a travel agent's. He would rather work abroad, though, because he is good at languages and doesn't enjoy his current job.

4. **Simon:** b; **Anja:** a

5. **a i** He did his **Abitur** five years ago, grade 3.9 (not very good). **ii** He worked for 18 months as an ambulance driver. **iii** He wasn't motivated. / He was bored. **iv** He eventually applied for a job in the library. **v** He worked on the computer a lot, but also with the public – taking books etc. **vi** He likes working in a team. / Speaks English quite well. **vii** He worked in a bar.

6. **1** , weil er gern anderen Menschen hilft.
 2 , weil sie sich für Bilder interessiert.
 3 , weil er sportlich ist. **4** , weil sie gern sehr spät ins Bett geht. **5** , weil er sich für Literatur interessiert.

7. **a** Geld **b** würden/möchten **c** liest **d** Stelle **e** kannst **f** wäschst **g** sucht **h** können **i** dich **j** bleiben

Unit 10

1. **a a** der **b** langweilig **c** würde **d** Ausland **e** Leben **f** Land **g** angenehmer **h** interessanter **i** will **j** Sprachkurs **k** Italienisch **l** ins **m** Erfahrungen **n** zurückkommt **o** verdient
 b Markus finds his work in the bookshop boring. He would like to work abroad. Life in a southern European country is more pleasant and the culture is more interesting. Markus wants to do a language course to learn Italian. He's going abroad to gain new experiences. When he comes back he will hopefully earn more money.

2. **a** will **b** muss **c** darf **d** kann **e** muss

3. **a** die Fahrradtour, das Dorf, der Bauernhof, der Wald, der See, der Strand, der Hafen **See** (f.) = sea, but **See** (m.) = a lake
 b Five (see section 3 of the Grammar Summary): Fahrrad<u>tour</u>en, <u>Dörf</u>er/<u>Wäld</u>er, Bauern<u>höf</u>e/<u>Ständ</u>e, <u>See</u>n, <u>Häf</u>en
 c malerische

4. **a** Job **b** können **c** gutes **d** mit **e** dem **f** teurer **g** Auto **h** fahren **i** zum **j** denn **k** das **l** sagt **m** gern

INDEX

APPENDIX

Additional glossary lists

*Verb strong in present tense

Unit 4 Am Wochenende

Aufgabe 14

bekommen	to get (here = to have)
die Tomatensuppe	tomato soup
das Huhn	chicken
die Sahnesauce	cream sauce
der Weißwein	white wine
die Nummer	number
sonst noch etwas?	anything else?
das ist alles	that's all
der Rotwein	red wine
das Vanilleeis	vanilla ice cream
das Schokoladeneis	chocolate ice cream

Extra!

die Woche	week
zusammen	together
allein	alone

Unit 5 Zu Hause

Aufgabe 8

das stimmt	that's right
kitschig	kitschy
altmodisch	old-fashioned
exklusiv	exclusive
teuer	expensive
kompakt	compact
der Kuchen (also *pl*)	cake
backen	to bake
köstlich	delicious
der Bäcker	baker
beim Bäcker	at the baker's
der Schokoladenkuchen	chocolate cake
die Idee	idea

Extra!/Grammatikübungen/Partnerarbeit

der Wohnort	place of residence
schon	already
einladen *sep*	to invite
die Toilette	toilet

Unit 6 In der Stadt

Aufgabe 12

tragen*	to wear
– er/sie trägt	wears/is wearing
der Anzug	suit
die Herrenabteilung	the men's dept
die Krawatte	tie
bunt	colourful

Aufgabe 13

langweilig	boring

Aufgabe 14

blau	blue
rot	red
grün	green
gelb	yellow
braun	brown
weiß	white
beige	beige

Unit 7 Fahren

Aufgabe 9

die Schnellwahl	rapid choice
das (Fahrt)ziel	destination
drücken	to press
entsprechend	appropriate
die Taste	button, key
erreichen	to get to
ein anderes Ziel	a different destination
suchen	to look for
das Verzeichnis	index
der Fahrpreis	fare
tippen	to type
wählen	to choose
gewünscht	desired
Erwachsene *pl*	adults
die Tageskarte	day ticket
der Automat	machine
die Zahlung	payment
Münzen *pl*	coins
Geldscheine *pl*	banknotes
zahlen	to pay
das Restgeld	change
zurückhalten* *sep*	to get back

Unit 9 Lebensläufe

Aufgabe 7

das Reisebüro	travel agency

Aufgabe 9

motiviert	motivated
enthusiastisch	enthusiastic
selbständig	independent
teamorientiert	team-orientated
flexibel	flexible
freundlich	friendly
kommunikativ	communicative
pünktlich	punctual
zuverlässig	reliable
organisiert	organised
die Fähigkeit	ability, capability
mobil	mobile
fleißig	hard-working
Flugreisen *pl*	air travel
europaweit	throughout Europe
die Kundenberatung	advising customers
Läden *pl*	shops, branches
besitzen	to possess
der Geist	spirit
bieten	to offer
das Arbeitsfeld	area of work

Aufgabe 10

der/die Übersetzer(in) (n/nen)	translator (m/f)
sich spezialisieren auf	to specialise in
technisch	technical
das Gehalt	salary
ausgezeichnet	excellent
die Bewerbung	application

Aufgabe 11

die Stellenanzeige	job advert
sich bewerben um*	to apply for
abgeschlossen	pp of abschließen
abschließen *sep*	to complete
Termine *pl*	deadlines
das Personal	personnel
das Metier	profession

Unit 10 Zukunftspläne

Aufgabe 11

die See	sea
aufs Land	to the country
die Nordsee	North Sea
die Ostsee	Baltic Sea
die Küste	coast
näher	nearer
bestimmt	definitely

Advert

die Vermietung	hire
Wanderungen	hikes, walks
Ausflüge *pl*	trips
Pensionen *pl*	boarding houses
Campingplätze *pl*	campsites

Aufgabe 12

Ski fahren	to ski
segeln	to sail
Kunstgalerien *pl*	art galleries
bergsteigen	to go mountain-climbing
wandern	to go on a hike, walk

p. 112

wen	whom

Overview

	Communication	Vocabulary	Grammar
1	Introducing and giving information about oneself. Understanding information about others. Asking questions (formal and informal) to elicit such information	Countries; nationalities; jobs	Pronouns **ich**, **du**, **er**, **sie**, **Sie**; present tense of weak verbs and **sein** (**ich-**, **du-**, **Sie-**, **er-**, **sie-** forms); forming questions.
2	Talking about daily routine. Frequency. Numbers. 24-hour clock	Campus locations and activities, evening leisure activities; mealtimes, food and drink; numbers 1–99; adverbs of frequency	Gender; prepositions (**in**, **an** + accusative); **haben**; separable verbs; **essen** as example of strong verb; definite and indefinite articles, word order: position of main verb, and adverbs
3	Understanding information about the family circumstances of others. Talking about your family. Talking about what you own and need. Healthy and unhealthy lifestyles	Family relationships, everyday objects	Accusative of indefinite article; **kein**; possessives in nominative and accusative; pronouns **wir**, **sie** ('they')
4	Saying what you like and don't like doing/eating/drinking. Stating preferences. Making and responding to suggestions, invitations. Understanding information about leisure activities. Ordering a meal. Telling the time ('five to')	Days of the week; leisure activities, food and drink	**Gern**, **lieber**, **am liebsten**; modal verbs – **müssen**, **können**, **wollen**; **man kann ...**; accusative of definite article; strong verbs **lesen** and **fahren**
5	Saying where you are/someone/something is. Giving and understanding information/opinions about where you and others live	Rooms; furniture/equipment; adjectives describing rooms and furniture	Recap articles and possessives: introduction of label 'nominative'; dative (articles and possessives) after prepositions; pronoun/possessive **ihr/euer**; **es gibt ...** ; adjectival endings in the accusative; adjectival endings before plural nouns

	Communication	Vocabulary	Grammar
6	Asking for and understanding directions Describing locations in a town centre Stating likes and dislikes	Shops, public buildings; clothes; colours	Imperative (**du-** and **Sie-** forms); prepositions with the dative/with the accusative; indirect object; **gefallen**; **dieser, welcher, jeder**
7	Trying to fix a date Saying when your birthday is Understanding information about accommodation Making travel enquiries Buying a ticket at the station Buying a ticket from a machine Booking a hotel room	Months; rail travel; about a ticket machine; accommodation	**Um ... zu**; subordinate clauses: **wenn, dass, weil**; dative plural; ordinal numbers; dative pronouns; **seit**
8	Talking about the recent past Describing how you feel	States of mind and emotions	Perfect tense; simple past tense used for **sein, haben**, modals; accusative pronouns
9	Years: brief lives of famous people Talking about your life, education and experience Saying what sort of job you would like Understanding information about jobs Constructing a CV Applying for a job	Language needed to write a CV/job application; qualities needed for a job	Perfect tense (verbs in **-ieren**, verbs with an inseparable prefix, mixed verbs); reflexive verbs; **würde gern/möchte gern**; subordinate clauses: **als, obwohl**
10	Expressing wishes and hopes Contrasting then and now Making holiday arrangements	Qualities of a potential partner; holiday activities and locations	The genitive; adjectives: the comparative; modal verb **dürfen**

From the publishers of *Breakthrough*

Foundations Languages

Meeting the language teaching needs of today

- Classroom courses

- Specifically designed for IWLPs and similar provision

- Tailored to the needs of a 20-24 week teaching year

- Focused on the needs of HE non-specialist language students including the growing number of international students

- A core classroom section is supported by ample self-study supplements to cater for all student abilities and timetabling provision

The price of cassettes includes a free site licence. Full set of tapescripts available on request, or downloadable from our website.

All course books are available on inspection to teaching staff where an adoption would result in the sale of at least 12 copies. Please email lecturerservices@palgrave.com

Contact:
Lecturer Services
Palgrave Macmillan, Houndmills, Basingstoke,
Hampshire RG21 6XS

tel : +44 (0) 1256 302866
fax : + 44 (0) 1256 330688
lecturerservices@palgrave.com

German 1
Tom Carty
Formerly Staffordshire University

Ilse Wührer
Keele University

French 1
Dounia Bissar
Cécile Tschirhart
London Metropolitan University

Helen Phillips
Bristol University

French 2
Kate Beeching
University of the West of England

Series Editor TOM CARTY
Formerly IWLP Programme Leader at Staffordshire University and the University of Wolverhampton

Italian 1
Mara Benetti
Imperial College and Goldsmiths College, London

Carmela Murtas
Project Coordinator:
Robert di Napoli
University of Westminster

Caterina Varchetta
London Metropolitan University

Spanish 1
Cathy Holden
Edinburgh University

www.palgrave.com/modernlanguages

 194

Breakthrough Languages

Ideal for self-study • Practise and develop your skills • Learn a new language

Level 1 beginner's courses

Easy-to-use book and cassette or CD* courses.

Available in French, Spanish, German, Italian, Greek and Chinese.

* CDs for French and Spanish only.

What is Breakthrough?

Breakthrough courses are aimed at the self-study learner. Each course offers:

* authentic, lively, conversational language
* a coherent and carefully structured approach
* an easy-to-follow sequence
* attractive photographs and illustrations
* cultural information
* between 3 and 4 hours of audio material

Taking it further

Level 2 in Spanish, French and German
Level 3 in French

Increase your vocabulary, fluency and confidence with these higher level book and cassette courses.

Extra practice

Activity Books with imaginative and varied exercises

Available for Level 1 French, Spanish and German

Available from all good bookshops, or direct from Palgrave Macmillan.
Please call Macmillan Direct on 01256 302866
All course books are available on inspection to teaching staff where an adoption would result in the sale of 12 or more copies. Please email lecturerservices@palgrave.com
For further information log on to www.palgrave.com/breakthrough